Prologues to Shakes]
Theatre

This is a clear, authoritative account that expands our understanding of the changing figure of the prologue in a range of Shakespearean and non-Shakespearean plays; Weimann and Bruster examine thoroughly, and incisively, the theatrical existence of the prologue, and situate it within the wider context of early modern theatre practice.

John Drakakis, University of Stirling

This eye-opening study draws attention to the largely neglected form of the early modern prologue. Reading the prologue in performed as well as printed contexts, Douglas Bruster and Robert Weimann take us beyond concepts of stability and autonomy in dramatic beginnings to reveal the crucial cultural functions performed by the prologue in Elizabethan England.

While its most basic task is to seize the attention of a noisy audience, the prologue's more significant threshold position is used to usher spectators and actors through a rite of passage. Engaging competing claims, expectations and offerings, the prologue introduces, authorizes and, critically, straddles the worlds of the actual theatrical event and the 'counterfeit' world on stage. In this way, prologues occupy a unique and powerful position between two orders of cultural practice and perception.

Close readings of prologues by Shakespeare and his contemporaries, including Marlowe, Peele and Lyly, demonstrate the prologue's role in representing both the world in the play and playing in the world. Through their detailed examination of this remarkable form and its functions, the authors provide a fascinating perspective on early modern drama, a perspective that enriches our knowledge of the plays' socio-cultural context and their mode of theatrical address and action.

Douglas Bruster is Associate Professor of English at The University of Texas at Austin, USA. **Robert Weimann** is Professor Emeritus in the Department of Drama, The University of California at Irvine, USA.

Prologues to Shakespeare's Theatre

Performance and liminality in early modern drama

Douglas Bruster and Robert Weimann

Routledge
Taylor & Francis Group

LONDON AND NEW YORK

First published 2004
by Routledge
2 Park Square, Milton Park, Abingdon, Oxon OX14 4RN

Simultaneously published in the USA and Canada
by Routledge
270 Madison Ave, New York, NY 10016

Routledge is an imprint of the Taylor & Francis Group

© 2004 Robert Weimann and Douglas Bruster

Typeset in Baskerville by The Running Head Limited, Cambridge
Printed and bound in Great Britain by Biddles Ltd, King's Lynn

British Library Cataloguing in Publication Data
A catalogue record for this book is available from the British Library

Library of Congress Cataloging in Publication Data
Weimann, Robert.
    Prologues to Shakespeare's theatre: performance and liminality in early
modern drama / Robert Weimann and Douglas Bruster.
      p.   cm.
      1. English drama—Early modern and Elizabethan, 1500–1600—
History and criticism. 2. English drama—17th century—History and
criticism. 3. Prologues and epilogues—History and criticism.
4. Shakespeare, William, 1564–1616—Technique. 5 Mimesis in literature.
6. Drama—Technique. 7. Openings (Rhetoric) I. Bruster, Douglas. II.
Title.
    PR658.P68W45 2004
    822.3'3—dc22   2004007537

ISBN 0–415–33442–X (hbk)
ISBN 0–415–33443–8 (pbk)

Contents

Preface

This study seeks to deepen our knowledge of representation and performance in the plays of Shakespeare and his early contemporaries. Building on chapters that take up the dramatic prologue from literary-historical and theoretical vantages, we examine the shapes and functions of prologues in plays by such authors as Christopher Marlowe, George Peele, John Lyly, and Shakespeare himself. It is our conviction that dramatic prologues of this era presented and commented upon some of the most dynamic issues relating to the early modern theatre. Elizabethan prologues, of course, spoke to their audiences sometimes heraldically, sometimes conversationally, and sometimes in supplication. This variety bespoke not only the various playwrights competing for status in the rapidly expanding entertainment industry in and around London during the later sixteenth century, but also the heterogeneity of theatrical resources (including genre and rhetorical models), of playhouse audiences themselves, and of the world outside the playhouses. Privileged introductions to the dramatic spectacles that followed, Elizabethan prologues provide us with some of the most concentrated, and most illuminating, accounts of what the early modern theatre was thought capable of achieving.

Over the centuries, prologues have almost stubbornly retained an important function in public life. Opening all sorts of discourses, ceremonies, and cultural or political events, they greet, inform, address, and, to a certain extent, seek to shape audiences' expectations. Prologues do so by appealing to potentially common interests and experiences. They thereby seek temporarily to project or control a socially significant space. In most cases their medium – a single speaker, writer, or textually arresting paragraph – is positioned somewhat apart; the utterance of the prologue, moreover, has a brief prominence dominating the unfolding occasion. There is in the air a covert claim on authority, even in the rhetoric of modesty or the graciously offered *captatio benevolentiae*.

We examine the workings of such authority by integrating our approach to the matter of performance in the early modern theatre. Drawing upon such methodologies as historicism, literary history, sociology, anthropology, and philology – to name only those most central to our concerns – we look to augment performance history with a historicized study of the early modern theatre's coming-into-consciousness of itself. In doing so, we address what remains one of the most vexing lacunae in English literary history: the hazy but momentous years of the 1580s and early 1590s when the Shakespearean theatre was emerging as a site of profound, notoriously complex theatrical performances. We should point out that our reference to Shakespeare in the last sentence is not meant to subsume other playwrights' differences within this more familiar dramatist's practice. Nor are we suggesting by our study's title that these writers be seen as merely helpful prologues to Shakespeare's achievement. On the contrary, we hope that our concentrated analysis of works by his predecessors and early contemporaries shows the importance of attending to these plays and playwrights with an eye to their own considerable achievements as well as the complexity of their contexts.

Our insights here have clear implications for these contexts, for the histories of playing and playgoing, and also for the analysis of a literary form written for oral delivery in aid of cultural mediation. The prologue is an embodied introduction to dramatic compositions, one that intermediates their production and reception in the theatre. The dramatic prologue typically addressed the complexity of these social relations in a discussion not available elsewhere in anything resembling the sustained mode it assumes in the prologue. It is, then, an irony of the critical tradition that, save for their attention to the well-known openings to *Romeo and Juliet* (1596) and *Henry V* (1599), scholars have generally overlooked the rich material in these prologues.

If the dramatic prologue was the more social cousin of the early modern lyric, it performed a function to which the lyric rarely aspired: that of providing a ritualized transition. In this case, the transition was one between the somewhat turbulent world of the playhouse and the equally energized but more focused representational world of the performed play. It is our argument here that many dramatic prologues functioned liminally, as threshold devices. The concepts of 'liminality' and 'threshold' take their theoretical dimensions, of course, from the work of such anthropologists as Arnold van Gennep and Victor Turner, where they are fundamental to the examination of ritual and cultural process. We propose that the early modern prologue can best be understood in relation to such concepts, that playing and playgoing at this time involved a powerful rite of passage facilitated and described by the prologue figure and by the performance of the prologue itself.

The concepts of liminality and threshold help clarify various instances of connection, transition, and difference between the early modern dramatic text and the circumstantial world and embodied space of its public presentation. In such a space the imaginary world in the play tends to be introduced and addressed by (but also drawn into complicity with) the material occasion for playing, writing, and watching in the world of sixteenth-century London. During this period prologues as theatrical beginnings assert intentions and decisions; they indicate relations of privilege, governance, and legitimacy; and they sort out potential continuities and discontinuities among diverging claims and expectations on the part of authors, performers, and spectators. Prologues authorize the theatre to produce and perform plays as well as the right of the audience to evaluate these practices.

In the moment of its staging, of course, a dramatic text is performed by moving, speaking bodies; such a performance delivers, in front of an audience, a visible, audible event. Although profoundly intertwined, then, 'text' and 'event' are not identical. On the early modern stage, the epistemological difference in question is particularly poignant in that it involves diverging parameters of social status and cultural production. As we will show, early modern prologues tend to serve as culturally significant sites on which this divergence is addressed. They thereby constitute a revealing nexus, comprising links as well as gaps between imaginary and material modes of representation. Our analysis treats such links and gaps in terms of divergent types of appeal; of the authorization between bodies and texts, orality and literacy; and of correlated modes of difference in cultural production and reception.

In taking up these questions, we have been influenced by changes within our own culture. More than ever before, literary modes of representation find themselves competing with media marked by visuality and a strong sense of performance. Today's theatre, in particular, is constantly negotiating its way among apertures and ruptures advanced by the illuminated screen – whether of cinema, television, computer, or various of the hand-held devices currently offering visual distraction. In view of their apparently self-sufficient visual strength and impact, the question that all these media raise is what do they actually mediate? What is their nexus? What kind of contact, if any, do they offer? These questions do not aim at any preconceived, wholesale critique of today's media. What they do suggest is the need for a new degree of awareness and self-orientation, a need that can perhaps be conveyed, even enhanced, by an understanding of how a great theatre of the past worked through and conceived different media. We recognize that to reap the rewards of such self-awareness neither theoretical postulate nor historical perspective is enough. To these we must add nuanced close readings of the prologues and plays themselves. It is on the basis of such readings that we hope to contribute to the understanding of what is past and yet potentially resilient in our own distractions between words and pictures, reading and viewing.

As far as such critical procedure deserves to be called conjunctural it is premised on the conviction that insight into the stages of the past cannot, ultimately, be discontinuous with the experience of our own living theatre. To a certain extent, the role of the prologue in various periods of theatre history – even its very presence or absence – helps indicate what kind of social energy, pressure, or constraint can best inspire a particular range of theatrical experience. The best way to comprehend the degree to which the Elizabethan prologue either stood for or challenged what Cornelius Castoriadis terms an 'ensemblist-ensemblizing dimension of social representing/ saying' is to minimize neither the area of difference nor the space of concurrence between then and now.[1] For instance, unless we seek to displace the historicity of our own perspective and experience, it seems difficult to forget about such major directions of the sixteenth- and seventeenth-century theatre as are very much alive to this day. There is, in Brecht's words, the 'battle between theatre and play', with divisive energies 'radically separating the elements', including the 'great struggle for supremacy between words, music and production'.[2] Brecht's alienating thrust against a univocal tradition of the theatre as *Gesamtkunstwerk*, together with Artaud's even more passionate revulsion from any purely textual authority therein was, of course, no more than an early prelude to what Beckett, Müller, Handke, not to mention Robert Wilson, Richard Foreman and others have developed. All these provide us with a context against which some of the most peculiar and peculiarly telling discourses of the Elizabethan theatre can be read in fresh perspective. Needless to say, it is a two-way perspective, one in which either period of theatre history can more incisively be envisaged against its difference from the other.

Owing to its demarcated subject matter, this volume offers itself to the reader as a self-sufficient study. At the same time, it develops a series of studies in early modern issues of authority, representation, print, and performance practice, as undertaken in Bruster's 'The Structural Transformation of Print in Late Elizabethan England' (in *Shakespeare and the Question of Culture* [2003]) and in Weimann's *Authority and Representation in Early Modern Discourse* (1996) and *Author's Pen and Actor's Voice* (2000). These links need to be recorded here because one section in the latter book has substantially enriched and been used in our chapter on Shakespeare's *Henry V*. A version of Chapter 5 here, devoted to the prologue to Lyly's *Midas*, has been published previously in the *European Journal of English Studies* (1997), I, no. 3, 310–28. Our thanks go to Victoria Cooper of Cambridge University Press and to the editors of the *European Journal of English Studies*.

While both authors wish to extend a sense of their indebtedness to several people, the greatest debt they owe is to each other. There was throughout the composition of this book a lively cooperation marked by plenty of give and take; although we have roughly divided responsibilities between authorship of the first three chapters (Douglas Bruster) and the last four (Robert Weimann), both authors have contributed to every part of this book.

Bruster wishes to thank his wife, Elizabeth Scala, and their two daughters, Madeleine and Claire, for their patience and love. He is grateful as well to his departmental chairman, James Garrison, for supporting the book, and to Abbey Maedgen and Dr Patricia Hanley, who provided expert and invaluable assistance in the project's final hours.

Weimann wishes to thank his wife Maja for prolonged forbearance and support as well as his son Robbi for endearing help on more than one level. He also wishes to express a deep and lasting indebtedness to two friends and colleagues who, having helped and edited earlier volumes in this larger project, also contributed to earlier drafts of the chapters on Marlowe, Peele, Lyly, and *Henry V*: William West, now at the University of Colorado, Boulder, and David Hillman, at Cambridge University, England. Finally, both authors wish to acknowledge a very special debt to Terry Hawkes who with characteristic generosity undertook not only to read most of these chapters in a draft version, but by a kind of 'heimlich manoeuvre' (a phrase prominently used in his book *Shakespeare in the Present*) helped make this publication possible.

A note on texts

Upon their first citation in each chapter of this book, play titles are accompanied with their approximate date of composition. These dates are most often taken from *Annals of English Drama, 975–1700*, 3rd edition, ed. Alfred Harbage, revised by S. Schoenbaum and Sylvia Stoler Wagonheim, London: Routledge, 1989. Unless otherwise noted, all quotations from Jonson here are from *Ben Jonson*, ed. C. H. Herford, Percy Simpson, and Evelyn Simpson, 11 vols, Oxford: Clarendon Press, 1925–52; those from Shakespeare are from *The Riverside Shakespeare*, 2nd edition, ed. G. Blakemore Evans *et al.* Boston: Houghton Mifflin, 1997. With a few exceptions, we have modernized the spelling and punctuation in the passages quoted here. Certain spellings have been brought into conformation with British usage.

1   The Elizabethan prologue

Text, actor, performance

Perhaps at no time, and nowhere, did prologues advance a more notable range of ambitions than in the plays of early modern England – the source of the prologues studied in this book. In fact, the myriad dimensions and issues implied by performance in sixteenth- and seventeenth-century play-houses and playing spaces require us to point out that, by 'prologue', we refer to a multifaceted phenomenon and term. Our use of 'prologue' acknowledges in particular three manifestations of the early modern pro-logue that, although closely intertwined, will reward serial examination in this chapter. These manifestations of 'prologue' include:

- the scripts for and textual traces of introductory performances that survive in printed playtexts and in other sources (sources which include mention of playhouse practices and expectations);
- the costumed actor who introduced plays in the theatres of Shake-speare's day; and
- the performance of those theatrical introductions.

Thus 'prologue' operates as text, actor, and performance.

The overlap of these meanings will be familiar to those who study the-atre history and those terms on which, in the words of Alan Dessen, early modern 'dramatists, actors, and spectators "agreed to meet"'.[1] The com-plexity of the dramatic prologues of this era qualifies them in strong relation to what Dessen has elsewhere described as the period's sometimes elusive 'theatrical vocabulary', such 'preinterpretive materials' as, for instance, 'theatrical strategy and techniques taken for granted by Shakespeare, his player-colleagues, and his playgoers . . . building blocks (analogous to nouns, verbs, and prepositions), particularly those alien to our literary and theatrical ways of thinking today and hence likely to be blurred or filtered out by editors, readers, and theatrical professionals'.[2] However focused we may be on early modern modes of performance, dramatic prologues of that era remain largely 'alien' to our ways of thinking about theatrical representation. And, despite their density and rich descriptions, dramatic prologues are – with the notable exceptions, of course, of the well-known prologues to *Romeo and Juliet* (1596) and *Henry V* (1599) – often passed over by critics otherwise interested in social and theatrical history.[3]

The reasons for such neglect are perhaps not far to seek. A number of widely held assumptions complicate any approach to prologues; adding to this problem is a certain critical reluctance to study conjunctures of dramatic form and social function. Together, these tendencies solidify an impression of the prologue as what an early twentieth-century commentator dubbed a 'non-organic element' of a dramatic text.[4] Prologues tend to be painted not only as awkward appendages, but as exemplars of a form archaic (from its classical and medieval heritage), artificial (from its highly formal nature, both as text and performance), redundant (from its apparent duplication of what the drama 'itself' is to present), uniform (from the common goals, language, and methods of many prologues), summary (from the prologue's reputation for rehearsing the details of plot), and obsequious (from its tendency to seek favour of the audience).[5]

Many of these characterizations are erroneous. Others have some truth in them. Early modern dramatic prologues, for instance, were indeed conventional and supplicatory. 'Only we entreat you think'; 'our begging tongues'; 'we shall desire you of patience': we hear these and other like phrases repeated frequently in prologues of this era. More valuable here than an apology for such features, however, is the simple point that it is precisely because dramatic prologues were asked to – among other things – introduce and request that they took up a position before and apparently 'outside' the world of the play. From this crucial position, prologues were able to function as interactive, liminal, boundary-breaking entities that negotiated charged thresholds between and among, variously, playwrights, actors, characters, audience members, playworlds, and the world outside the playhouse. The conventional nature of early modern prologues facilitated rather than diminished their ability to comment meaningfully on the complex relations of playing and the twin worlds implied by the resonant phrase *theatrum mundi*. The privileged and liminal position that prologues enjoyed – their place before the dramatic spectacle – produced one of their greatest attractions for those interested in how these plays were designed to appeal to, and mean for, their audiences. In the absence of extensive records of contemporary responses to specific plays, prologues offer cultural historicism some of the most significant characterizations of the early modern theatre.[6]

Implying not only a 'poetics', but, in many cases, a poetics of theatre, even of culture, these prologues work to define the contours of theatrical representation in early modern England.

Prologue as text

We have said that prologues can be seen as persons, performances, and texts. Because much of our information about the prologue-as-actor and prologue-as-performance comes from printed texts – especially the printed dramatic text – it will be helpful to ascertain what we know, most basically, about the prologue-as-text. We could start by pointing out that traces of several dramatic prologues from this era exist *in potentia*, prior to their composition *as* texts, as recorded in Philip Henslowe's invaluable *Diary*. Three entries there note the entrepreneur's payments for the composition of prologues. Each stipulates that a playwright provide both a prologue and an epilogue:

> pd vnto Thomas decke*rs* at th*e* apoyntmente
> of the company for A prologe & a epiloge for $\left.\right\}$ $\begin{array}{c} + \\ \text{xs} \end{array}$
> the play*e* of ponescioue*s* pillet th*e* 12 of
> Janewary 1601 th*e* some of . . .

Here Henslowe enters the details of a payment of 10 shillings ('xs') for a prologue and epilogue to a play now lost, presumably titled *Pontius Pilate* (1597). Later Henslowe would record that 5 shillings had been lent 'to paye unto m^r mydelton for a prologe & A epeloge for th*e* playe of bacon for th*e* corte', and, two weeks later, 5 shillings 'to paye unto harey chettell for a prologe & a epyloge for th*e* corte'.[7] As is so often the case, Henslowe's *Diary* sketches in outline form the material basis of the early modern theatre; however varied – depending on the circumstances of the transaction – prologues (and epilogues) in these entries have a monetary value. Recognizing that prologues were commodities of a sort serves to remind us that the business of theatre during this period strongly correlated texts, performance practices, and the cultural worlds in and outside early modern plays. If prologues were never 'merely' texts, we nevertheless stand to see things about them that could otherwise escape notice by approaching them first in their textual form.

To begin with, we could ask how many plays had prologues? Thinking over titles of plays from this era, one can recall a number with remarkable prologues, but one can also think of many canonical plays without them: *King Lear* (1605), *The Revenger's Tragedy* (1606), *The Tempest* (1611), and *The Changeling* (1622), to name only a few. Were such plays, plays without prologues, the exception or the norm? Perhaps it would be most useful to ask, simply, How many dramatic prologues survive from the early modern era?

So far, the best answer to this question has been the figure advanced by

Autrey Wiley, who offered, after counting works available to her: 'From 1558 to 1642 the popularity of stage-orations increased, and about forty-eight per cent of the plays of this period had prologues and epilogues'.[8] Although Wiley notes that the popularity of dramatic prologues fluctuated during this period, we lack more specifics about such fluctuation. How popular were prologues, and how much did their popularity vary over time? Posing this question prompts us to delimit our inquiry to a particular range of years. If we wish to examine a period that borders the rise of the commercial theatres in England and their closing, the years 1560 to 1639 offer a convenient area of focus. For these eight decades, the indispensable *Index of Characters in Early Modern English Drama: Printed Plays, 1500–1660* lists some 671 surviving plays.[9] Of these 671 plays, according to the list of characters compiled by the *Index*, some 268 have a prologue (or, more accurately, a 'prologue' figure usually – but not invariably – before the play). For the period in question, then, figures provided by the *Index* suggest that something like 40 per cent of the surviving playtexts feature a prologue.

We should notice, though, that this number varies significantly over time: according to figures derived from the *Index*, a high of 64 per cent of surviving plays originally performed from 1580 to 1589 have prologues, in contrast with a low of 31 per cent of surviving plays performed from 1590 to 1599. Although the total number of plays involved in this calculation is not so large that we can make confident pronouncements, it seems no coincidence that the decade with an apparently low number of prologues also sponsored a number of remarks, in and out of plays, about the patent artificiality (and apparently unfashionable nature) of prologues.

By the time of *Romeo and Juliet* in 1596, for instance, in response to Romeo's query about a 'speech . . . spoke for our excuse', Benvolio would declare:

> The date is out of such prolixity:
> We'll have no Cupid hoodwink'd with a scarf,
> Bearing a Tartar's painted bow of lath,   5
> Scaring the ladies like a crow-keeper,
> Nor no without-book prologue, faintly spoke
> After the prompter, for our entrance;
> But let them measure us by what they will . . .
>
> (1.4.1–9)

That two of these lines ('Nor no without-book prologue . . . / . . . for our entrance') exist only in the Quarto of 1597 (the so-called 'bad' quarto) may well be a part of what one editor has called this text's unusually sustained engagement with 'contemporary stage business'.[10]

In any case, Benvolio's opinion would be echoed by the Stagekeeper of *The Return from Parnassus*, Part One (1600), who interrupts a boy prologue and indicts the form for being old-fashioned:

> *Prologue:*   Gentle–
> *Stagekeeper:*   How, *gentle* say you, cringing parasite?
> That scraping leg, that dopping courtesy,
> That fawning bow, those sycophant's smooth terms
> Gained our stage much favour, did they not?
> Surely it made our poet a staid man,
> Kept his proud neck from baser lambskin's wear,
> Had like to have made him senior sophister.
> . . . .
> Sirrah be gone, you play no prologue here,
> Call no rude hearer *gentle, debonair*.
> We'll spend no flattering on this carping crowd,
> Nor with gold terms make each rude dullard proud.
> A Christmas toy thou hast; carp till thy death,
> Our muse's praise depends not on thy breath.
>
> (Pro. 1–7, 14–19)[11]

The Stagekeeper criticizes the prologue after, and because of, a single word: 'Gentle'. His indictment of this prologue comes, that is, on the basis of a linguistic register (*'gentle, debonair'*) that implies a 'dopping courtesy' as insincere as it is unctuous (to 'dop' is to stoop, as in a curtsey). It is a register, and a repertoire, apparently so familiar that even a single word sketches out the entire routine. To the Stagekeeper, the tradition of the formal prologue is a sycophantic one best discontinued.

We hear something like an opposite account of the prologue's associations used by the '*Prologus Laureatus*' to *The Birth of Hercules* (1604). He notes the old-fashioned nature of the form with some approval:

> I am a Prologue, should I not tell you so
> You would scarce know me; 'tis so long ago
> Since Prologues were in use: men put behind
> Now, that they were wont to put before.
> Th' epilogue is in fashion; prologues no more.
> But as an old City woman well
> Becomes her white cap still: an old priest
> His shaved crown: A cross, an old church door:
> So well befits a Prologue an old play . . .[12]

In contrast to the sycophantic, Osric-like quality that the Stagekeeper of *The Return from Parnassus*, Part One ascribed to the prologue, this speaker from *The Birth of Hercules* – while admitting the prologue's outdated feel – groups dramatic prologues in a homely, nostalgic place with white caps, shaved crowns, and crosses. Perhaps disagreeing on the cause of its obsolescence, each speaker notes that the prologue seems outdated in London at the beginning of the seventeenth century. Although such statements need to be examined in much more detailed context than can be afforded here, when considered alongside the figures for prologues in plays surviving from the 1590s they seem to confirm a decline in the popularity of dramatic prologues during the later sixteenth and early seventeenth century.

Following this apparent decline, the percentages recover: from 31 per cent in the 1590s, the number rises to around 37 per cent for the 1600s and 1610s, 33 per cent for the 1620s, and 46 per cent for plays surviving from the 1630s. Significantly, remarks printed in other plays coincide with these figures as well. By the end of the 1630s, for instance, we have Suckling mentioning, in his prologue to *The Goblins* (1638), a new vogue for witty prologues: 'Wit in a prologue poets justly may / Style a new imposition on a play;' and in the Dedication to his *Unnatural Combat* (printed in 1639, but written a decade earlier), Massinger informs the reader that 'I present you with this old Tragedy, without Prologue, or Epilogue, it being composed in a time (and that too, peradventure, as knowing as this) when such by-ornaments were not advanced above the fabric of the whole work'.[13] Each of these quotations gives us a playwright of the 1630s commenting directly on positive expectations, on the part of contemporary audiences, concerning prologues. It seems no coincidence, then, that the 1630s also witnessed the first publication of prologues *as* prologues, in Thomas Heywood's *Pleasant Dialogues and Dramas* (1637). Heywood's collection was followed by a remarkable quarto of 1642 – remarkable because it anticipated Restoration practice – that reproduced the prologue and epilogue (and illustration of an actor who appears to deliver these speeches) to a comedy performed for Prince Charles at Cambridge a year earlier.[14]

Thus while the numbers behind the percentages given in the preceding are too modest to make much of (it is quite possible, for instance, that vagaries of survival joined with printing-house and publishing practices to influence the figures derived here), they square in the main with discussion of prologues from the period itself. The marked decline in the percentage of surviving plays featuring prologues – from 64 per cent in the 1580s to 31 per cent in the 1590s – appears to show a changing dynamic not only in the survival and printing of plays, but in the composition and performance of prologues as well.

Such figures make several things clear. First, the prologues known best to posterity – the prologues, again, to *Romeo and Juliet* and *Henry V* – came at what appears to have been the nadir of the form's popularity in early modern England. Like the belated publication of his Sonnets in 1609 (well after such sonnet sequences and collections had proved attractive), and like his rewriting of the 'Hamlet' story in 1601 (almost a decade after revenge tragedy had become somewhat passé), Shakespeare displayed his absolute mastery of a form – in this case, the prologue – precisely when that form had passed the crest of its popularity. Second, these figures suggest that we must not conceive of the early modern dramatic prologue as a uniform thing. Clearly prologues, and audience expectations inflected therein, varied widely. Such variety notwithstanding, however, it is apparent that early modern dramatic prologues possessed a family resemblance, from their composition and structure to their performance and reception. It is to such commonalities that we now turn.

We should start by acknowledging the 'in between' nature of the prologue as constituting both a literary form and a theatrical practice. On one side, the prologue is bordered by the summarizing *argumentum* and by the epigraphic motto. For only one example of the latter, we could offer the quotation from Horace's *Epistles* on the title page of Webster's *The Duchess of Malfi* (1614, printed 1623) as a prologue-like text that introduces and frames the playtext that follows: '*Si quid . . . / Candidus Imperti si non his utere mecum*' ('If you know wiser precepts than these, be kind and tell me; if not, practice mine with me'). An epigraph of this sort would hint, to prospective buyers, of the gnomic wisdom and *sententiae* to be found in the printed playtext.[15] Brief and pithy, such epigraphs could become as central to authorial self-fashioning in relation to the printed text as the prologue was to the positioning of the dramatic performance in the playhouse itself.[16]

Less formally sententious, the literary 'prologues' to two modern Shakespearean films strive for a similar resonance. Laurence Olivier's *Hamlet* of 1948, for instance, begins with a subtitle taken from the play: Hamlet's 'So, oft it chances in particular men' speech (1.4.23–38). Olivier famously glosses the film with a voiced-over summary simultaneously moral, psychoanalytic, and reductive: 'This is the tragedy of a man who could not make up his mind'.[17] In a happier but equally pedagogical way, Kenneth Branagh's film version of *Much Ado About Nothing* (released 1996) also begins with a subtitle from the play itself; in this case, with typographical segments of Balthasar's song lyrics from Act 2 Scene 3 flashed at intervals on the screen. Emma Thompson, as Beatrice, speaks over a soft lute as words and phrases join first to make lines, then the song's complete first stanza. We use spaces here to represent the intervals this ingenious prologue deploys:

Sigh no more   ladies,
Sigh no more,
Men   were deceivers   ever,
One foot in sea,
And one on shore,
To one thing   constant   never,
Then sigh not so,
But let them go,
And be you blithe   and bonny,
Converting all   your sounds of woe,
Into hey   nonny   nonny!

It goes without saying in both instances, perhaps, that the transposition of words from their original contexts to these places of prominence at the beginning of the films changes what and how the words mean, as well as our relation to the events and dialogue that follow. For instance, to have Beatrice speak lyrics about male perfidy and inconstancy – lyrics otherwise heard only in a sequence populated by male characters – helps to advance a theme important to the production in question. In each of these films, the prologue-like subtitles are called upon to lend a kind of scriptural, even lapidary authority to the ensuing scenes, grounding the visual image in the epigraphic word.

If on one side the dramatic prologue is bordered by the scriptural dimensions of the epigraphic, on the other it abuts the orally delivered first act of dramatic performance itself, where the single prologue figure gives way to multiple speakers. We should point out that increasing the number of speakers within a prolocutory sequence can lead to a change in literary kind as well. For instance, when prologues begin to multiply their figures or characters and add dialogue, action, even conflict, they become dramatic 'induction' – an episodic, introductory sequence featuring more than one character, often involving debate.[18] *The Taming of the Shrew* (1592) features what is perhaps the most famous example of the dramatic induction, as Christopher Sly's story melts into the play of Katherina and Petruchio. Here it seems worth speculating whether the decline in the prologue's popularity was related (in however complex a way) to the rise, during the later sixteenth and early seventeenth century, of the dramatic induction. E. K. Chambers, for his part, suggested that the induction was an 'attempt to give new life to a waning convention'.[19] A familiar instance of the prologue appearing to evolve into this larger form occurs as early as *The Spanish Tragedy* (1587), where a long Senecan speech by the ghost of Andrea is punctuated by the figure of Revenge, who counsels and guides Andrea, transforming his monologic speech into dialogue. We see this as well in a play we have already examined, the first part of *The Return from Parnassus*, where the splenetic Stagekeeper interrupts the boy prologue. The Stage-keeper's lines are in turn complicated by a conversation amongst Momus and Defensor before the latter delivers a more traditional prologue in what he insists are 'blank verse' couplets.

This irony of description – 'blank verse' that rhymes – is perhaps inten-tional, relying as it does on early modern prologues' gravitation toward such formal language. To be sure, many prologues were written in prose; the prologue of Lyly's *Midas* (1589), treated later in this study, is but one instance of the prose prologue in early modern drama. The majority of prologues were written in verse, however, and many of these showed their attraction to rhyme – especially through a feature common to many, the 'capping couplet' familiar as well in a related form, the dramatic soliloquy. We could note that when Shakespeare condenses the prologue for the equally condensed play-within-the-play in *Hamlet* (1601), he gives us some-thing like the 'thing itself' in three rhyming tetrameter lines: 'For us, and for our tragedy, / Here stooping to your clemency, / We beg your hearing patiently' (3.2.149–151). Hamlet's glib response – 'Is this a prologue, or the posy of a ring?' (152) – reminds us that prologues not only possessed affilia-tions with other forms of creative writing, but that, like ring posies, they often depended on rhyme to consolidate meaning, convey forceful mes-sages to audiences, and – in the case of many prologues, soliloquies, and sonnets – formally signal their conclusion.[20]

Hamlet condenses its 'interior' prologue so that it correlates with the length of the performance it introduces. This correlation applies to other prologues as well. For instance, even as prologues in the early modern the-atre gravitate toward verse, they tend to fall within a particular range in terms of length. The majority of prologues from dramas of the commercial playhouses are between 15 and 35 lines long, with some early prologues for these venues shorter than that.[21] Marlowe's prologues to *1* and *2 Tam-burlaine* (1587, 1588), for instance, total 8 and 9 lines, respectively. And Lyly's prologue to *Endymion* (1588) is 11 lines long. But most prologues were longer than this, as is suggested by the following table of line-lengths for prologues to Shakespeare's plays (some of which plays were, of course, written collaboratively):

Play	Year	Length of prologue, in lines
Romeo and Juliet	1596	14
2 Henry IV	1598	40
Henry V	1599	34

Troilus and Cressida	1602	31
Pericles	1608	42
The Two Noble Kinsmen	1613	32
Henry VIII	1613	32

What seems significant about these figures is that, with the exception of *Romeo and Juliet* (whose sonnet-prologue is not only a perfect fit with the petrarchan conceits that drive the play's action but in keeping with Benvolio's misgivings about 'prolixity'), most of the prologues to plays with which Shakespeare was associated are around 32 lines in length, with 6 out of 7 falling between 31 and 42 lines long. To these figures we could add two more Shakespearean 'prologues' of like length: the prologue-like appearance of Time at the beginning of Act 4 in *The Winter's Tale* (1610), which has 32 lines; and the 35 lines of Quince's prologue speeches before the play of *Pyramus and Thisby* in *A Midsummer Night's Dream* (1596). Thus while even Shakespeare's practice shows some variety, the basic duration of prologues connected with his plays was quite uniform, with a length of approximately 32 lines seeming to be standard. The sonnet prefacing *Romeo and Juliet* gives us a useful reference: many prologues from this era shared the lyric's rhetorical ambition and density of meaning, but Shakespeare's prologues tended to be over twice as long as the typical Elizabethan sonnet.

The dramatic prologue became more abbreviated as the seventeenth century progressed, however. For instance, the seven prologues that appear to have preceded staged plays that Thomas Heywood collected in his 1637 compilation, *Pleasant Dialogues and Dramas*, average approximately 21 lines apiece, a length that 14 of Jonson's prologues, with an average of 25 lines apiece, only slightly exceed. Of five prologues in plays connected with John Ford, the average is 19 lines, while five connected with Middleton are shorter still, with an average of approximately 15 lines, including very brief prologues to *A Game at Chess* (1624), with 10 lines, and *The Widow* (1616), with 6 lines.

Earlier in this chapter we saw that Henslowe recorded a payment of 5 shillings to Middleton for writing a prologue and epilogue for a court performance. If it is accurate in representing the playwright's feelings, a later prologue to Middleton's *The Nice Valour* (1616) – almost surely written for a performance in the decade or so after the playwright's death (1627) and before the closing of the playhouses, and printed with the Beaumont and Fletcher Folio in 1647 – may explain his brevity in the form:

> It's grown in fashion of late in these days,
> To come and beg a sufferance to our Plays;
> Faith, Gentlemen, our Poet ever writ

Language so good, mixt with such sprightly wit,
He made the Theatre so sovereign   5
With his rare Scenes, he scorn'd this crouching vein:
We stabb'd him with keen daggers when we pray'd
Him write a Preface to a Play well made.
He could not write these toys; 'twas easier far
To bring a Felon to appear at th'Bar,   10
So much he hated baseness; which this day,
His Scenes will best convince you of in's Play.[22]

Here the prologue refers to prologues themselves as 'toys' (9), and ascribes its own existence to the original playwright's distaste for the form. Whether this prologue – penned for a later revival of a 1616 play – accurately characterizes a playwright's sentiments (and whether that playwright was Middleton or Fletcher), it suggests that the reluctance over prologues we have seen in the 1590s remained with playwrights for whom that period must have been formative.

Another insight implied by line-lengths for prologues of this period involves a potential difference between prologues written for public performance and those for delivery at court. Prologues delivered at court appear to have been much shorter than their public counterparts – in many cases, almost exactly half the length. Admittedly, such prologues often assumed the double burden of singling out the monarch and members of the royal family in addition to introducing the play, and as such may be considered a separate form from that of the prologue for public performances. Too, these prologues may have been delivered in addition to the play's more standard prologue. In any case, it is worth pointing out that Jonson's prologue for a court performance of *Bartholomew Fair* (1 November 1614) is only 12 lines, exactly half the length of his 24-line prologue to *The Alchemist* (1610), and that the complete (that is, non-inductional) prologue to *The Staple of News* (1626) is 30 lines in length, almost exactly twice as long as the 14-line prologue he penned for a performance of this play at court. Although such evidence must be treated carefully, these figures appear to jibe with contemporary remarks about the prologues' kneeling at court in the royal presence and suggest that playwrights and actors alike were extremely modest when introducing their plays to the monarch and court.

If the early modern prologue can be compared, in length, to the sonnet (to which, as we have seen, it sometimes gravitated in terms of form), another useful comparison here could be to the soliloquy. We have already pointed out a common attraction to the capping couplet. And prologues were like dramatic soliloquies, of course, in being delivered most often by single actors isolated onstage. Like soliloquies, prologues were often highly organized as to rhetorical structure and goal; and, as did soliloquies, prologues typically anticipated and described action that followed. Not surprisingly then, does one find that many of Shakespeare's major soliloquies fall within the same parameters of length as his prologues. The opening soliloquy to *Richard III* (1592), for instance, is a speech of 41 lines. Perhaps appropriately, then – and in light of its expository function – it has often been held a disguised prologue.[23] Hamlet's 'O that this too too sallied flesh' (31 lines), 'To be or not to be' (33.5 lines), and 'How all occasions do inform against me' (35 lines) jibe with the line-lengths we have seen for Shakespeare's prologues, and suggest a Shakespearean template for the monological address. Whether the figure or character spoke, within the context of the dramatic fiction, 'privately' (that is, in soliloquy) or 'publicly' (more directly, to the playhouse audience itself), 30-odd lines formed a standard unit of communication.

What was communicated in and by the prologue, as far as we can study it as a printed text? As Manfred Pfister points out, dramatic prologues most basically 'comment and reflect on the ensuing action through a mediating communication system, thereby placing it in a certain perspective'.[24] What we have observed to this point would indicate that such a 'mediating communication system' was often highly traditionalistic in nature. The early modern dramatic prologue had a conventional rhetorical structure, for instance, that supported but was not necessarily identical with the implications of (and the ways it was accentuated in) its performance – implications which we will explore in the next chapter. Dramatic prologues traditionally provided information about the plot, theme, genre, and location of the dramatic story, and sought the goodwill of the audience.

Rhetorically, prologues embodied what the pseudo-Cicernonian *Rhetorica ad Herennium* called the 'principium' or 'direct opening' (in Greek, the προοίμιον) as opposed to the 'insinuatio' or 'subtle approach'. As is related in that popular handbook, 'The Direct Opening straightway prepares the hearer to attend to our speech. Its purpose is to enable us to have hearers who are attentive, receptive, and well-disposed'.[25] We have called the play-within-the-play's prologue in *Hamlet* the 'thing itself' because it flags many of these functions within its three short lines: 'For us, and for our tragedy, / Here stooping to your clemency, / We beg your hearing patiently'. '[S]tooping', 'clemency', and 'beg' suggest, of course, the prologue's humbling of itself in requesting the patient 'hearing' of the audience. Announcing this quintessential prologue's basis in performance, the somatic references ('stooping', 'hearing') not only implicate audience ('your') and player ('our', 'We') alike in a community of participation, but also undermine any strict distinctions among printed text, the potential range or quality of its impact on readers, and the effect of what is orally delivered in performance.

The rich array of resources that informed the early modern prologue drew Chambers's notice: 'The prologue appears to be a composite figure, partly representing the poet, and deriving also in part from the presenter of dumb-shows, in part from the Chorus of neo-classic tragedy, and in part from the 'exposytour in doctorys wede', developed by miracle-plays and moralities out of the Augustine of the *Prophetae*'.[26] We will discuss more fully the range of resources and traditions that early modern prologues drew upon in Chapter 3, but for the moment it is worth confirming Chambers's observation by acknowledging that a valuable rhetorical resource for the early modern prologue came in the various subgenres of the classical and medieval prologue. For their 'resources of kind' regarding dramatic prologues, many early modern playwrights would indeed have looked to residual traces of a medieval tradition that had seen *vexilators* and 'Doctor' figures introducing plays with grave authority.[27] Nor should we pass over the important role of the 'presenter' in such medieval cyclical plays as the *Ludus Coventriae*. Yet however salient a resource the domestic tradition may have proved, an undeniable influence on the early modern prologue was the Latin drama that formed part of the school tradition: in particular, not only the choruses of neo-classic tragedy that Chambers mentions, but the prologues to the plays of Plautus and Terence, most of which feature significant introductory speeches.

As part of his commentary on Terence, the grammarian Aelius Donatus (*fl.* 354 AD) developed a brief poetics of comedy that pays some attention to the role of the prologue – the prologue constituting, in his view, one of the four essential parts of a comedy.[28] Donatus says the following about prologues:

> The prologue is the first speech, called by the Greeks *ho pro tou dramatos logos*, or the speech coming before the real substance of the play. There are four types of prologue: *sustatikos* or introductory [*commendativus*], in which either the poet or the play is recommended; *epitimetikos* or critical [*relativus*], in which either a curse is pronounced against a rival or thanks is given to the audience; *dramatikos* or narrative [*argumentativus*], explaining the plot of the play; *mixtos* or mixed [*mixtus*], containing all of these things.[29]

Using Donatus's schema, one can make a general distinction in the kinds of classical prologues available to early modern playwrights. Plautus's comedies most frequently feature what Donatus calls the 'narrative' prologue – the *argumentativus* form that sets out the plot of the play – whereas Terence's prologues routinely eschew the narration of plot-centred information and instead unfold within the 'critical' or *relativus* form that allows Terence to respond to criticism of his dramatic style and practice.[30]

Although the great number and variety of early modern prologues make it difficult to generalize about this issue, many prologues from Shakespeare's time can be identified with the 'mixed' or *mixtus* category. They not only introduce and recommend their plays (sometimes doing so, of course, within a larger gesture of humility) and relate their plays' plots, but also engage the 'critical' or *relativus* discourse that allowed various imaginative apprehensions of the worlds of playing, playgoing, and playwriting. Indeed, as this study will show, the most remarkable prologues from this era were decidedly 'mixed' in their genre, taking upon themselves numerous functions and attempting both to satisfy and provoke, through creative interrelation, various of the playhouse constituencies: actors, audience members, and playwrights alike.

We can see the essentially 'mixed' nature of the early modern prologue in the sonnet-prologue of Thomas Heywood's *A Woman Killed with Kindness* (1603):

> I come but like a harbinger, being sent
> To tell you what these preparations mean.
> Look for no glorious state; our muse is bent
> Upon a barren subject, a bare scene.
> We could afford this twig a timber-tree   5
> Whose strength might boldly on your favours build;
> Our russet, tissue; a drone, a honey-bee;
> Our barren plot, a large and spacious field;
> Our coarse fare, banquets; our thin water, wine;
> Our brook, a sea; our bat's eyes, eagle's sight;   10
> Our poet's dull and earthly muse, divine;
> Our ravens, doves; our crow's black feathers, white.
> But gentle thoughts, when they may give the foil,
> Save them that yield, and spare where they may spoil.[31]

From its beginning, this prologue displays a mixed modality as well as a varied set of inheritances and goals. In its self-negation ('I come but like . . .'), for instance, the opening sentence recalls the *sermo humilis* so much a part of medieval literature (the modesty topos here will continue, of course, throughout the prologue). This sentence also offers the oddly uneven vocabulary ('. . . a *harbinger*, being sent / To tell you what these *preparations* mean') that so famously marks the beginning of *Mankind* (*c.* 1464–71), where Mercy's aureate terms similarly articulate a numinous verbal authority.

Lines 3–4, of course, give us an identification of register if not of genre or plot: 'our muse is bent / Upon a barren subject, a bare scene'. But more of this prologue's energy falls within the critical or *relativus* genre than within the narrative or *argumentativus*. Like so many early modern prologues, the prologue to *A Woman Killed with Kindness* focuses less on the shapes of the dramatic narrative – on identifying, that is, characters, setting, and action – than on the relations among playing, playgoing, and the writing of plays, especially as they pertain to the materiality of the early modern stage. When this prologue announces 'We could afford this twig a timber-tree / Whose strength might boldly on your favours build' (5–6), for instance, he recalls the 'imaginary puissance' that the prologue to *Henry V* had mentioned some four years earlier, and begins a string of anaphoric lines that declare the speech's quintessentially Renaissance rhetoric. Indeed, it is characteristic of the Renaissance love of copia that this formulation stretches across six lines and two quatrains of the poem, the elegant production of tropes seemingly distracting the prologue's author from the larger end of the speech. Much in the manner of the prologue to *Henry V* – without which, it is fair to say, this prologue would not have been written as it was – these lines work by contrast; the mundane, even paltry actualities of the platform stage can be augmented only by the 'favours' (6) and 'gentle thoughts' (13) of a cooperative spectatorship.

The density of the prologue's final lines contributes to its 'mixed' nature. More at home, perhaps, in the formal sonnet than in a sonnet-prologue, such density is nonetheless appropriate for the complexity of the issues the couplet addresses, and even attempts to solve: 'But gentle thoughts, when they may give the foil, / Save them that yield, and spare where they may spoil' (13–14). This couplet, encapsulating a theory of reception, can be read as offering something like 'Spectators, when you give us your forgiving thoughts in the face of unhappy performances, these thoughts enrich those who give them, and are merciful wherever the performers happen to be destructive'. The meaning is compressed in a couplet that aspires to gnomic wisdom, which helps characterize the prologue as learned. We may hear a biblical echo, of course, in the 'spare . . . spoil' conjunction. But the most important word in the couplet is doubtless 'gentle', which of course does not mean here only, or even perhaps primarily, 'good' or 'kind'. It has these valences, to be sure, but much more strongly connotes social class, as in 'gentleman'. And as such, it once more recalls for us the prologues to *The Return from Parnassus* and *Henry V*, the latter of which famously intones 'Pardon, gentles all' (and, as we will see, quite deliberately tends to level connotations of superior class).

Like so many prologues examined in this book, Heywood's prologue inserts itself into a charged milieu and attempts, by means of equally charged and provocative language, to describe, define, and manipulate elements within that milieu to the advantage of the playwright, acting company, theatrical production, and dramatic narrative. These constituencies lay behind the artful execution of this prologue, a text whose intertextuality with Shakespeare's earlier speech remains only one of a host of complicating elements in it. With its combination of concerns and strategies, and even its formal attraction to the sonnet, this introductory speech to *A Woman Killed with Kindness* stands as a fairly representative early modern dramatic prologue. For its 'mixed' nature comes not only in its complex rhetorical goals, but also its compositional elements and intensively social networks. This modality would be commonplace across prologues during this period. What made this mixed mode especially attractive to early modern playwrights – as we will see in the next chapter – was its accommodation to the largely unexplored needs and possibilities of a fledgling institution finding its way, and voice, within a burgeoning entertainment industry in early modern London.

Prologue as actor

Any approach to the prologue in its written, almost invariably printed form remains incomplete as long as the oral uses of the dramatic prologue are left out of the picture. Although for obvious reasons we know little about the precise modalities of its performance, there is no doubt that it was delivered by a presenter and that, in the process, a second level of signifying practice – that of the speaking actor's voice and body – affected the text's impact on spectators.

Who, among these early actors, typically gave the prologue? Evidence concerning the prologue's status within sixteenth- and seventeenth-century acting companies comes primarily from three sources: the casting suggestions provided in printed plays and interludes 'offered for acting'; the information recorded in playhouse documents (including plots and playbooks); and names recorded in printed playtexts. Because these sources of information deal with what can be seen as distinctive if contiguous phases in the history of the English theatre, and thus with various types of theatrical activity, they offer perspectives on the prologue that may be understood best when examined separately. Where the casting suggestions of printed plays and interludes offered for acting provide evidence concerning the prologue's role in relation to other roles in casts spread thinly over a small troupe of actors – the nostalgic glance back in *The Book of Sir Thomas More* (1595) describes these groups as consisting of 'Four men and a boy' (3.2.72)[32] – the information detailed in playhouse documents, in contrast, tends to specify, by name, which actors are to deliver the prologues in the plays these documents concern.

Of various texts of plays and interludes offered for acting (in print and manuscript alike) prior to 1600, at least 14 rise to notice for their suggestion of casting arrangements specifying which roles the performer of the prologue is to take in addition to the opening speech. The works are, in approximate chronological order: *The Croxton Play of the Sacrament* (1461–1500); *The Longer Thou Livest the More Fool Thou Art* (1559), by William Wager; *Patient and Meek Grissell* (1559), by John Phillip; *Enough is as Good as a Feast* (1560), by William Wager; *Misogonus* (c. 1560–77; MS), by Laurentius Bariona; *Cambises* (1561), by Thomas Preston; *Horestes* (1567), by John Pickering; *The Trial of Treasure* (1567); *Like Will to Like* (1568), by Ulpian Fulwell; *Virtuous and Godly Susanna* (1569), by Thomas Garter; *New Custom* (1571); *The Conflict of Conscience* (1572), by Nathaniel Woodes; *The Marriage of Wit and Wisdom* (c. 1571–8; MS), by Francis Merbury; *The Tide Tarrieth No Man* (1576), by George Wapull; and *Mucedorus* (1590). This list takes us from a fifteenth-century Miracle play – *The Croxton Play of the Sacrament* – to a work, *Mucedorus*, popular in the commercial theatres, and with readers, well into the seventeenth century. What can we learn about dramatic prologues from these plays?

First, these plays confirm one's sense that the prologue had the general responsibility of quieting the audience while gaining their good will, introducing the play and its particulars (including its themes and moral messages), and, last, begging the audience's indulgence for the performance's imperfections. So much, as we have seen, would be standard for prologues throughout the sixteenth and seventeenth centuries. But the printed texts of these plays are significant as well for making suggestions about the distribution of roles, going so far as to list the parts that actors could take so as to most efficiently use the company's labour. For example, Woodes's *Conflict of Conscience* provides 'The Actors names, divided into six parts, most convenient for such as be disposed, either to shew this Comedy in private houses, or otherwise'.[33] Two of the actors' suggested parts are as follows:

Prologue / Mathetes / Conscience / Paphinitius } for one   Satan / Tyranny / Spirit / Horror / Eusebius } for one

Here, as in play after play during these years, we find the prologue assigned to an actor who is not required to appear in the performance immediately after delivering the prologue. This confirms the casting suggestions' tendency to give the prologue to an actor who does not play one of the work's main characters – meaning that, in many of these plays, the prologue does not play either the hero or the Vice.

In fact, what one sees repeatedly is the moral and poetic authority of the prologue giving way to the turbulent entrance of the Vice – or, at least, to an unregenerate *humanum genus* figure. An incompatibility between the prologue and such figures can be perceived in the almost embarrassed remarks of the prologue to *Enough is as Good as a Feast*:

> The Worldly Man is frolic, lusty and strong,
> Who will show his qualities before you;
> Stout he is and in any wise will not bow.
> Behold, yonder he cometh into this place;
> Therefore, thus I finish our simple preface.

$$(88-92)^{34}$$

Of course, part of this prologue's embarrassment is over the length of what he has just acknowledged to be a 'too long' (86) preface. But there is also a sense of two characters not being able to occupy the same moral or theatrical space at the same time. We see this repeated so frequently that it seems almost a rule of these plays' imaginative construction.[35] In *The Conflict of Conscience*, the prologue exits and Satan enters; presumably following its prologue, the Vice of *Horestes* speaks first (no prologue is printed with the play, even though the text assigns an actor that part); in Lewis Wager's *Life and Repentance of Mary Magdalen* (1558), the prologue exits as the Vice enters; this pattern is followed by Fulwell's *Like Will to Like* when Nichol Newfangle, the Vice, comes onstage following the prologue; Moros, the fool, enters following the departure of the prologue in *The Longer Thou Livest*; Merbury's *Marriage of Wit and Wisdom* has a trio of Vices enter following the prologue; in *New Custom*, too, the prologue exits just prior to the entrance of Perversedoctrine and Ignorance.

What this pattern implies, we would suggest, is something concerning the relative status – and, perhaps, talent – of the performer directed to deliver the prologue. If the Vice figure – whose role appears to have grown in complexity and popularity throughout the late-fifteenth and sixteenth centuries – can be presumed to have been played by the group's most talented performer, with the second strongest actor taking the *humanum genus* or hero role, we can conclude that the prologue was, for many plays prior to 1600, a formal role given to a competent but lesser actor in the group.[36] Thus, to keep to *Enough is as Good as a Feast*, of the seven actors required in the text's suggested casting, Covetousness the Vice is played by one actor, Worldly Man by another, with the prologue's part given to what can be assumed (on the basis of parts assigned) to have been the third or fourth actor in the troupe. We see this as well in *Misogonus*, where the prologue is assigned to the fourth actor. And although in some plays the actor assigned the prologue is to speak the epilogue as well – for instance, in *The Marriage of Wit and Wisdom* and *Virtuous and Godly Susanna* (where he is still identified as 'the prologue' while delivering the epilogue) – in two plays – *Cambises* and *Patient and Meek Grissell* – the leading actor is asked to give the epilogue, even though it is feasible for the actor who had given the prologue to do so. In these instances we may suspect that the playwrights imagined a troupe capitalizing on the good will that the performances' leading actors had generated by having these performers continue on through the closing of the dramatic frame.

The status of the prologue manifests certain parallels to the rise of the commercial playhouses themselves. If the small-company interludes typically had assigned the performance of the prologue to a lesser actor, the larger companies of the sixteenth century and after were increasingly likely to give the prologue's role to a leading actor in the company. By the time of the Restoration theatre, of course, prologues and epilogues alike had come to be seen, by the players, as possessing enviable status, and were thus highly desirable parts to speak. As Wiley put it, in the period after the playhouses reopened in 1660 'The best actors were jealous of the prerogative to deliver prologues and epilogues'.[37] But this eventuality was not yet a given in the acting companies of the Elizabethan era. How did the prologue came to hold this status?

A half-dozen or so references to particular individuals assuming the prologue's role survive for the period from 1597 through 1635. Although these references do not point in a single direction only, the story they tell has a discernible trajectory: during the era that witnessed the consolidation of performance in the commercial playhouses, the prologue appears to have been given to talented actors – juvenile and adult alike – with some emphasis on those who, in a transitional phase of their careers, were achieving higher status in the company (and, presumably, special regard with their audiences). The prologue thus appears to have served as a vehicle for a rite of passage, a passage simultaneously personal and professional.

The first individual we have found named in relation to the performance of prologues in the commercial playhouses is one Richard Alleyn, apparently no relation to Edward Alleyn, the more famous actor of his day. Richard Alleyn may have been a member of the Queen's Men during the early 1590s and was certainly connected with the Lord Admiral's Men from at least 1597 until his death in November of 1601.[38] Alleyn's name is mentioned in conjunction with the prologue's role in two documents pertaining to distinct plays. In the preserved plot of a lost play titled *Frederick and Basilea* (1597), he is slated to give the prologue and epilogue to the play, as well as what appears to have been a prominent male role, that of Frederick.[39] It is interesting to note that, according to the plot for this performance, Alleyn would appear to be required to deliver the prologue, exit, and then almost immediately – perhaps after a change of costume – reappear as Frederick for the play's first scene. Because other actors would have been available to give the prologue and then have more time for any change of costume, such contiguity may indicate that Alleyn was specially wanted to deliver the prologue. The likelihood of this would seem to be confirmed by the fact that Alleyn is also recorded in the surviving plot for *The Battle of Alcazar*, a play originally written around 1589, but the plot for which was probably prepared for a revival at the Rose in late 1598 and early 1599. For this performance, he is identified as taking the role of Portingall-Presenter and that of the Governor of Lisbon (as T. J. King observes, these may actually have been the same roles).[40] In terms of lines, Alleyn's appears to have been the second-largest role, rivalling even the lead part; he probably would have delivered 209 lines in comparison to the largest role of Muly Mahamet (taken by Edward Alleyn, the company's leading actor) with 213 lines and that of Sebastian, with 196 lines.[41]

Richard Alleyn seems to have been 'hired' by Henslowe rather than a sharer in the company: on 25 March 1598, he bound himself to Henslowe for two years in an agreement witnessed by various shareholders in the Admiral's Men.[42] We point this out because it hints he may have possessed a kind of liminal status in relation to the company: a talented actor given significant roles but little financial stake in the company. Such a status – that of the actor 'between' professional positions – is strongly implied by other documents of the time that identify the actor giving the prologue in particular performances. For instance, in the transcript of the plot for *1 Tamar Cham*, a play written at around 1592 and apparently revived by the Admiral's Men some time in 1602 – for which revival the plot was most likely prepared – the part of the Chorus is given to Richard (Dick) Juby. In 1598, Juby had been the right age to be given both a female role (Abdula Rais) and a male role (Christopher de Tavera) in the Admiral's Men's production of *The Battle of Alcazar*. That Juby would, after four years' time, be given the prominent role of Chorus to *1 Tamar Cham* suggests a kind of 'arrival' for him as an actor. Although the evidence is scanty, the fact that the company had the confidence to give Juby both female and male roles in a single production, and then the role of Chorus in *1 Tamar Cham* suggests that, like Alleyn, he may well have been a talented actor experiencing a transition of status within the company – and, presumably, with London's playgoers.

We know that the prologue would be given to extremely talented actors as the decades passed. One can see this when examining the list of 'Persons (and) Actors' for John Clavell's 1629–30 play, *The Soddered Citizen*. Here the prologue and epilogue, along with the fourth-largest role – that of Sir Wittworth – are given to Richard Sharp. Sharp, like Juby before him, had worked his way into the company (in this case, the King's Men) by playing female roles. In the 1623 quarto of *The Duchess of Malfi*, Sharp is recorded as having acted the part of the Duchess herself. At 556 lines, this is the second-largest part (after Bosola's 824-line role), and, as any reader or play-goer knows, the role of the Duchess is the emotional and aesthetic centre of this play. Given the talent and charisma that the Duchess's role obviously demands, it is perhaps no surprise to find that Sharp succeeded as an adult player in the King's Men, where he became, in time, and alternately, the third-, second-, and first actor in various productions. For him to be given the prologue to *The Soddered Citizen* around 1630, then, may testify to a kind of 'coming of age' in the acting company.

Another actor associated with the delivery of prologues in plays from this time had experience with female roles as well. Theophilus Bird (or Bourne) is known to have acted the roles of Paulina in Massinger's *Renegado*, a play written in 1624, that of Toota, the Queen of Fesse, in Heywood's *2 Fair Maid of the West* (1631), and Massanissa in Nabbes's *Hannibal and Scipio* (1635). His name is given at the end of the prologue to *The Witch of Edmonton* (written 1621), and similarly at the end of the prologue to Ford's *Lady's Trial*, which was acted at the Cockpit in May of 1638. Most of his acting appears to have been done at the Cockpit; after Queen Henrietta's players disbanded in 1637, Bird may have joined Beeston's Boys to perform there. He was a member of the King's Men by 1642, and appears to have been thought of as an eminent actor until his death in 1663. Like Sharp, Bird must have succeeded in playing female roles; similarly, he was graduated thereafter to a more secure status in the company. Like Sharp too, Bird's graduation involved the performance of prologues.

We can confirm that the delivery of a prologue constituted a theatrical rite of passage in the mind of at least one early modern playwright when we look at a text written specifically for Ezekiel Fenn. Fenn was a London actor who – like several of the individuals we have seen to be associated with prologues during the first three decades of the 1600s – broke into the industry as a boy player performing female roles. We know that Fenn took the part of Sophonisba in Nabbes's *Hannibal and Scipio* in 1635, and, because his name appears just after the epilogue to *The Witch of Edmonton* – a part spoken by the character of Winnifrede, a maid – it seems safe to conclude that Fenn took this role as well. Significantly, in the late 1630s Fenn would be given another liminal speech – this time by the poet and playwright Henry Glapthorne. This speech was liminal in two ways, for not only does it analogize the act of performance (and, by extension, the reception of that performance) to a sea journey, but also Glapthorne composed his special prologue as a coming-of-age celebration for the young man. Included in Glapthorne's 1639 *Pöems*, the piece is titled 'For *Ezekiel Fen* at his first Acting a Man's Part'.[43] We reproduce it here in its entirety:

> Suppose a Merchant when he launches forth
> An untried Vessel, doubtful of its worth,
> Dare not adventure on that infant Piece
> The glorious fetching of a golden Fleece
> From the remot'st Indies. 'Tis so with me,   5
> Whose Innocence and timorous Modesty
> Does blush at my own shadow, prone to fear
> Each Wave a Billow that arises here;
> The Company's my merchant, nor dare they
> Expose my weak frame on so rough a Sea,   10
> 'Less you (their skillful Pilots) please to steer
> By mild direction of your Eye and Ear
> Their new-rigg'd Bark. This is their hopes and mine
> Promise my self; if you like North-star's shine,
> I like a daring, and adventrous Man,   15
> Seeking new paths i'th' angry Ocean,
> In threatening Tempests, when the surges rise
> And give salt kisses to the neighb'ring Skies,
> When blustering *Boreas* with impetuous breath
> Gives the spread Sails a wound to let in Death,   20
> Cracks the tall Mast, forcing the ship (though loath)
> On its carv'd Prow to wear a Crown of froth;
> Will face all perils boldly, to attain
> Harbour in safety; then set forth again.

Although Glapthorne wrote many plays for Whitehall and the Cockpit – of which four survive – we cannot know whether Fenn's prologue was ever delivered in playhouse. But certainly there is nothing that would argue against such a possibility: its diction, rhetoric, and conceits are entirely consonant with what one finds in other prologues of this era. Worth special attention here, however, are the biographical implications of the piece. One could notice the care, for instance, with which Glapthorne augments the actor-as-ship metaphor with concern for Fenn's sexual maturation. The female roles that Fenn had played are, as Nungezer remarked, doubtless glanced at in the series of references to the actor's innocence and frailty: 'infant Piece' (1); 'Innocence and timorous Modesty' (6); 'blush at my own shadow, prone to fear' (7); 'my weak frame' (10).

Because Glapthorne's 'prologue' appeared in print in 1639, and because we know that Fenn had been playing female roles as late as 1635, we can say with some certainty that Fenn took his first 'Man's Part' in the latter half of the 1630s.[44] The prologue celebrates his transition, in the eyes of the acting company and its patrons, from boy to adult and concomitantly from playing female roles to playing male roles. The 'in between' nature of the prologue itself – its position, as form and event, between the audience and the players, the world outside the playhouse and the world of the play, and even, as a text, between the reader and the imagined playworld – must have seemed not only apt but absolutely fitting as a vehicle with which to mark Fenn's physical and professional rite of passage.

Fenn's coming of age via the prologue offers a parallel for the form's own history. To the extent that the prologue appears to have been delivered by lesser actors (and, perhaps, boys) during the era of the Tudor interlude, and, a century later, by leading actors in the Restoration theatre, it experienced its own transitional era between the rise of the commercial playhouses and their forced closing in 1642. During this period, prologues appear to have been delivered by talented actors on the cusp of success as adult players. The marginal status of the 'hired' Richard Alleyn found consonance in the proximate nature of talented boy actors and younger adult players who had successfully performed female roles: Dick Juby, Richard Sharp, Theophilus Bird (Bourne), and Ezekiel Fenn. Although such is conjectural, these players' success at female roles may imply not only a range of performance skills – including flexibility, charm, and charisma – but also an 'in between' status relative to the appearance of gender as well. If such was indeed the case, it would mark the prologue as a zone of multiple transitions.

What did such players look like when delivering their prologues? We cannot be sure, of course, as to the physical appearance of any prologue from this era. Yet this is not to say that we cannot, from its subsequent history, presume certain elements of the prologue's visual ensemble on stage. Even today, many readers and playgoers have a generalized image of what a prologue looks like: a sombre and darkly clad actor, in full possession of what Kevin Dunn has called 'prefatory authority'.[45] This image has historical support, for modern productions of Shakespeare's plays – productions theatrical and cinematic alike – often use special costuming for their prologues that derives from remarks about prologues in early modern documents.

A ready example comes with Derek Jacobi's prologue in Kenneth Branagh's landmark 1989 film of *Henry V*. Jacobi's prologue begins by lighting a match that provides the only illumination for a darkened screen in what may be an equally dark cinema. As he progresses through the initial lines of the prologue, he turns on a bank of floodlights to reveal a cluttered film studio. As though illustrating Mayakovsky's observations about the material basis of artistic fabrication, the camera glides past not only various properties of the production to follow (including banners, candles, shields, and swords) but also equipment necessary to – but otherwise unseen in – that filmed drama: ladders, scaffolding, cameras, work stations, and coffee cups.[46]

Jacobi's prologue to *Henry V* cleverly moulds the original lines' interest in the praxis of playing with the modernity of film's apparatus. We can see what, behind the scene, allows the scene to exist. Significant as well is this production's choice regarding its prologue's costume. Dressed almost wholly in black – from a black scarf to a long black coat and black gloves – Jacobi's prologue could seem merely to reproduce the fashionable dress of a stage- or movie actor. But his garb actually replicates something we know about the clothing of prologues in the early modern playhouse, where our information about performance practice comes from a variety of contemporary sources, chief among them plays and dramatic prologues themselves. To cite only one instance out of many such sources, the prose prologue to Fletcher's *The Woman Hater* (1606) begins 'Gentlemen, inductions are out of date, and a Prologue in Verse, is as stale as a black Velvet Cloak, and a Bay Garland'.[47] Even in such a brief passage we see encapsulated reference to the (temporary) decline in popularity of the prologue and two features that would frequently be associated with the traditional costuming of the prologue actor: black velvet cloaks and bay garlands.

In what remains the most extensive study of the staging of prologues in the early modern era, James Gousseff sifts the available evidence – a large number of references to and descriptions of prologues – and comes to the following conclusion about the typical appearance of the actor playing the prologue in plays of the era:

> When the conventional prologue speaker made his entrance, he presented a distinctive appearance. He was dressed in black from head to foot. His suit was of fashionable cut. It was surmounted by a long, black, velvet cloak. His hat was swept from his head in a gesture of respect. Around his brow was a wreath of bay leaves in token of his task as representative of the play's poet. In contrast to the custom of the gentlemen of the period, he wore no sword. His face may have appeared a bit white from stage fright, but aside from a formally trimmed little beard, he apparently wore no makeup. In one of his hands it is quite likely that he carried a book, a scroll, or one or more sheets of paper. In other cases he apparently carried a staff, a banner with the name of the play inscribed upon it, or a placard of some sort giving the same piece of information.[48]

Gousseff's research acknowledges that dramatic prologues were by no means uniform during this period: from mythological personae and female prologues to the 'interrupted' prologues that, as we have seen, become dramatic inductions, playwrights demonstrated great ingenuity in varying the standard prologue form. Too, the passage quoted from *The Woman Hater* suggests that conventions of dress and mode were malleable – even that they are typically recorded in the very face of change. And few texts from the period bother to rehearse many of the details summarized in the foregoing description. Yet instead of suggesting a lack of convention to the prologue's ensemble, the overwhelmingly casual reference to details of dress and stage properties may imply that the appearance and deportment of prologues was largely taken for granted.

Indeed, the details glanced at in a number of sources cohere in such a way as to suggest that the prologue had just such a conventional appearance. The female prologue to Shirley's *The Coronation* (1635) summarizes a tradition broken by her very appearance:

> Since 'tis become the Title of our Play,
> A woman once in a Coronation may,
> With pardon, speak the *Prologue*, give as free
> A welcome to the Theatre, as he
> That with a little beard, a long black cloak,
> With a starch'd face, and a supple leg hath spoke
> Before the Plays the twelvemonth . . .

> (Prol. 1–7)[49]

As this prologue suggests, and far before the 'twelvemonth' to which its speaker refers, the early modern prologue's outward show appears to have routinely included a 'long, black, velvet cloak', hat, and beard, as well as papers, book, scroll, or other property conveying an authority behind the information communicated to the playgoer. The various items here draw on diverse realms of authority. The prologue's black velvet robe, for instance, suggests academic, ecclesiastical, or judicial authority. The bay garland he may have worn on his head symbolizes poetic authority and tradition. The items that the prologue may have held – whether book, scroll, papers, or staff – could have signified not only literary authority but the *skeptron* of political power extending over theatrical affairs as well. After all, the speaker almost certainly was one of the players, one who would typically be in association with whatever histrionic politics the troupe tended to pursue.

Taken together, the early modern prologue's accoutrements spoke to both an overdetermination of symbolic authority and a fundamental ambivalence concerning that very authority. We can perhaps see traces of the most literal kind of this ambivalence in the oft-noted trepidation exhibited by actors delivering the prologue – trepidation clearly motivated when one considers the various interruptions metadramatic prologues are confronted with in such plays as *Love's Labour's Lost* (1595) and the first part of *The Return from Parnassus* (1600). Thus when the prologue to *Troilus and Cressida* identifies himself as 'armed – but not in confidence' (23), he perhaps accidentally characterizes the manner in which early modern prologue figures were typically, and often uneasily, 'armed' with the vestures of power, literary and governmental alike. Of course, the prologue in question may well have been clad as a soldier primarily to introduce this Trojan War play. But we can take any military garb as not a divergence from but rather an extension of the standard prologue costume, which worked to authorize a figure that had, nevertheless, to seek the goodwill of others even as he commented upon a theatrical environment made newly turbulent by the confrontational energies of the War of the Theatres.[50]

Prologue as performance

If the prologue's costume, accoutrements, and presumably this entire habitus asserted a novel kind of authority in the early modern playhouse, it was a prefatory authority between and among various groups rather than over any particular constituency. As we will see in Chapter 2, such 'betweeness', or *liminality*, characterized every aspect of the prologue's performance, rendering the prologue a powerful threshold figure. This liminality also, as we will note, dovetailed with, even as it was a product of, the prologue's essentially ambivalent relationship to theatrical power. For now, however, we may inquire as to the shapes of the prologue as performance.

The performance of the prologue appears to have followed a traditional pattern of movement and gesture. To be sure, some plays of the early seventeenth century – perhaps in response to the decline of the prologue's popularity – experimented with novel forms of prologue, introducing mythological or other allegorical personae and sometimes (as we have seen) expanding the prologue into dramatic induction. Yet on the whole the prologue's staging, as Gousseff relates, 'was fairly well developed by the 1590s and apparently changed but little from that time to the closing of the theatres'.[51] Gousseff describes a typical performance as follows:

> The entrance of the conventional prologue speaker was – at least in many cases – introduced by three short trumpet calls at intervals of unknown length. At the third such sounding, the prologue actor entered the principal acting area of the theatre or hall in which the

performance was being given . . . Having reached the stage, the
speaker took his stand near the lateral center of the tiring house
façade. He began his performance by making three bows (in an exact
manner prescribed by the latest courtly fashion) to his audience. The
bows completed, he was ready to address the assembled spectators.[52]

A brief qualification to this portrait may be offered. Gousseff appears to
base his remarks about the stage position of the prologue ('near the lateral
center of the tiring house façade') on illustrations, early modern and
medieval, of prologue and presenter figures. So numerous are the dramatic
cues for proximity of presenting-actors (prologue and epilogue alike) to
audience, however, that it seems likely the prologue would have been positioned *downstage*, where one could make use of the *platea* area of the stage
and that area's proximity to the audience.

As Tom Clayton suggests concerning Puck's epilogue to *A Midsummer
Night's Dream*,

> Perhaps a pause cueing applause was intended or practiced between
> 'So goodnight unto you all' – which has a terminal ring – and the clos-
> ing couplet, 'Give me your hands', which is affably forthcoming – and
> does mean 'applaud', of course, the practical purport of all epilogues.
> But here the phrase must surely have been intended also to initiate
> hand-shaking. It is used in that way by Shakespeare many times with
> 'hand' and four to six other times with 'hands' . . . The gesture of
> taking hands is exactly right for Robin here, and it must have been the
> business of public performance in Shakespeare's day . . . With an ele-
> vated platform like the new Bankside Globe's, the natural action
> accompanying the lines would be the speaker's bending or kneeling to
> take the hands of spectators closest to the platform, whether right to
> right hand, or more likely, one by each hand, two by two.[53]

Of course, this interpretation of a phrase from Puck's epilogic speech
should not be taken prescriptively. While prologues and epilogues shared
many functions, epilogues would have been able to capitalize on an *ethos*
generated by the communal participation of an audience in a theatrical
performance. Too, prologues were often described as (understandably) ner-
vous, something that perhaps suggests a psychological distance from an
audience.[54] Yet the process of initiating the dramatic community of players
and spectators must have begun with at least a gesture, on the part of the
prologue-actor, of immersion in and acquaintance with an audience that
was being considered, and was being asked to consider itself, in new
relation to a playworld and to the players who brought that world to lively

being. However much the prologue represented authority elsewhere connected with the *locus* area of the stage, the liminality implied in and by the
prologue's 'moment' would find no better home than in the richly marginal
space of the *platea*.

To this description we could also add a remark about the duration of
prologues. Although we cannot know for certain the pace at which lines
were spoken in the early modern playhouses, it is worth pointing out that
the standard Shakespearean unit of 30-odd lines would appear to have
taken approximately two minutes to deliver. For instance, in each of the
two major films of *Henry V* – Olivier's and Branagh's – the Prologue's
speech is delivered in almost exactly two minutes. And while a modern film
could seem insufficient evidence for reckoning the duration of theatrical
performance, it is difficult to feel that early modern actors would have
delivered these prologues at a greatly faster or slower rate. A duration of
approximately two minutes, then (and even less for shorter prologues), may
well have been the norm for dramatic prologues.

As Gousseff points out, however, the speech itself was only a part of the
performed prologue. In addition to a significant ensemble of costume and
properties, the prologue appears to have involved a highly conventional set
of gestures and movements, all of which unfolded within a larger milieu of
sight and sound. Many prologues from this period, and accounts of theatrical prologues, for instance, mention the sounding of the trumpets that
preceded the prologue's entry. We have heard several sources take note of
the traditional bows directed toward various parts of the playhouse:
Hamlet's 'stooping to your clemency', *The Return from Parnassus*'s 'cringing
parasite? / That scraping leg, that dopping courtesy, / That fawning bow
. . .'. At court, again, kneeling appears to have substituted for these conventional bows. Perhaps needless to say, across the many references to
prologues in dramatic and extra-dramatic texts of this era runs an acknowledgment of the prologue's deep connections to the interests and protocols
of *formality*. Whatever else they did, early modern prologues functioned in
strong relationship to existing authority, however ambivalent they were to
and within the authority they represented themselves.

Such reminds us that the prologue and induction in plays of this period
did not exist in isolation. Prologues were, among other forms for mustering
attention, part of a constellation of heraldic devices surrounding the performance of plays in the early modern era. Among such attention-rousing
devices were playbills, which appear to have been routinely posted in various locations to announce dramatic productions.[55] Notable too are the
flags that regularly adorned public amphitheatres on the days of performance and are included in contemporary illustrations of London's urban
landscape. If we add to these heraldic devices less tangible elements, such

as word-of-mouth about dramatic performances, and actors' reputations, even celebrity, the prologue can be seen as having assumed a place, and an important one, within a rich array of attention-soliciting devices in the developing entertainment institutions of early modern London. Poised, historically, between community and market, the prologue bore witness to the collision, the mutual engagement, of traditional and commercial strategies in a burgeoning national centre.

Finally, it is worth noting that, however conventional their performance during the early modern era – and however standard they became during the Restoration and early eighteenth century – dramatic prologues historically underwent a long eclipse that is only recently showing signs of reversal.[56] The prologue and choruses to *Henry V*, as Emma Smith notes, were not included in the 1600 Quarto of the play, and were 'omitted in a number of eighteenth- and nineteenth-century productions'.[57] During much of the eighteenth and nineteenth centuries, the prologue to *Romeo and Juliet* had not been given in most performances either. As James Loehlin observes, Henry Irving is 'generally credited with having restored it, at the Lyceum in 1882'.[58] Yet even after its restoration, this prologue has shown the felt pressures to find a modern equivalent for its presentational status. According to Loehlin, the Irving production had Howard Russell, 'costumed as Dante', deliver the prologue 'in front of fantastically embroidered curtains'. We can see in this choice a desire for an authorial prologue, an Italian poet for an Italian story, presumably. Whatever its *raison d'être*, Russell's prologue was harbinger to numerous twentieth-century experiments. For instance, both John Gielgud and Orson Welles, in separate productions in the mid-1930s, wore gold masks as they delivered the prologue. This attempt to present a gilded, authoritative speaker was made only slightly less literal when, in a 1954 film version, Gielgud, 'made up as Shakespeare, speaks directly to the camera with a book in his hand'. And Baz Luhrmann's *Romeo + Juliet* film of 1996 has the prologue delivered twice: 'first by a banal television news anchor, then offscreen over a montage of urban violence and conspicuous consumption'.

Whether advancing Dante, Shakespeare himself, the patina of gold, or the authority of a news anchor, modern productions of *Romeo and Juliet* have accepted the integrity of the prologue without having a repeatable figure for its conveyance. The experiments that Loehlin chronicles are indeed ingenious, and speak to the changing expectations and experiences of the play's audiences. Indeed, no single solution to the prologue's appearance has 'taken'. Nor, perhaps, should we expect such, so substantial have been changes to the field of theatrical representation during the last century. It is unlikely, for instance, that youthful moviegoers of 1996 would have identified a 'Dante'-prologue – only slightly more likely, perhaps, than it would have been for a Lyceum audience to understand a 'news anchor'-prologue.

Each of the productions discussed above fastened upon something at hand, a ready figure of authority, even prestige. Together, they testify to assumptions concerning the prologue's perceived core of authority and privilege. Yet the attempts to secure an appropriate prologue say something about the pressures of various media upon the modern theatre. In their divergence, in fact, modern productions reveal the near obsolescence of the theatrical tradition studied in this book. For even though (as we have seen in Branagh's film of *Henry V*) certain vestiges of this conventional prologue survive in various modern productions, on the whole the tradition of the dramatic prologue exists mainly in textual traces. These traces form the basis of our subsequent chapters and provide the stimulus for attending to a number of questions important for the history of the Elizabethan theatre and Shakespeare's position in it – questions that, in the past, have not received the attention they deserve.

Which aims did the early modern dramatic prologue pursue? What tasks did it seek to accomplish? Such prologues were of course more than packaging, and more than advertisement. They did more than provide utilitarian information about the performance to follow. As this study will show, it was in the dramatic prologue that playwrights felt called upon – even, perhaps, pressured – to address a host of issues. Owing to the new, largely experimental quality of work in the Elizabethan theatre, some of these issues seem to have been open questions to the prologues themselves: What are verbal artifacts delivered to multitudes on bare platforms capable of showing? What interests and responsibilities do humanist-trained writers, plebeian actors, and mixed audiences share? On what grounds and in which areas would differences and divisions prevail? How to accommodate royalty, the 'worthiness' of those above, on this 'unworthy' stage?

The show of fiction and illusion, its role in the delivery of what was held to be truthful, was further to be explored. But then the question was: How to begin to mediate the deep gap between the imaginary world in the play and the physically present world of actors and spectators? How, in particular, to cope with what is socially, culturally, conventionally different between the two worlds? How is the authority, desperately needed to accomplish this task, to be defined, displayed, and negotiated? These are only a few of the concerns that at times motivated the composition of dramatic prologues. It is in answer to such questions that fresh insight into the early modern theatre may be sought.

2 Prologue as threshold and usher

Early modern writers drew on a host of ready associations to describe theatrical prologues. A noteworthy analogy for what prologues did, and were asked to do, arose with the office of the 'usher' – or 'huisher', as it was variously spelled.[1] Ben Jonson's *Entertainment at Althrope* (1603), for example, sees the figure of 'No-body' come forward to declare 'We are the Huisher to a Morris'.[2] In William Lower's *The Phoenix in Her Flames* (1622–39), Amandus also draws upon the connection to describe 'affection . . . / . . . which serves as a prologue / To usher in our welcome'.[3] In Jasper Mayne's *The City Match* (1637), Warehouse promises Dorcas that 'you shall have your Usher, Dame, to stalk / Before you like a buskined Prologue, in / A stately, high, majestic motion, bare'.[4] Perhaps most tellingly for our purposes here, however, Nathan Field's contribution to *Four Plays, or Moral Representations, in One* (1613) sees Don Frigozo turn to the audience at the end of a conversational Induction to deliver a formal speech beginning: 'Prologues are Huishers bare before the wise; / Why may not then an Huisher Prologize?'[5] With its obvious neologism, 'prologize', the rhetorical question here marks a change in the character's perceived role. Significantly, Frigozo has earlier complained about his responsibilities as a courtier, self-importantly remarking, upon his blustery entrance to the stage, that 'A man in Authority is but as a candle in the wind, sooner wasted or blown out than under a bushel'. By having Frigozo declare, lament, then cede authority – a sequence that has a 'man in Authority' quickly becoming an 'Usher' in the playhouse – the Induction and prologue to *Four Plays, or Moral Representations, in One* explicitly stage the divisions within authority that productively complicated the early modern dramatic prologue.

Field's conceit takes the prologue to be an usher. That his text's conjunction of these two roles ('Prologues are Huishers') was more than happenstance can be seen in the overlap between them in various private theatrical venues of early modern England. E. K. Chambers reminds us, for instance, that the banqueting-house where court masks were performed was 'under the supervision of the Lord Chamberlain and the officers of the Chamber, headed by the Gentleman Usher'. Chambers describes some of their duties as follows: 'They seated the audience, kept the doors against the turbulent crowds knocking for admission, cleared the dancing-place when the King was seated, and supplied the principal guests with programmes or abstracts of the device prepared by the poet'.[6] When we recall the expository function that some prologues assumed – providing information, that is, about the plot, setting, characters, or genre of a play – the Gentleman Usher's supplying guests with 'programmes or abstracts' of the masking entertainment would seem to make the conjunction of these roles a natural one, the pairing of prologues with ushers more of an identification than an analogy.

Of course, in early modern England there were various types of ushers, and the term was defined in various ways. Thomas Thomas's Latin–English dictionary of 1587 recognizes one version of this role, for instance, when it speaks of an 'usher or treader that goeth before his master or mistress'.[7] Similarly, Randle Cotgrave's dictionary of 1611 notes that 'an Usher, or Cryer is also, in some Courts, termed *Audiencier*, but with the addition of Huissier'.[8] At the elite end of this scale we find the gentlemen usher, a figure that oversaw noble households and was 'probably the most active man in the entire household personnel'.[9] The term 'usher', then, could describe figures as various as those from the ranks of simple household servants who answered the door and those who managed large, aristocratic households. Yet whether acting as porters, treaders, criers, or overseeing servants, ushers in early modern England clearly shared something at their core: the role of the 'go-between'. Positioned between, on one hand, his master or mistress, and, on the other, a visitor seeking access to a domicile (or, conversely, another person whose attention was sought by the usher's master or mistress), the usher – occupying a liminal position betwixt and between – was responsible for inspecting, evaluating, introducing – in a word, for *mediating* – separate parties.

In an essay titled 'The Go-between', Stephen Greenblatt describes the figure of the go-between as an 'interpreter' and 'translator', one who 'passes from one representational form to another, who mediates between systems, who inhabits the inbetween'.[10] As we will see, this sense of the 'inbetween' would be as central to the theatrical prologue as to the early modern usher. Both roles involve extensive mediation, interpretation, and even translation. Both roles involve a paradoxical relationship to power: the usher and prologue found themselves vested with a kind of authority, yet an authority that (as we have already noted in the case of the theatrical prologue) was neither permanent nor simply given. Going, quite literally, *between* parties, ushers and prologues inhabited an 'inbetween' place. As we will maintain, the place of the prologue in the early modern theatre was not just between: in its very 'betweenness', in its liminality, it was distinct, and implicated through this distinction in differences of authority and representation.

Like Frigozo's 'candle in the wind', prologues tended to perform such differences even as they were affected by them. To the extent that ushers were asked to serve as mediating figures, for instance, sometimes this mediation involved gestures of subservience to acknowledge differences in status or power. It is precisely such formal decorum that Frigozo describes when he refers to ushers making themselves 'bare before the wise' – that is, deferentially removing their caps in a gesture often noticed in descriptions of the theatrical prologue. That such subservience could strike observers as involving obsequious rituals of humiliation becomes clear in Jonson's *Sejanus* (1603) when Arruntius criticizes those who declaim, 'like servile huishers, make / Way for my lord! proclaim his idol lord-ship, / More than ten criers, or six noise of trumpets!' (5.450–2). Like 'criers', 'trumpets', and theatrical prologues (who, as we observed in the last chapter, typically followed three 'noise of trumpets'), ushers introduced and strove for attention. In doing so, of course, they variously put forward, for approval and acceptance, an awareness of, even acquaintance with, the parties introduced; they tended to characterize any existing relationship between those parties; and suggested a potential relationship or relationships. As Field's conceit suggests, all these actions closely coincide with the office of the prologue.

Yet at the same time that the prologue can be seen as exercising the formal deference that traditionally accompanied the tendered *captatio benevolentiae*, it functioned within a habitus that – from costume to properties to vocabulary – could suggest a strong connection to authority and power. Participating in a theatrical tradition that had seen prolocutors, messengers, and other servant characters speak before and in the interests of power, the early modern prologue could be – and often was – alternately deferential and commanding. For instance, given the task of quieting the assembled audience (a potentially imperious role) even as he needed to gain that audience's good will (a role largely deferential in nature), the prologue was asked, in the words of *Henry V*'s churchman, to 'work contrariously' (1.2.206).

Indeed, if the 'prologue as usher'-conceit touches on issues as central to early modern prologues themselves as to our understanding of those prologues and the social and theatrical relations they routinely addressed, it also poses a significant and puzzling question. We could phrase this query as follows: To the extent that a prologue is an usher, who is being ushered before whom? Does the prologue, that is, 'serve' the audience?

The acting company? The playwright or playwrights? Dramatic tradition? The 'theatre', conceived generally? Precisely where do authority and power lie, in relationship to the prologue? If we take the prologue-usher as a kind of porter figure (among the many aspects of the prologue's role that we could consider), just who is the authority figure of the 'house' and in which ways and directions is this figure being served by the prologue? Is the authority figure (or figures) best understood as, on one hand, supportive of or in deference to the actors, playwright(s), and other theatrical workers, or, on the other, as serving or enhancing the position of the audience members themselves, from 'lord' to 'lown'?[11] From the prologue's point of view: Whose position is the more commanding in the playhouse? Who is the presiding master or mistress? Whose interests, we could ask, are negotiated, whose cultural and economic profits are advanced or at stake? If, finally, the authority in question is − like a 'candle in the wind' − indistinct, divided, or inconsistent, what are we to make of such variation?

We put these questions so bluntly in part because they touch on the complexity that characterized the relations of power and authority in the theatrical prologues of early modern drama (and on the ways, of course, in which prologues themselves represented these relations) and in part because they ask us to consider a recent, and alternate account of the prologue's role. In *The Acoustic World of Early Modern England* Bruce Smith turns to the theatrical prologue as part of his attempt to recapture the 'soundscape' of the early modern playhouse and its social environment. Smith's 'historical phenomenology of listening' takes up the ways in which early modern subjects (and, especially, playgoers) might have listened to and heard their surroundings, and the ways in which elements of that 'soundscape' can be discerned in various details of early modern playtexts.[12] Smith identifies the Elizabethan prologue with the long line of prolocutor figures in medieval and late-medieval drama, pointing out that the latter 'define an auditory circle that encompasses both actors and audience' and by doing so 'extend' an 'auditory dominion' that was sometimes charged with political symbolism: 'Standing or seated within the same acoustic circle as the speaker/king, the audience become his political subjects as well as his auditory subjects'.[13]

In what remains the most extensive critical imagining of the theatrical 'scene' of the performed prologue, Smith represents the performance as a powerful exercise in what he calls 'auditory dominion':

[W]e can 'see' the acoustic field by imagining the Prologue standing at the front edge of the stage, near the geometric centre of The Globe. As he projects his voice in all directions, he defines a circle. Beyond the reach of his voice stretches a horizon of silence. Along with the speaker, the auditors stand well within the circle defined by that horizon. Actor and audience share the same field of sound. If the actor stands at the centre of that shared acoustic space, each individual auditor stands nonetheless at the centre of his or her own field of hearing – a field that includes the actor's voice but is not limited to it. The radius of sounds each auditor can hear is defined by its own encircling horizon of silence. For the space of the play, each individual auditor's radius of hearing is narrowed. As each of the 'gentles all' focuses his or her attention on the speakers onstage, sounds outside the acoustic field of the play become, quite literally, peripheral. The result is, or can be, a totalizing experience of sound that surrounds each hearer completely, penetrating his or her body through the ears, immersing him or her in the playful patterning of speech. When a listener heeds the Prologue's commands, the play fills that listener's entire auditory field . . . [T]he playgoer willingly makes herself subject to the spoken word's gestalt of force.[14]

The imaginative portrait Smith paints here reflects the importance we have ascribed to the theatrical prologue. Like the present study, Smith sees the prologue as standing in a liminal area near the edge of the stage and sharing 'acoustic space' with the gathered assembly of playgoers. Like the present study too, Smith sees the prologue as coming at a crucial moment in the theatrical performance, and assuming a central role in the inauguration of that performance.

But in privileging the sonic and aural dimensions of the performed prologue – what one could call the 'how' of its saying – Smith leaves open the 'what' of early modern prologues' functioning. That is, his extensive portrait does not address prologues' frequent, and sometimes profound imaginings of the interrelations of audiences, actors, playwrights, playworlds, and the extra-theatrical world itself. Part of the difficulty resides in Smith's concentration on the sonic dimension of the prologue. For Smith, the spoken word has a 'gestalt of force;' but what force it has does not inform, or find itself realized in, a range of meanings, descriptions, or propositions. As though fully in possession of that irresistible magniloquence that Marlowe's tragedic figures routinely seek, Smith's prologue dominates rather this side of a full spectrum of functions. And although, after acknowledging that 'plays are staged conversations', Smith goes on to admit that 'The effect of introducing a second speaker, then a third, then a fourth, then a fifth is to *decenter* the aural field, to set up a competition for mastery over that field – and hence over the listeners' subjectivity', his characterization of that very subjectivity takes it to be a passive or responsive thing, easily gained through and controlled by sensory stimulation.[15]

Smith's Prospero-like prologue broadcasts sound that 'penetrate[es]' and 'immers[es]' the audience, seemingly without their consent. Thus where he describes *Titus Andronicus* (1593) as a 'competition among voices for dominance of the auditory field', in his discussion of the early modern theatrical soliloquy Smith reverts to the language of what is quite literally univocal power: 'In soliloquies . . . [the voice] can be heard by the audience in the same way they might hear music, as a totalizing volume of sound that shuts out all other sounds and fills the listener's very body'.[16] Smith seems to 'hear' the early modern prologue the way one could hear an electronically amplified loudspeaker at a twenty-first century concert – a picture scarcely consistent with the 'unperfect actor' (the phrase is Shakespeare's, from Sonnet 23. 1) or even the 'without-book prologue, faintly spoke / After the prompter' (*Romeo* 1.4.7–8) that Dekker describes more explicitly in his reference to a 'quaking prologue' who 'hath (by rubbing) got cullor into his cheeks'.[17]

The theatrical implications of such an 'unperfect actor' have recently drawn the attention of David Schalkwyk in his study of performative language in Shakespeare's sonnets and plays. Schalkwyk reads sonnet 23 alongside Spenser's sonnet 54 from the *Amoretti*, noting that each poem employs, as an analogy to the situation of 'Petrarchan suitor and beloved', the 'unequal power relations' of the playhouse. This was an environment in which – according to Shakespeare's lyric – 'both the silence of the spectator and [the actor's] own dumb-struck stage-fright are marks of his exposure and vulnerability'.[18] Thus if, in the rhythm of their language and delivery, prologues could attain musical status, we have seen that they also had a dimension not only less than dominating, but in fact extremely tentative – tentative because actorly, and performed, with all the vulnerabilities and incapacities (as well as the wonders and strengths) that accrue to theatrical labour. Yet it was precisely through the contingencies of such performance that prologues meaningfully addressed audiences and asked them, as a social body, to consider issues salient both within and without the early modern playhouse.

In the previous chapter, we observed that prologues were given to actors who possessed a kind of liminal status in relation to the company: Richard Alleyn was apparently a hired man; Dick Juby was a young actor who on at least one occasion took both male and female roles; Richard Sharp had taken the very challenging role of the Duchess of Malfi as a boy actor before assuming adult male roles; the same trajectory marked the careers of Theophilus Bird (or Bourne) and Ezekiel Fenn. Taken together, we suggested, these examples indicate a graduation or rite of passage for the actors, a transition marked by their delivery of prologues in the commercial playhouses. As such, the performance of prologues may have constituted a kind of professional threshold for actors, a performance by which their 'in between' status was acknowledged and drawn on. Such a professional threshold correlated to a larger, boundary-crossing action in the theatre itself.

In ushering between stage and audience the prologue inhabited and defined a *threshold*, a liminal space between the actual and the potential that characterized the 'playing holidays' (*1 Henry IV* [1597], 1.2.204) of dramatic fiction in the early modern playhouse. At the outset of dramatic performances, the prologue ushered its early modern audience over an imaginary threshold – a threshold both of and for the imagination as well as one both of and for the specifically dramatic, theatrical uses of the 'wooden O'. This differentiating function of the prologue helped isolate dramatic from non-verbal types of performances. The importance of these performances for our argument becomes clear in Terence Hawkes's *Shakespeare in the Present*, which demonstrates that the dramatically oriented perspective on London's amphitheatrical buildings has traditionally underestimated the presence of various non-verbal practices such as bear-baiting. As Hawkes argues, 'that disturbing conjunction' of baiting and play-acting underlines a 'relationship that not only goes to the savage heart of Shakespeare's work but raises questions about what wrenching it from its intertextual ligaments has done to the notion of "playing" itself'.[19] To play with a ferocious choice between life and death of a creature was one thing; it was an entirely different matter in the same arena to play *as if* the choice were the player's own, as hidden under a fixed persona. To go from one to another was a huge step; in fact, it involved a transition that stipulated a remarkable transformation – in many ways a new psychology and epistemology – in the structure of audience responses. Key to preparing the spectators for the purely imaginative, verbally rendered playworlds of the dramatic fictions within the early modern amphitheatrical arena, however, was the prologue's status as threshold. It was over this threshold that the prologue invited the audience to move, to participate in and reflect upon a set of new, and newly imagined, possible worlds that had at their base the conjunctures of authority characterizing the larger social, cognitive, cartographic, and – politically – international spaces of early modern representation.

Our characterization of the prologue as a liminal space involves associations of the word 'liminal' itself, which derives of course from Latin *limen*, or 'threshold'. In fact we advance these conjoined terms, 'liminal' and 'threshold', in part to discuss several influential theories concerned with liminality and transition. One of these theoretical statements comes in the work of Gérard Genette, particularly in his 1986 study *Seuils* ('Thresholds'), published in English as *Paratexts: Thresholds of Interpretation* in 1997. A kind of gossipy Aristotelian, Genette surveys many hundreds of literary works to

address the importance of what he labels 'paratexts:' 'verbal or other productions, such as an author's name, a title, a preface, [or] illustrations' that
enable 'a text to become a book and to be offered as such to its readers
and, more generally, to the public'.[20] *Paratexts* makes a signal contribution
to our understanding of the role that various parts of texts assume in relation to what could otherwise be thought an undifferentiated whole. The
study's implications for appreciating the prefatory authority of the prologue
seem clear. One of Genette's central themes (clearly evident in the original
title of his book) concerns the liminal status and functioning of paratexts –
of such units as, again, prefaces, footnotes, titles, and publisher's blurbs.
'More than a boundary or sealed border', Genette holds, 'the paratext is,
rather, a *threshold* that works to constitute 'a zone between text and off-text,
a zone not only of transition but of *transaction*: a privileged place of a prag-
matics and a strategy, of an influence on the public, an influence that –
whether well or poorly understood and achieved – is at the service of a
better reception for a text and a more pertinent reading of it (more pertinent, of course, in the eyes of the author and his allies)'.[21]

As the preceding passage may suggest, Genette's description of the paratext is rich in its implications for understanding the complicated workings
of literary texts and their many parts. Perhaps no better introduction exists
to the disparate contributions of such features as prologues, epilogues, and
titles when considered part of a printed work. Yet for all our admiration of
Genette's theory, we believe it remains limited for our purposes in its
acceptance of modern literary authority as a norm. For Genette, that is,
'the' text is most often a novel, and most often the product of a highly self-
conscious *deus alter*. If Genette's audience is public, the text this author
produces is for a *reading* public. Genette comes closest to our interest in the
dramatic prologue in his section on the 'public epitext' – that is, 'any paratextual element not materially appended to the text within the same
volume but circulating, as it were, freely, in a virtually limitless physical
and social space'.[22] But even here he displays little interest in acts or
instances of prefatory discourse that transpire outside the firm control of a
responsible author: 'I will not dwell on the publisher's epitext: its basically
marketing and "promotional" function does not always involve the responsibility of the author in a very meaningful way; most often he is satisfied
just to close his eyes officially to the value-inflating hyperbole inseparable
from the needs of the trade'.[23] And although Genette comes tantalizingly
near to acknowledging a plural literary scene when he describes the 'social
game' of the author's interview (the phrase is ultimately that of Roland
Barthes),[24] *Paratexts* is too wedded to a novelistic model of literary production to account for the complexities of collaboration involved in the early
modern theatre. In this theatre, of course, players combined with play-

wrights and audience members in a shared dramatic performance; the 'public epitext' of the prologues performed there often functioned as not only the place and time where these collaborative relations were addressed, but also the means by which dramatic process of threshold-crossing was facilitated.

Such a threshold-crossing resembled nothing so much as an evocative passage from one place and state to another. For this sense of liminal activity we turn from the textual theories of Genette to accounts of liminality in anthropological theory. Of course, regarding this subject no work has been more foundational than Arnold van Gennep's famous description of the *rites de passage*. Originally published in 1908, van Gennep's *Les Rites de Passage* was translated into English in 1960, and became one of the most influential works of anthropological theory during the 1960s and 1970s. In this study van Gennep argues that all societies have certain rituals connected with important, even crucial changes and events – birth, death, marriage, adoption, initiation, aging, to name just a few. These changes and events, in van Gennep's view, are typically marked by a three-part process involving separation, transition, and reincorporation. Van Gennep glosses these stages as follows: 'I propose to call the rites of separation from a previous world, *preliminal rites*, those executed during the transitional stage *liminal* (*or threshold*) rites, and the ceremonies of incorporation into the new world *postliminal rites*'.[25]

The threshold remains central to van Gennep's account of the rites of passage. He employs it to describe what separates the neutral ('a previous world') from the sacred ('the new world'). Those who pass from one zone to the other waver 'between two worlds' in a 'symbolic and spatial area of transition'.[26] In the secular world of early modern dramatic performances, the prologue serves in its own way as a separating or differentiating function. As against nonverbal practice, the prologue both inhabits and helps reduce this 'area of transition' to the incipient operation of the newly symbolic code of dramatic fiction. Expanding van Gennep's anthropological insights in an important essay titled 'Variations on a Theme of Liminality', Victor Turner – one of van Gennep's most influential interpreters – repeats this key image and concept in noting that 'A *limen* is a threshold . . . a corridor almost, or a tunnel'.[27] Turner's conclusions in this essay also support our characterization of the prologue's paradoxical status. For instance, our description of the prologue as a kind of 'go between' itself inhabiting an 'inbetween' space finds confirmation in Turner's declaration that the transitional (or, in his phrase, 'midliminal') state is often marked by the paradoxical: 'the most characteristic midliminal symbolism is that of paradox, or being *both* this *and* that'.[28]

The concept of liminality, and the 'rites of passage' from which it is drawn, have been employed to meaningful effect in criticism concerned with early modern drama. Many of the critics who have used van Gennep testify, in their criticism, to the study's deep influence upon a generation of scholars who entered the profession since the book's translation into English in 1960. One thinks, for instance, of Marjorie Garber's *Coming of Age in Shakespeare* (1981), Edward Berry's *Shakespeare's Comic Rites* (1984), and Brian Vickers's 'Rites of Passage in Shakespeare's Prose' (1986), all of which deploy van Gennep's account of the rites of passage to cast light on elements of Shakespeare's plays.[29] Garber's study is largely representative here in its use of van Gennep's three-part process – of separation, transition, and reincorporation – to explain how 'Through their repetitions of motif, incident and phrase, the plays offer us a cumulative portrait of what it means to be a successful adult in a Shakespearean world – and, just possibly, in our own'.[30] Blending van Gennep's theory with an anthropological interest shaped (as her title indicates) by Margaret Meade's *Coming of Age in Samoa* (1928), Garber explores the manner in which rites of passage – and, in particular, the act of 'crossing the threshold' – become, for Shakespeare, a way of showing 'the individual's ability to grow and change'.[31] Garber is by no means alone in this emphasis on individual rites of passage, as most of the critics who have taken up this concept have focused on specific characters and their passage through playworld rites.[32]

It is here that we encounter an apparent element of incongruity between critical uses of the rites of passage and the ushering, threshold-role we are suggesting for the theatrical prologue. For if rites of passages are essentially applied to a reading of individuals or individual characters, how can we explain the group dynamics that we have posited for the prologue's performance and rhetoric in the early modern playhouse? Perhaps the best way of addressing this question is to consider whether its initial assumption is valid. Are rites of passage indeed so individual in nature and import? Garber's study would seem to suggest that they are: for instance, even when examining the complicated interrelation of the 'twin' couples in, respectively, *The Comedy of Errors* (1592) and *Twelfth Night* (1601), she stresses the ways in which pressures of 'individuation' and 'self-knowledge' move each character, in these comedies' rites of passage, 'from the confused and mingled identity of twinship, which thwarts fertile pairing, toward productive courtship and marriage'.[33]

In response to critical emphases on individualized rites of passage, we should note that van Gennep's own study was by no means so exclusive concerning the threshold or rites of passage. In his book's third chapter, 'Individuals and Groups', for instance, he declares that 'The operation of rites is the same for groups as for individuals', and later states clearly that 'For groups, as well as for individuals, life itself means to separate and to be reunited, to change form and condition, to die and to be reborn. It is to act and to cease, to wait and rest, and then to begin acting again, but in a different way. And there are always new thresholds to cross: the thresholds of summer and winter, of a season or a year, of a month or a night . . .'.[34] Likewise in his 1982 study, *From Ritual to Theatre: The Human Seriousness of Play*, Victor Turner sees a decidedly social extension to the theory: '[W]hen persons, groups, sets of ideas, etc., move from one level or style of organization or regulation of the interdependence of their parts or elements to another level, there has to be an interfacial region or, to change the metaphor, an interval, however brief, of *margin* or *limen*, when the past is momentarily negated, suspended, or abrogated, and the future has not yet begun, an instant of pure potentiality when everything, as it were, trembles in the balance'.[35] And while Stephen Greenblatt echoes rites-criticism in Shakespearean scholarship generally in claiming that 'A rite of passage is something that happens to an individual – and as such, is a particularly intense personal experience', he goes on to acknowledge that 'it is at the same time social and in most cases institutional. A private rite of passage is like an unattended wedding: it can mime the form of the ritual, but it misses the mark. The significance of the transition derives from collective understandings that accumulate around the performed acts'.[36]

The invocation here of 'collective understandings' will help us to describe the manner in which early modern audiences participated in and responded to the advent of verbally sustained dramatic performances in the sixteenth-century public playhouses. Rather than the threshold being crossed simply by the prologue as an individual actor, the standard, thoroughly embracing plurals of the prologue's speech – for instance, '*your* thoughts . . . must deck *our* kings' (*Henry V* [1599] Pro. 28) – speak, on behalf of a community of actors, to a community of imaginers on equal footing with one another, and with the actors, a community necessary to the success of the impending representation. As M. C. Bradbrook described this community, 'Spectators of a play, who participate in its collective action, together with the actors, go through a curve of experience traced for them by the author . . . . To become absorbed in such an experience collectively is a natural strengthening of personal security; it affirms their *existenz* to each of the participants, at the same time that it offers them a common cohesion'.[37] What Bradbrook calls the 'curve of experience' here is described to similar effect in M. M. Mahood's examination of Shakespeare's 'transposers', which speaks to this togetherness of the theatrical community by analogizing the experience of a performance to an airplane flight. Mahood intriguingly describes prologues and epilogues as the 'Take-off and landing' that constitute 'critical moments in the flight of the imagination by which a playwright transposes a story to the stage'.[38] Seeing the audience as thus conjoined in a larger community with the players need not imply, of course, that we should consider them (or, for that matter, any ritual participants or observers) either uniform or pliant. Nor do we wish to downplay the differences between and among the public and private play-houses, their reportorial systems, and performance habits. The question here is one that Anthony Dawson and Paul Yachnin usefully debate in their lively collaboration, *The Culture of Playgoing in Shakespeare's England*.[30] In this balanced exchange of models and arguments, Yachnin holds that the marketplace (in particular, the market for 'populuxe' goods) offers the best analogy for playgoing in London during the early modern era; in contrast, Dawson sees the participatory dynamic of religious observance and cere-mony as the social function most resembling the experience of attending plays.

We would suggest that a truth may lie somewhere in the middle of these positions; one can see in various dramatic prologues, that is, a process that owes greatly (and sometimes alternately) to participation and selection. To illustrate these aspects, let us look at what may well serve as a *locus classicus* for the perceived differences among the various playhouses, their clientele and favourite subject matter. Characteristically, in *Turners dish of Lenten stuff* (1612), we encounter a virtual catalogue of playgoing types and topics:

> That's the fat fool of the Curtain,
> and the lean fool of the Bull:
> Since *Shank* did leave to sing his rhymes,
> he is counted but a gull.
> The players of the Bank side
> The round Globe and the Swan,
> Will teach you idle tricks of love,
> But the Bull will play the man.[40]

Such differences – more than stylistic, surely, unless we take 'style' to include such aspects of social life as ideology and politics – may well have had an effect upon the various ways liminality was experienced. Taken in the context of the individualistic dynamic we have seen attached to rites of passage theory by several recent critics, the divergences among repertories and audience members declared by *Turners dish of Lenten stuff* would seem to posit a narrowly-drawn, if not isolated, set of theatrical experiences and playgoers in early modern England. Did prologues, then, speak mainly to and about the typical individuals we hear mentioned – 'the fat fool of the Curtain, / and the lean fool of the Bull'?

Playgoing was of course by no means a monadic experience. We would suggest that what one encounters in this passage from *Turners dish* is less a claim about absolute differences among the various playhouses, repertories, and audiences, and more an implicit celebration of generic diversity within a well-known and predictable theatrical environment. Whether a 'fat' or a 'lean' fool, the audience member is here described as having a choice (however 'foolishly' applied) of repertorial styles and even content in four playhouses that can be freely visited – even as they can be contrasted in this description – *precisely because they are so similar and dependable.* Turner is able to collocate these various playhouses, in fact, precisely because his readers could recognize their family resemblance. However diverse, even dissimilar, playgoers and playhouses seem from such an account, we know from various sources that the fluidity of the entertainment industry, the frequently emulative reportorial system, and even theatre architecture itself led to deep continuities in not only theatrical fashion and generic preferences, but also the overall experience of playgoing.[41] The commonalities of the prologue's performance that we explored in the preceding chapter – commonalities of costume, rhetoric, and stage praxis – testify in themselves to such continuity among repertories. If not a uniform set of experiences, then at least an open unity of shared assumptions and feelings relating to attendance at plays must have underwritten the average playgoer's relationship to and understanding of playgoing. At the same time, one must consider not only the potential for diversity in this experience, but the possibility that – owing in part to the waning hold of London's 'duopoly' companies – such diversity increased over time.[42] Nor can we subscribe to what earlier scholars concerned with Shakespeare's audience considered to be a 'unity of taste'.[43] Even while emphasizing a groundswell of responses informed by a socially shared sense of 'separation', 'transition', and – particularly, perhaps – 'incorporation', then, we need to be aware of a considerable range of discrepancy between social and individual acts of reception.

With this in mind, Michael Bristol's emphasis on the 'intensification of collective life represented and experienced in the theatre'[44] can lead us to a complex understanding of early modern playgoing. Such an understanding would allow for potentially marked differentiations *within* the collectivity ushered across the threshold of the dramatic representation by the prologue figure and his performance. Here, the crucial question is what role prologues could have played in relationship to such a collectivity. We can start to answer this question by referring to Louis Montrose's *The Purpose of Playing*, which explores the depth of Shakespeare's interest in 'points of transition in the life cycle – birth, puberty, marriage, death (and, by extension, inheritance and succession) – where discontinuities arise and where adjustments are necessary to basic interrelationships in the family, the household, and the society at large'.[45] Going beyond the traditional range of criticism concerned with rites of passage in Shakespeare's plays,

Montrose suggests an anthropological extension that has clear relevance for the argument at hand:

> The theatrical analogy to transition rites is not limited to the fictional space–time within the play. The actual process of theatrical performance, marked off in both time and space from the normal flow and loci of social activity, offered to its audience – and, of course, to its performers – an imaginative experience that partially and temporarily removed them from their normal places, their ascribed subject positions. In this sense, for the Queen's common subjects, to go to the public playhouse to see a play was to undergo a marginal experience; it was to visit the interstices of the Elizabethan social and cognitive order.[46]

Montrose here connects the theatrical equivalent of 'transition rites' with an experiential order of representation. The 'place' of the latter was an imaginative one, 'partially and temporarily removed' from the social and political positions that audience members typically inhabited.

By invoking the concept of marginality, Montrose touches on what Steven Mullaney has described as 'the place of the stage' in a study of that title.[47] Mullaney argues, in short, that the political marginality of London's liberties – where many of the commercial playhouses were situated – fostered a theatrical tradition that was itself dedicated to marginality, and to the subversion of that social and political orthodoxy against which the license of the liberties was defined. The point that we wish to make is that both the experiential order of representation and geographical–political marginality were deeply assimilated and yet partially intercepted in many Elizabethan prologues. For them to cope with liminality, with a passage not only between different locations but among various orders of discourse, epistemology, and experience was a formidable task. Yet it was one informed and sustained by an institutionalized place within its own 'threshold' or 'limbo' area relative to the centres of London's commercial and political power. Prologues were vitally keyed to the needs of that larger passage. By facilitating the transition from everyday world to playworld, from ordinary perception to imaginary reception, they reconstituted their own liminality in terms of textual and performative strategies. They thus helped conduct theatre-goers over the threshold of a fictional world that allowed new perspectives on a host of issues relating to these centres of power and their affect on playgoers' lives.

Playgoers indeed had a larger ensemble of activities and experiences in common than the enumeration of their differences would indicate. These commonalities sprang from the physical and intellectual commitments that playgoing demanded. Having heard of a production by word of mouth, or seeing it advertised by an ephemeral playbill, for instance, a playgoer would have to factor in time and means for getting to the playhouse, as going to plays invariably involved a journey of some kind, whether by foot, boat, or other conveyance, or a combination of these. The long trip to the Red Lion outside Stepney – a playhouse erected in 1567 – was shortened, of course, for playgoers who walked to The Theatre after its construction in 1576. And during the 1580s and 1590s the building and opening of playhouses closer in to London made such journeys shorter still. Yet, as *The Alchemist* (1610) reminds us, even going to a play in (and about) one's own parish would entail a trip of some kind. Sometimes this meant a significant crossing of natural boundaries, such as the Thames, which could be traversed via a waterman's boat or by walking across London Bridge. The significance of such a crossing – a physical threshold to be crossed before encountering, and traversing, thresholds within the playhouse – would be pressed home as the playgoer was charged for the crossing, whether by water or by bridge.

Once at a playhouse itself, another kind of crossing had occurred, and was made apparent to the playgoer when he or she paid for entry at the door, and then again, sometimes, for admittance to select areas within the playhouse itself. In the previous chapter, we noted how prologues were typically asked to quiet and gain the attention of a noisy audience, an audience that already possessed a group identity via its participation in and experience of the clamour and 'hurly-burly' generated by many hundreds – sometimes thousands – of fellow playgoers. Three soundings of a trumpet would usually announce the impending beginning of a play, and when a prologue figure strode front and centre the audience's transition through the most central of what was in fact a series of transitional moments began to take place. Deliberately leaving their working-day lives through a physical journey that ended in the presence of the stage, these playgoers were ushered, by the prologue, into what Montrose calls an 'imaginative experience' that engaged 'the interstices of the Elizabethan social and cognitive order'. What began as a physical trip whose stages registered upon the mind of the playgoers found transformation, through the ushering agency of a prologue, into a mental journey whose visible, audible directions were nonetheless registered upon the senses of the participating playgoer.

So far we have in fairly general terms discussed the material and imaginative process of ushering associated with the early modern prologue – a process that very nearly consummated a secular rite of passage for, presumably, most Elizabethan spectators. In the space that remains we will examine the prologue's ushering function more specifically in relation to two plays – *A Midsummer Night's Dream* (1596) and *2 Henry IV* (1598) – each apparently written within a two-year span, and each possessing its own

version of the prologue figure. We will begin with the prologue or prologues internal to *A Midsummer Night's Dream* – that is, with the two-part
speech that Peter Quince makes before the courtly audience of Athenian
aristocrats in the fifth act of the comedy.

Quince's prologue to the Mechanicals' play of *Pyramus and Thisby* is
known more for the comic trick of its mispunctuation than anything else.
We reproduce it here with the punctuation that Quince follows when he
addresses the onstage audience:

> If we offend, it is with our good will.
> That you should think, we come not to offend,
> But with good will. To show our simple skill,   110
> That is the true beginning of our end.
> Consider then, we come but in despite.
> We do not come, as minding to content you,
> Our true intent is. All for your delight
> We are not here. That you should here repent you,   115
> The actors are at hand; and, by their show,
> You shall know all, that you are like to know.
>
> (5.1.108–17)

Although the play titles itself a 'Dream', and although it begins with Hippolyta reassuring her anxious fiancé that 'Four nights will quickly dream
away the time; / And then the moon, like to a silver bow / New bent in
heaven, shall behold the night / Of our solemnities' (1.1.8–11), nothing,
perhaps, could seem less dream-like, less prone to inducing the easy slip-
ping of the critical imagination into a drowsy forbearance than Quince's
mispointed prologue. Instead of sleep, the listener is required to be at full
attention, asked to keep not one prologue but two in mind, the figure and
its disfigurement (to use the play's own phrase) – with the former prologue
sounding (or looking) something like the following:

> If we offend, it is with our good will
> That you should think we come, not to offend,
> But with good will to show our simple skill:
> That is the true beginning of our end.
> Consider then, we come (but in despite
> We do not come) as minding to content you;
> Our true intent is all for your delight:
> We are not here that you should here repent you.
> The actors are at hand; and, by their show,
> You shall know all that you are like to know.

With a half-dozen or so infelicitous changes to the punctuation of the immediately preceding lines, Quince manages to make his speech, in the words of Theseus, 'like a tangled chain; nothing impair'd, but all disor-der'd' (5.1.125–6). Most likely recalling a similarly mispunctuated letter in *Ralph Roister Doister* (1552), Shakespeare, in self-projecting the prologue's reception, expects his spectators not to dream but, as it were, to copy-edit a speech – or, one could say, to disfigure the disfiguration. Hearing the pro-logue demands attentiveness rather than drowsiness. In what way, then, could this prologue be said to function as an usher for the audience as well as for the (staged) audience within the play? And what could be meant, even, by 'audience' here? That is, even if we define audience broadly, as neither *only* onstage characters nor paying spectators in the larger theatre, but rather as a combination of all those attending to *Pyramus and Thisby*, what threshold is crossed – even in terms of a metatheatrical representa-tion, a portrayal of a rite-of-passage in miniature – within *A Midsummer Night's Dream*? And what role does Quince have in the passage?

In presenting a mispunctuated speech that causes a kind of cognitive friction in the audience (onstage as well as off), Quince effectively licenses those listeners to place themselves in a position of superiority that Theseus and Oberon have been scripting throughout the play. Part critic and aristo-cratic humanist, Theseus has already delineated the power of the poet in his famous speech on the imagination:

> The poet's eye, in a fine frenzy rolling,
> Doth glance from heaven to earth, from earth to heaven;
> And as imagination bodies forth
> The forms of things unknown, the poet's pen
> Turns them to shapes, and gives to aery nothing
> A local habitation and a name.
>
> (5.1.12–17)

The whole of Act 5 preceding Quince's prologue can be said, in fact, to establish imaginative writing generally, and the hearing of plays in particu-lar, as an active and important form of cultural practice. The rehearsal of four titles for possible performance to 'wear away this long age of three hours' (33–4) before the aristocrats go to bed leads, of course, to Theseus's seemingly perverse insistence on hearing *Pyramus and Thisby*. As Theseus claims, 'never any thing can be amiss, / When simpleness and duty tender it' (82–3).

Hippolyta, significantly, employs this very analytical strategy when she observes that something about the lovers' fantastic stories 'More witnesseth than fancy's images, / And grows to something of great constancy' (25–6).

Her willingness to credit '*something*' where Theseus sees 'aery *nothing*' is important, if in part because it is precisely the critical process that Theseus will claim as his own in the momentary disagreement that erupts over *Pyramus and Thisby*. Philostrate tells Theseus pointedly 'No, my noble lord, / It is not for you. I have heard it over, / And it is nothing, nothing in the world; / Unless you can find sport in their intents, / Extremely stretch'd, and conn'd with cruel pain, / To do you service' (76–81). After Theseus insists on the play in question, Hippolyta states that 'I love not to see wretchedness o'ercharged, / And duty in his service perishing' (85–6). And to her subsequent insistence that '[Philostrate] says they can do nothing in this kind', Theseus responds with what can be read as mid-1590s defence of a form – the theatrical prologue – that every year seemed increasingly antique. This speech begins as follows:

> The kinder we, to give them thanks for nothing.
> Our sport shall be to take what they mistake;
> And what poor duty cannot do, noble respect
> Takes it in might, not merit.

> (5.1.89–92)

One could pause here to note that the challenge for the audience (onstage and off) to *figure* what the comedy in performative practice *dis*figures is viewed and authorized as 'sport', as part of the cultural practice in a theatre where literary and non-literary modes of communication mingle-mangle in a new fashion. The two types of audience (offstage and onstage) are expected to respond *with a difference*. It is fascinating as well as satisfying that the onstage courtly audience in their response is designed to be less sensitive, less creative, more limited. It is the offstage audience, in contrast, that is expected fully to enjoy and comically to 'take' the illiteracy in 'mistaken' punctuation. They are expected to see through the metaparody, to disfigure the disfigurement.

It is worth noticing that Theseus continues the distinction between hearing and seeing that had characterized his and Hippolyta's debate over desirable theatre. Where both Philostrate (68) and Hippolyta (85) have used the visual to describe playgoing, Theseus has twice used the aural ('we will hear it' [76]; 'I will hear that play' [81]), and will go on to collect the two apprehensive modes in a trope of reading sounds: 'I read as much as from the rattling tongue / Of saucy and audacious eloquence' (102–3). This paradox would seem less puzzling, of course, to an audience accustomed to discussion of *ekphrasis*. But the claim remains striking nonetheless in relation to the preceding divisions posited between sight and sound; these divisions are articulated within the meta-discourse of Theseus's speech on the imagination (where the madman 'sees', the lover 'Sees', and the poet 'Doth glance' [9–13]), and, as we have seen, within the debates on likely plays for performance at the nuptial banquet.

If the great majority of the dialogue and action preceding Quince's prologue can be read as a meta-discursive exploration of theatricality, representation, and the sensuous apprehension and comprehension of performance, Theseus's pronouncement on the 'capacity' (105) of an experienced playgoer to 'take' (90, 92) and 'read' (102; there in the past tense) what has been 'premeditated' (94) can itself be read as a kind of commentary on the early modern prologue. Yet his admittedly condescending terms do not mesh with (let alone intercept) the bewildering, inverted language of the prologue. In particular, the claim for 'sport' (90) reaches out to an audience larger than the one drawing their aristocratic pleasure from a benign tolerance of the exercise of 'poor' and 'fearful duty' (91, 101). Thus, the prologue in its 'mistake[n]' form is doubly taken: first by Theseus as benevolent sponsor, and, second, by the actual offstage audience members who are made to respond to both the polite version and the impolite inversion of liminality in a comedy.

Once the differences are acknowledged whereby thresholds offstage and onstage subtly interact, resemblances between them can be explored. Like the onstage observers, those in the offstage, playhouse audience are ushered over a threshold mindful of issues of representation, performance, and the experience of playgoing itself. Theseus's prologue to Quince's prologue can be read as a licence for the audience to practise a hermeneutics not only benevolent but critical as well. The mistakes that Quince makes reinforce this initial assumption of a magisterial role, as does Quince's noticeably archaic diction in the second half of his prologue, which glosses what appears to be a dumb show of *Pyramus and Thisby*'s essential actions.[48] This archaic diction includes (but is by no means limited to) such words as terminal 'certain' (130) and the rustic phrase 'no scorn' (137), the four instances of 'did' used as the emphatic periphrastic auxiliary of the past indicative (141–3), and the comically excessive alliteration of 'with blade, with bloody blameful blade, / He bravely broach'd his boiling bloody breast' (146–7). This is comic, surely, but not necessarily condescending on Shakespeare's part. For however archaic such forms of dramatic language may have seemed to sophisticated playgoers in the 1590s, such an audience would be asked to recognize – with the characteristically mixed feelings that accompany awareness of formerly popular literary styles – a common past, and a current position in a theatrical environment that had evolved from the seemingly naïve theatre of Quince and the Mechanicals.

It is precisely the audience's *involvement* with the amateur agents of this common type of performance practice that leads them to feel not superior to but complicit with the production of *Pyramus and Thisby* that follows. There is, of course, a staggering complexity in the play-within-the-play's confusions between the materiality of the production and two entirely different playworlds. These, together with a mutually intersecting layering of presentation and imaginary representation (that is, of the play's performance, its critique, and fictional audience response), do not allow Elizabethan spectators, either onstage or off, to remain distanced from or superior to the performance. As Weimann has noted in a discussion of how social difference and duplicity inform the staging of disfigurement, 'the full range and tenor of the parody' onstage in *A Midsummer Night's Dream* implicate the questioning of an 'unformulated poetics on either side', that is, the poetics of both onstage spectators and amateur players.[49] Coupled with the complexity of the issues involved is the players' willingness to break the bounds of their dramatic fiction to respond, to the onstage audience, in such a manner as to indicate not only awareness of that audience's own responsiveness but also these players' eager anticipation of just such responses and concerns. More than mere 'shadows' in the theatre (the word is both Theseus's and Puck's [5.1.211, 423]), the Mechanicals speak back to the aristocrats. When Bottom hears Theseus remark that 'The wall methinks, being sensible, should curse again', he replies directly to the Duke: 'No, in truth, sir, he should not. "Deceiving me" is Thisby's cue. She is to enter now, and I am to spy her through the wall. You shall see it will fall pat as I told you. Yonder she comes' (184–7). In this contradiction we see a kind of audacious, and – for the Athenian world we have seen – unprecedented dialogue started. Bottom will later respond in a similar manner to Demetrius; when the latter remarks that 'Wall' remains to bury the dead, Bottom starts up and corrects him: 'No, I assure you, the wall is down that parted their fathers'. He then turns to Theseus and characteristically mixes the senses when asking the ruler 'Will it please you to see the epilogue, or to hear a Bergomask dance between two of our company?' (351–4).

If the offstage audience members have assumed the role of *magister* in relation to the play-within-the-play, they are confronted with the limits of that role's authority when the performers onstage talk back to the initial playworld audience at their production. Where Theseus has hoped for some 'play / To ease the anguish of a torturing hour' and 'beguile / The lazy time . . . with some delight' (5.1.36–7, 39–40), the chosen play, beginning with its prologue, asks for a diligent, attentive awareness rather than the courtly horizon of expectation and consumption that the reasons given for his choice imply. But to achieve this awareness, the audience onstage and off are both made to submit to a challenge which the former (and, no doubt, a considerable section of the latter) fail to meet. The challenge is most acute when both audiences are ushered into the play within the play. At this moment, they are taken across a threshold within the theatre proper. It is a passage prepared for by the rehearsal scenes, to a mingle-mangle order of compact imaginations and threadbare histrionics. No better transition to this order than the 'tangled chain' of Quince's prologue: having 'all disorder'd' the artful decorum of its own socially respectful form, the authority of the convention itself is made to shift. Rather than effectively projecting the traditional act of ushering and welcoming, the prologue sets out comically to disfigure the rules of literary punctuation, even composition. The resulting confusion in the order of 'disorder'd' order bewilders precisely because the 'tangled chain' demands spectators able to disfigure (and enjoy) the disfigurement itself. Such ability is required at the point where the order of representational writing ironically collides with the extemporal thrust of traditionally playing bodies. What Quince's prologue finally does is juggle the differences between humanistic and plebeian modes of cultural authority.

From Quince's prologue we turn now to the prologue or induction to *2 Henry IV*, more familiar for its bold figural conceit than for its specific discussion of theatrical conventions. The conceit in question, of course, is the allegorical figure of Rumour, who is described as entering 'painted full of tongues'. As James Gousseff points out in his study of the early modern prologue, such allegorically conceived and costumed prologues were not uncommon during the era. Shakespeare's Rumour, by no means idiosyncratic in its conception, is nonetheless remarkable for the consistency of its attention to the 'rumour' trope throughout its spoken prologue. We reproduce it in full here:

> Open your ears; for which of you will stop
> The vent of hearing when loud Rumour speaks?
> I, from the orient to the drooping west
> (Making the wind my post-horse), still unfold
> The acts commenced on this ball of earth.   5
> Upon my tongues continual slanders ride,
> The which in every language I pronounce,
> Stuffing the ears of men with false reports.
> I speak of peace, while covert enmity
> Under the smile of safety wounds the world;   10
> And who but Rumour, who but only I,
> Make fearful musters and prepar'd defence,
> Whiles the big year, swoll'n with some other grief,
> Is thought with child by the stern tyrant war,
> And no such matter? Rumour is a pipe   15

Blown by surmises, jealousies, conjectures,
And of so easy and so plain a stop
That the blunt monster with uncounted heads,
The still-discordant wav'ring multitude,
Can play upon it. But what need I thus   20
My well-known body to anatomize
Among my household? Why is Rumour here?
I run before King Harry's victory,
Who in a bloody field by Shrewsbury
Hath beaten down young Hotspur and his troops,   25
Quenching the flame of bold rebellion
Even with the rebels' blood. But what mean I
To speak so true at first? My office is
To noise abroad that Harry Monmouth fell
Under the wrath of noble Hotspur's sword,   30
And that the King before the Douglas' rage
Stoop'd his anointed head as low as death.
This have I rumour'd through the peasant towns
Between that royal field of Shrewsbury
And this worm-eaten hold of ragged stone,   35
Where Hotspur's father, old Northumberland,
Lies crafty-sick. The posts come tiring on,
And not a man of them brings other news
Than they have learnt of me. From Rumour's tongues
They bring smooth comforts false, worse than true wrongs. 40

It will prove helpful to a reading of this prologue to describe its various sections. Beginning with a three-word, heraldic command ('Open your ears',
l. 1), the prologue Rumour engages in a characterization of the audience
that is simultaneously moral, aesthetic, and social (2–3) then offers 15 lines
of self-characterization (3–17) before adding three lines that again characterize the audience (18–20). There follow two rhetorical questions that
function as a moment of metatheatrical transition (20–2) preceding 5 lines
of 'true' exposition (23–7); yet another rhetorical question that functions as
a metatheatrical transition (27–8); 12 lines that perform a true exposition of
the 'false' exposition that Rumour has performed within the playworld
itself (28–39); and a capping couplet that sententiously summarizes the
paradoxes of the many-tongued prologue (39–40).

In what we have called the true exposition of the 'false' exposition that
Rumour has performed, one sees Rumour effectively taking the 'mistake'
mentioned in *Dream* in its true (inverted) order. Likewise the transitions
noted in Rumour's prologue recall the various instances of threshold-

crossing we have examined in *Dream*'s fifth act. Like these crossings in *Dream*, the transitions spelled out above involve not only divisions within composition, but movement between different epistemologies and reception strategies. Shakespeare's choice of allegorical figuration for this prologue, of course, strongly contributed to both its tone and its content. That is, Rumour remains decidedly 'in character' for the duration of its speech and performance. More than half of Rumour's line are given over to self-description, with the prologue divided almost exactly at line 22, after which begins a compressed exposition. So in character does Rumour remain, however, that this exposition is interrupted by the assertive self-presentation that occupies the first half of his prologue. We could notice the strong verbs that follow the first person pronoun throughout the prologue: 'I . . . unfold' (3–4); 'I pronounce' (7); 'I speak' (9); 'I / Make' (11–12); 'I run' (23). (Such assertiveness, we will see later in this study, was a part of the Marlovian tradition of the prologue that Shakespeare learned from.) Indeed, Rumour is so wont to be carried away by the imaginative power of his descriptions that we could analogize his prologue to Mercutio's Queen Mab speech in *Romeo and Juliet* ([1596] 1.4.53–95, 96–103). Like Mab, Rumour is portrayed as a figure with tremendous powers of movement and instigation. Even Rumour's frequent rhetorical questions here (1–2; 11–15; 20–2; 22; 27–8) are assertive, and sometimes aggressively so.

On the surface, nothing could seem less like the ushering prologue and its tendered *captatio benevolentiae* that we saw described by Field in his claim that 'Prologues are Huishers bare before the wise'. If anything, Rumour seems to go out of the way to chastise, if not insult, the audience. In what way, then, can such a prologue be conceived as initiating any rite of passage for a playhouse audience, preparing them to transverse the *limen* between the two epistemologies of 'false reports' (8) and 'true' (28) representations? We would suggest that it is precisely in the act of connecting the individual audience members through their *participation* in 'rumour' that this prologue ushers them over the threshold of the 'true wrongs' (40) of the dramatic history that there commences. Rumour begins its prologue with a command, 'Open your ears', that carries with it both the implicit physical consequence of obeying that command (that is, those who 'Open [their] ears' will also 'close [their] mouths'), and the explicit justification of and reward for such obedience: 'for which of you will stop / The vent of hearing when loud Rumour speaks?' The question is, once again, a rhetorical one. And in its nature as a rhetorical question we can see that – as with all rhetorical questions – it masks a statement or claim. In this case, the claim could be phrased as follows: 'None of you differs from the others where rumour is concerned; you will, each of you, willfully listen to rumours'. Such common greediness of the ear is supported by tropes of roundness and of gluttonous engrossment that occur in the prologue; the earth is a 'ball' (5); Rumour describes itself as 'Stuffing the ears of men' (8), and as a 'pipe / Blown' (15–16); the year is 'big . . . swoll'n' and 'with child' (13, 14); Northumberland's palace is 'worm-eaten' (35). If Rumour's tongues represent speech, they also represent eating, and the desire to ingest. Such desire is portrayed, in the prologue, as both a process that can devour the attending playgoers and one that remains a large part of who they are.

Indeed, what this prologue uses to initiate the play's rite of passage is less a deferential bid for good will than a strategic and satirical claim about the common weaknesses – about the weaknesses in common – of the audience before it. The audience is ushered over the threshold not as a social or political superior, but as itself a 'well-known body' anatomized, by Rumour, in relation to that body's social, aural, and cognitive greediness. We should note, however, that Rumour inverts the aesthetic and political relationship of its satirical remarks in a famous image that has often been taken as a representation of the playhouse audience itself:

> Rumour is a pipe   15
> Blown by surmises, jealousies, conjectures,
> And of so easy and so plain a stop
> That the blunt monster with uncounted heads,
> The still-discordant wav'ring multitude,
> Can play upon it.   20

It is difficult to hear these lines, of course, without anticipating Hamlet's equally well-known rebuke of Guildenstern:

> Why, look you now, how unworthy a thing you make of me! You would play upon me, you would seem to know my stops, you would pluck out the heart of my mystery, you would sound me from my lowest note to the top of my compass; and there is much music, excellent voice, in this little organ, yet cannot you make it speak. 'Sblood, do you think I am easier to be play'd on than a pipe? Call me what instrument you will, though you fret me, yet you cannot play upon me.
>
> (3.2.363–2)

What seems to be the repetition of a striking metaphor of the easily played-upon instrument, however, is actually a repetition with an important difference. Hamlet chides his friends for thinking him 'easier to be play'd on than a pipe'. Rumour, in contrast, advertises itself as a 'pipe' that is 'of so easy and so plain a stop / That the blunt monster with uncounted heads, / The still-discordant wav'ring multitude, / Can play upon it'. As opposed to the self-conscious leading man fending off attempts to penetrate and manipulate, Rumour openly reifies itself ('Rumour is a pipe') as an instrument for the use ('play upon it') of the playhouse audience. Yet what should we make of this image, that of the 'blunt monster with uncounted heads'?[50] Does Rumour's description of 'The still-discordant wav'ring multitude', for instance, ask to be read alongside Coriolanus's 'many-headed multitude' (2.3.16) in portraying an almost Jonsonian reluctance, on the part of the playwright, over crowds?

Rumour's characterization of large groups provides reason for such suspicion. In addition to the 'wav'ring multitude' and 'uncounted heads' of this section of the prologue, for instance, we hear of 'fearful musters and prepar'd defence' (12), of an indistinguishable, 'bloody field' (24), of 'rebels' blood' (27), of 'peasant towns' (33), and of 'news' that 'not a man' brings from any other source than Rumour itself (37–9). In this prologue Shakespeare seems to suggest that it is in the very nature of Rumour to collapse the distinctions between and among persons, and in so doing to precipitate violent acts that further undermine any integrity and safety remaining to them. But in asking a transitional question at the midpoint of the prologue – '[W]hat need I thus / My well-known body to anatomize / Among my household?' (20–2) – Rumour implicitly acknowledges that the playgoers who are now a part of the *theatrical* 'household' are equally empowered as participants in both the theatrical performance to follow and in the world that will 'unfold' (4) differently after that performance. Playgoers, that is, routinely open their ears for the speeches and sounds of the performances that follow, and, as physical participants ('still discordant', 'wav'ring') in the seats and the yards of the playhouses, metaphorically 'play' within those theatrical 'households'. Likewise through their declared extra-theatrical participation in 'surmises, jealousies, [and] conjectures', and even in the political units of 'fearful musters and prepar'd defence', these playgoers are reminded of their agency in socially meaningful groups outside the playhouses themselves. The prologue speaks of 'acts commenced upon this ball of earth', and – no less than modern readers aware that, soon after this play's composition, the Lord Chamberlain's Men would be performing within a playhouse renamed for 'this ball of earth' – playgoers accustomed to the *theatrum mundi* metaphor perhaps could be expected to have recognized a leading significance to the metaphor.

In its blunt, even aggressively condescending prologue before the play of *2 Henry IV*, Rumour can be said to revisit – though not exceed – the limit to prologic assertiveness that Marlowe had established years before in his well-known prologues to *Tamburlaine* (1587; 1588) and *The Jew of Malta* (1589). Coming at the opposite end of the spectrum of politeness from

Peter Quince in *A Midsummer Night's Dream* – from which it was separated by only two years – Rumour's critical prologue to *2 Henry IV* winds up performing an identical function. Each of these prologues ushers its audience over a threshold and alerts them to their responsibilities in the reception of theatrical representations. Rumour accomplishes this not by complimenting but by indicting the play's audience, and demonstrating its involvement in matters of social dialogue and representation. If, as Hippolyta claims, Quince has 'play'd on this prologue like a child on a recorder – a sound, but not in government' (5.1.122–4), both prologues ask their audiences to consider, even as they experience, their own relations to issues of theatrical and social participation within and without the early modern playhouse.

3 Authority and authorization in the pre-Shakespearean prologue

In the previous chapter we heard one of Nathan Field's prologue-figures liken 'A man in Authority' to 'a candle in the wind'. Of course, authority itself is a pressing topic in most early modern plays. As Marjorie Garber has noted, it has long been a commonplace that Shakespeare's plays, for instance, 'are full of questions of authority, legitimacy, usurpation, authorship, and interpretation'. Garber attributes some of this interest to the dispersed authority of drama itself, which, in her words, 'as a genre not only permits but also encodes the dissemination of authority'.[1] Surely attention to form helps us begin to understand why it was that, while authority remained of continual interest to early modern playwrights, they addressed the subject most regularly in their drama's liminal introductions. As we saw in Chapter 1, prologues appear to have been written after the composition of a play – sometimes long after, and sometimes by a playwright not connected to the work's original composition – but were, of course, delivered and, when printed, placed before the play in question. Separated from the play 'itself', sometimes even in terms of authorship, prologues nonetheless assumed a position of authority in relation to it. From its formal location and provenance, then, the prologue was likely to be a site of inquiry concerning authority.

Yet the force of authority as an issue in early modern prologues was extremely overdetermined. There are several reasons that prologues were recurrently confronted with issues of authority and authorization, with the need for validating various, only partially overlapping cultural interests and practices within the theatre. During the later sixteenth century, of course, there was also a need – and a different one, to be sure – for meeting such questions of legitimacy as were negotiated outside the theatre, at various points among and between City, Church and Crown. Since the question of authority in early modern discourse was both a burning issue and one in the process of confusing readjustments and revaluations, the sources of authorization were exposed to a welter of contingent factors and circumstances. In an attempt to do justice to an extremely complex situation, we will distinguish briefly here some four or five historical circumstances that must have stimulated and enhanced the significance of the question of authority, especially in the opening of plays in public performances.

To begin with, we should note that, as Edward Said has shown, 'authority cannot reside simply in the speaker's anterior privilege'.[2] '*Auctoritas* is production, invention, cause', something or someone who 'originates or gives existence to something;' in cultural discourses, authority is an 'enabling relationship' informing a range of choices, especially when 'explicit and implicit rules of pertinence' are called for at a moment of launching, unfolding a course of doings and resolutions.[3] Prologues may therefore depend upon 'anterior privilege' but are also faced with the reality of generating authority through performance. Here, we could refer to Kierkegaard's sense of a 'possibility of a beginning' which 'is not generated from previous conditions' – to counterpoint theatrical beginnings in prologue-form where, precisely, 'the subject' is *not* 'free' to choose, because obligated to many agencies.[4]

This overdetermination of prologic discourse in the Elizabethan theatre was subjected to two disparate sources circumscribing the range of initially 'enabling relationship[s]'. One of these sources wielding an invisible influence, support coupled with censorship, was the demand for plays that could be performed before the Queen. The Crown's support was an important political factor in the larger practice of legitimation, albeit an indirect and mediated one. Far more important was the audience's direct impact on those 'rules of pertinence' at stake in each play's opening. As a commercial institution, the theatre participated in market relations that, in the teeth of the theatre's ties to a more traditional type of popular culture, established proto-contractual relations between what was offered on stages and what, before the show began, was paid for. It was on these grounds that prologues (and epilogues as well) asked for and negotiated terms of an unwritten, unspecified contract offering gratification and promising acceptance and satisfaction to be expressed, finally, through applause.

Prologues, being the foremost vessel of invitations to and acknowledgments of this relationship, were more profoundly representative of these proto-contractual relations than any other person or figure in the playhouse. The speaker of the prologue was indeed, in Hobbes's phrase, the 'Actor' who was a 'Representative' or 'Representer' in that he (like the 'Attorney' or 'procurator' in emergent civil society) must be 'considered as representing the words and actions of an other'.[5] For Hobbes, the point in bracketing 'any representer of speech and action, as well in tribunals, as theatres' is that such 'actor acteth by authority' – by what authority, that is, others bestow upon him.

Under the circumstances of the pre-Shakespearean playhouse the pro-

logue fulfilled a crucial role in terms of the theatre's authority and accountability. The prologue constituted the best possible instrument through
which unprecedented innovations on the road from pre-dramatic shows to
dramatic spectacles could be advocated, introduced, and explained. Thus,
as Leeds Barroll has maintained, the early Shakespearean (let alone the
preShakespearean) stage was a 'largely untried and new focus of public
expression' – 'so turbulently new to London that no comfortable conceptual models' were available for its placement.[6] It was the prologue that
provided a platform to initiate and accompany spectators in the (for some)
bewildering process of viewing the world as movable, audible, visible picture – as though seen in a dream or fiction. Even while prologues helped
spectators enter strange and distant worlds, they validated the need for an
'experimental medium' by guiding audiences toward 'feeling their way
round a problematic of exchange' that involved, in the process, 'a peculiarly shape-shifting practice'.[7] Thus prologues could be positioned at the
crossroads of market-dominated exchange and the purely imaginary site of
aliquid stat pro aliquo. At this conjuncture they authorized, by helping to
cross, thresholds of imaginary representation whose meaning and whose
experience themselves had become marketable.

In ushering spectators into a new world as an imaginary representation,
prologues themselves were transformed into representatives commissioned
to speak for the theatre in general but for the dramatist in particular. The
growing availability of print and its transformation into, increasingly, an
authorial product initiated a groundswell of cultural change in the course
of which locations of authority and effects of authorization became inseparable from written and printed language. By the late 1590s, a social
horizon marked by religious dissent had been clouded as well by economic
hardship. The licence that a younger, more notorious, and highly competitive generation of writers took in their works – licence that included
personal satire and erotic, even pornographic fictions – contributed to a
larger transformation of print culture during this turbulent era.[8] Not surprisingly, the playhouse served as the platform for the dynamic exploration
of changes that print would undergo during the later years of Elizabeth's
reign.

To the degree that prologues seem to have been increasingly pulled
between two locations of authority, they by and large participated in a situation characteristic of the early modern world at large. More than any
single actor in performance, prologues were assailed by colliding claims. As
far as their office and functions were affected, their position testified to the
situation of authority during the early modern period. For, perhaps more
than ever before, authority itself at this time became a highly numinous,
and thoroughly contested, topic and process. Weimann has noted elsewhere

that, 'As the traditional system of lineage relations, with their family loyal-
ties and fealty, and the universal order of the old church gave way,
centuries-old sources of validity came into disarray. Among the divisive
forces in discursive action, the sixteenth-century European Reformation
looms largest; here, the problem of authority appears especially acute
where the old church was defied and where the resulting schism was
directly as well as indirectly confronted with an explosion of largely unauthorized and partially uncontrollable tracts, printed sermons, and
preachings'.[9]

Indeed it seems impossible to overstate the momentous nature of the
political, social, and cultural changes transpiring in the wake of the Reformation. It can even be argued that the resulting effects upon the literary
field are still being registered. For Brian Cummings, the 'Pressure on writing and on meaning' during this era can be discerned in the 'vexatious
creativity of Reformation language' itself.[10] Alongside tracts, sermons, and
preachings, the theatre immediately as well as substantially served as both
a platform for and a medium of the era's changes – as has been shown in
the work of such critics as, among others, David Bevington, Paul Whitfield
White, and Greg Walker.[11] Such transformations would be especially pressing, of course, to an England that, in contrast to parts of the Continent,
was feeling the effects of the reformist activities and texts at the same time
it was experiencing the energies that subsequently have been gathered
under the banner of the 'Renaissance'. Timothy Reiss has usefully defined
one effect of such energies as a developing, 'aesthetic rationalism' which
testified to a 'change . . . in what was taken to be the nature of *discovery*: not
a finding of something that already existed, but a making of a new rational
order for the comprehension of what existed'.[12]

We can see something like this attempt newly to gain a 'comprehension
of what existed' in the self-conscious prologues of what was among the
most innovative institutions of the early modern era in England: the commercial playhouse. Devoted more to a ludic order than to the rational
system Reiss explores, the early modern playhouses nonetheless functioned
as sites of discursive interrogation and explanation. The theatre was particularly suited to serve this function once its own generic structure had come
to conjoin two socially and culturally distinct media and traditions: com-
bining the authority of the word with the sensuous impact and validity of
its bodily delivery, the theatre, as no other cultural institution of the time,
harboured a twofold, contestatory mode of authorization. Here, as
Weimann has noted elsewhere, 'two modes and sources of signification –
writing and playing – came together to multiply, and make dynamic, the
theatrical process itself. As the new signifying potential in the dramatist's
use of language was mediated, intercepted or enhanced through voices and

bodies, the unsanctioned double-bind in the authorization of performed meanings must have achieved an unprecedented density'.[13]

The following chapters will examine the ways and degrees to which the 'density' of authorization's 'double-bind', its paradoxical status within the signifying economy of the early modern theatre, was not only a subject of many early modern prologues but also a prompt. This 'double-bind' provided some of prologues' most vital stimuli, an engrossing cultural thrust. Such self-contestatory space allowed two culturally and generically different sources of theatrical impact to collide but also to coalesce, and sometimes to enhance their mutually interactive effects. The emergence, within the early modern prologue, of a newly energized 'bi-fold authority' (to anticipate the prologue to *Troilus and Cressida* [1602]) cannot, of course, be traced as a gradually unfolding, linear pattern of development. Yet the process in question has elements of a genealogy which deserves to be noted. Hence we will examine, in this chapter, various pre-Shakespearean prologues that significantly project diverse sources of theatrical authority. Beginning with several classical prologues, we take up various instances of authorization within classical as well as medieval and late-medieval prologues before turning to two sixteenth-century prologues. These sixteenth-century prologues hint at the diversity, as well as the density, of authorization's double-bind in their articulation of almost diametrically opposed positions, strategies, and preferences.

The dramatic prologue in early modern England helped to project what Rosalie Colie has called the habituation to 'mixed genre as a mode of *thought*'.[14] Few better examples of this tendency existed than the form in question: the early modern prologue's typical attraction to *genera mista* bespoke not only the playhouses' heterogeneous audiences and dramatic themes, but also the need to accommodate itself to the multiple sources of entertainment and knowledge that were so much a part of new forms of cultural 'discovery' in Reiss' sense of the word. As we will see, conventional theatrical prologues indeed formed 'resources of kind' for early modern playwrights and performers. Yet such antecedents were neither uncritically adopted nor thoughtlessly discarded. Instead, these prologues' general features were adapted so as to conform to the diversity of experience as it was portrayed and understood in the early modern playhouse. The authority of the classical prologue in particular was both deepened and divided as it was recast to represent an authority that, like the flame of Field's candle, was visible, vulnerable, and in every way as contingent upon its conditions of production as it was mindful of them.

Our examination of authorization in the prologues that early modern playwrights and players inherited begins with the prologue to *Menaechmi*. Of the 20 or so comedies surviving by Titus Maccius Plautus (*c.* 250–184

BC), most feature prologues. And, as Timothy Moore points out, Plautus's penchant for and talent at writing monologues (a dominant form in his drama) translated into a rich variety in these speeches.[15] In addition to some of the standard functions that characterize prologues (providing exposition, seeking goodwill), Plautus's prologues are remarkable, according to Moore, for their close attention to the real and potential physical difficulties implied by the playing space, and for their similarly anxious recognition of the 'vulnerability of the actors'.[16] Such vulnerability found itself figured intriguingly in the prologue to *Menaechmi*. A major resource, of course, for Shakespeare's *Comedy of Errors* (1592), this Roman New Comedy begins with a prologue spoken by Peniculus, a slave. We quote William Warner's English translation of 1595:

> Peniculus was given me for my name when I was young, because like a broom I swept all clean away, where so ere I become: Namely all the victuals which are set before me. Now in my judgment, men that clap iron bolts on such captives as they would keep safe, and tie those servants in chains, who they think will run away, they commit an exceeding great folly: my reason is, these poor wretches enduring one misery upon an other, never cease devising how by wrenching asunder their gyves, or by some subtlety or other they may escape such cursed bands. If then ye would keep a man without all suspicion of running away from ye, the surest way is to tie him with meat, drink, and ease: Let him ever be idle, eat his belly full, and carouse while his skin will hold, and he shall never I warrant ye, stir a foot. These strings to tie one by the teeth, pass all the bands of iron, steel, or what metal so ever, for the more slack and easy ye make them, the faster still they tie the party which is in them. I speak this upon experience of my self, who am now going for *Menaechmus*, there willingly to be tied to his good cheer: he is commonly so exceeding bountiful and liberal in his fare, as no marvel though such guests as my self be drawn to his Table, and tied there in his dishes. Now because I have lately been a stranger there, I mean to visit him at dinner: for my stomach me-thinks even thrusts me into the fetters of his dainty fare. But yonder I [see] his door open, and himself ready to come forth.[17]

Plautus's slave – or 'parasite', in Warner's translation – opens his prologue by appealing to the circular signification of his name. Dubbed, for his great appetite, Peniculus (which we could translate, variously, as 'Sponge' or 'Little Broom' – the word is a diminutive of *pēnis*), he unfolds his character-based prologue on the basis of a playfully involved authority that likewise springs from the sheer physicality of his needs and appetite.

More important, perhaps, is the way in which this prologue bases itself on Peniculus' and his audience's common understanding of the theatrically potent relation of desire and acquiescence. Making a servant's 'belly full' will 'tie' him tighter than 'chains', according to Peniculus. Articulating what seems a proverbial and practical truth, however, this prologue takes what he calls the 'experience of my self' and extrapolates from it a series of materially verifiable statements that leads him and his audience into the drama proper. One could note the concatenation of assertions and egoistic formulations in his prologue: 'I swept all;' 'in my judgment;' 'my reason is;' 'I warrant ye;' 'I mean to visit'. Paradoxically, although appetite remains the 'tie' that binds him to service, it is also what authorizes his activity within both the playworld and the world of playing itself. In his liminality, the prologue speaker/character 'willingly' submits to the festive practicality of 'good cheer' that, bridging the prologue's threshold, metatheatrically involves the audience's own goals in the theatre. Indeed, in a gesture that we have already encountered in Rumour's satirical prologue to *2 Henry IV* (1598), Peniculus authorizes his prologue's observations in a manner that 'ties' the audience by means of a pervasive, shared, and satisfying understanding of human motivation.

Plautus's prologue to *Menaechmi* engages in a strategy that would be a common feature of later prologues. Articulating an aphoristic truth – in his case, a truth of the body – Peniculus solicits an imaginative consensus and the subsequent theatrical participation such consensus can imply. The prologue's mode of authorizing the theatrical occasion thus depends on a kind of embodied knowledge that cannot adequately be defined as either *sermo simplex* or even *sermo humilis*, but rather as taking its place in a subgenre of rhetoric that stretches from Plautus to Rabelais to the 'belly fable' of Menenius in Shakespeare's *Coriolanus* (1608) and beyond.[18] We can perhaps hear, in Peniculus's body-authorized remarks, hints of the Elizabethan popular clown and what a contemporary commentator in reference to his liminal, double-bound status would call this clown's 'self-resembled show'.[19] There is a difference, clearly, between Peniculus's 'experience of my self' as persona and the actual actor's 'self-resembled show', but it may be a difference in perspective rather than kind. To provide an early modern analogy, Hamlet's indictment of an egoistic, self-directed clown who diverges from some 'necessary question' of a carefully scripted production would oppose itself to the authority of the comedic body within the early modern theatre (*Hamlet* [1601], 3.2.42). In contrast, the actor Will Kemp's profoundly physicalized comedy – to cite only this example, which may have been included in Hamlet's critique – extended the corporeal themes manifest in the remarks, and dramatic practice, of Plautus's hungry slave.[20]

The basis of this prologue in character and appetite contrasts strongly with our next text, the *Andria* of Terence (185?–159 BC). In distinction to Peniculus's body-authorized remarks, Terence's prologue to this play advances an extra-theatrical, strongly literary, and sophisticated discussion of plays, playmaking, and the reception of plays. Our selection here is from Richard Bernard's 1598 translation, *Terence in English*:

> When first the Poet gave his mind to setting forth of comedies, he thought surely that he had nothing else to look unto but this, to wit, that the comedies he made might please the people: but he sees it to fall out far otherwise. For in writing of prologues he bestows his labour to a wrong end; who doth not tell you the matter of the comedy, but answereth to the railing speeches of the malicious cankered old Poet. And now, I beseech you, hearken what it is he finds fault withal. The Greek poet *Menander* set forth two comedies, one called *Andria*, the other *Perinthia*, he that knows either of them well, knows them both: which albeit they differ little in the subject matter: yet notwithstanding they are unlike in composition and form of speech: Now Terence confesseth that what things agreed to his purpose, those he hath taken out of *Perinthia* and brought them into this his comedy of *Andria*, and so to have used them for his own. Now that is the fact they find fault withal, and reason of it, saying, that a mingle mangle should not be made of comedies. But verily in showing themselves to be so wise, they manifest their folly. Who when they reprehend this our Poet, they find also fault with *Nævius*, *Plautus*, and *Ennius*, whom this our poet followeth, and wisheth rather to emulate their negligence, than the diligence of those fellows which breeds obscurities. Henceforth I advise them to keep themselves quiet hereafter, and leave off to rail on me, lest they should have their ill deeds blazed abroad. I pray you keep silence, use not partiality, and diligently weigh the matter, that you may every way understand, what hope remains of the rest of the comedies which hereafter eftsoons we will act, to wit, whether they shall be worthy the beholding, before they be justly barred the stage of you.[21]

The marginal glosses in Latin that Bernard includes with the text here identify this prologue generically: '*Hic prologus est relativus: sive defensorius*'. Critical or defensive (in the sense of a formal 'apology'), the prologue to *Andria* takes as its authorizing foundation not the appetite of the body – although what 'might please the people' seems important to the speaker – but rather the playwright's and play's relation to literary–historical lineage.

As the prologue makes clear, 'Terence confesseth' that his comedy draws on and thus mingles two plays by Menander. Instead of apologizing for using these resources, Terence's prologue boasts of a lineage that includes Menander in addition to '*Nævius, Plautus,* and *Ennius,* whom this our poet followeth, and wisheth rather to emulate their negligence, than the diligence of those fellows which breeds obscurities'. The rhetorical tactic here is worth noting. Even as the epistle before the second state of the Quarto of Shakespeare's *Troilus and Cressida* (publ. 1609) invokes images of censorious misreading as an anticipation of an imagined time when his plays could well be unavailable, so does Terence's prologue draw on a string of negative characterizations – 'wrong end;' 'malicious;' 'finds fault' (three times used); 'folly;' 'negligence;' 'obscurities;' 'rail' (used twice); 'ill deeds;' 'partiality' – critically to implore his audience better to calculate the likelihood that 'the rest of the comedies which hereafter eftsoons we will act' will 'be worthy the beholding, before they be justly barred the stage of you'. This prologue counterposes the unbroken line of literary and theatrical heritage – a line, it is implied, that may well be extended by future productions within this very venue – with the potential disruption that 'partiality' and its negative counterparts could effect. The phrase 'whom this our poet followeth' thus seems at the centre of a strategy of authorization that is sanctioned by, just as it sanctions, the act of providing, or opening up matter, an occasion, a space for entertainment. Such are the grounds of authority granted the playwright and translated into such words and phrases as 'setting forth of comedies', 'comedies he made', and 'bestows his labour' in the service of a request for a similarly active, similarly consequential 'diligen[ce]' on the part of the audience.

At this point, let us throw a glance equally brief on the practice of authorization and authority in the opening of medieval plays. As distinct from late classical antiquity, the material realities of medieval theatre would alter in such a way that prologues would no longer be able to offer this kind of literary authority for ensuing productions. Partially at least, the movement was from playing in fixed, fairly urban spaces to performing itinerantly in various, more 'open' venues. The different locations led to a kind of prologue that sought authorization not in the lineage of a history which could be associated with traditional dramatic structures and theatre spaces nor in the expectation of a judicious reception, but rather through the homiletic invocation of religious and secular authority. We can see this in the 'Banns' of *The Castle of Perseverance*, the almost epic-sized morality play originally composed *c.* 1405–25. In alternating speeches that themselves are constructed of carefully chained lines, two 'vexillators' (banner-bearers) step forward to declare at length the story and spiritual context of the drama. Their 156-line prologue begins as follows:

1 Vexillator: Glorious God, in all degrees Lord most of myth
That hevene and erthe made of mowth, both se and lond–

> The aungelys in hevene, him to serve bryth,
> And [man]kinde in midylerd he made with his hond–
> And [our lo]fty Lady, that lanterne is of lyth,   5
> Save oure lege lord the kinge, the leder of this londe,
> And all the ryall[ys] of this revme, and rede hem the ryth,
> And all the good comowns of this towne that beforn us stoned
> In this place!
> We mustyr you with menschepe,   10
> And freyne you of freely frenchepe.
> Crist safe you all from schenchepe,
> That knowyn wil our case![22]

This prologue begins with a prayer and invocation that descends what Genesis 28:12 calls the 'ladder' of sanctity. Beginning with 'Glorious God' and continuing through a catalogue that includes, in order, angels, mankind, Mary, the king, nobles, and commons, the first vexillator anticipates, with this vertical representation of the great chain of being, the verticality of the subsequent performance's impressive collocation of scaffolds and castle. Contrasting with this rhetorical and ideational verticality, of course, was the energized movement of actors (and, perhaps, audience members who wished physically to follow such action) from scaffold to scaffold, a movement that occurred horizontally across the playing space. In such a way did the various orders of bodily performance and imaginary representation potentially clash, at the very least offering bifold modes of authority.

The catalogue's orderliness underlies what is potentially a strong instance of authorization in this first stanza. The catalogue, that is, ends with an address to those 'that beforn us stoned / In this place!' (8–9), and states that 'We mustyr you with menschepe' (10). '[M]enschepe' can be glossed as 'honour', and the verb 'mustyr' here could mean something like 'To show, to show forth, display, exhibit; to show up, report, tell, explain' (*OED* v.1.1a). Thus one gloss for this line could hold it to mean: 'We report [to] you honourably'. Yet in the context of the performance this verb is perhaps more likely to mean 'muster' in the sense familiar from military contexts: 'To collect or assemble (*primarily* soldiers) for ascertainment or verification of numbers, inspection as to condition and equipment, exercise, display, or introduction into service' (*OED* v.1.2.a). The *OED* records this sense as obtaining from around 1420, which coincides with the likely date of composition for the play. If this is indeed a possible, even likely, implication for this verb, it helps explain the heraldic declaration of authority in the Banns' beginning: the audience is gathered and defined with the same authority that power exercises to compel service.

Significantly, the prologue's final two stanzas turn from the invocation of authority and from narrating the story of its audience's common spiritual life to the discussion of the play *as* play. Here the heraldic declaration of authority in the prologue's beginning gives way to a more ingratiating conversation with an audience that is defined prospectively:

1 Vexillator: Grace if God wil graunte us, of his mikyl myth,
These parcel[ys] in propyrtes we purpose us to playe 1 132
This day sevenenyt, before you in syth,
At —— on the grene, in ryal array.

. . . .

2 Vexillator: Os oure livys we love you, thus takande our leve.
Ye manly men of ——, ther Crist save you all! 145
He mainten youre mirthys, and kepe you from greve,
That born was of Mary mild in an ox stall.
Now, mery be all ——, and wel mote ye cheve,
All our feythful frendys, ther faire mote ye fall!

We recognize from these lines that this 'prologue' to *The Castle of Perseverance* is greatly proleptic. Separated from the performance a 'sevenenyt' (133), the Banns are delivered by actors who travel ahead of their troupe to advertise what the company's members 'purpose . . . to playe' (132). This separation was most likely necessitated in part by the intensive labour required to prepare the towers called for in the play. The dashes in the passage quoted above are of course placeholders for the names of villages, towns, and cities that could be counted on for prospective audiences. Even as it specifies time and place, then, this prologue exchanges the more abstract authorities of its initial catalogue for the concrete flattery of direct and specific address. If it begins as a quasi-official 'mustyr' of citizens, the prologue testifies to the acting company's inability to do more than mime, with 'These parcel[ys] in propyrtes' (132), the authority of the sacred and secular entities they invoke.

Chaining proliferates in the prologue-like Banns to *The Castle of Perseverance*, from its invocation of an authoritative chain of sacred and secular order to the internally chained rhymes of the vexillators' speeches to the intertwined speeches themselves. So conjoined are these prologic vexillators, however, that their alternating speeches cannot be said to represent dialogue. Instead, they present an occasion, and in doing so speak with identical purpose and voice. In one of the many moralities that can be said to have sprung out of the almost encyclopedic achievement of *The Castle of Perseverance*, however, the prologue initiates – albeit unwittingly – a dialogical response that suggests new pressures on the authority, and on the process of authorization, that supported the morality tradition.

In the anonymously authored *Mankind* (*c.* 1464–71), the figure of Mercy addresses the gathered assembly with a long prologue. He begins with the story of Man's disobedience and Christ's benevolent sacrifice, and introduces himself before turning to admonish the audience as follows:

> O ye sovereigns that sit and ye brothern that stand right up,
> Prick not your felicities in things transitory!   30
> Behold not the earth, but lift your eye up!
> See how the head the members daily do magnify.
> Who is the head? Forsooth, I shall you certify:
> I mean our Saviour, that was likened to a lamb;
> And his saints be the members that daily he doth satisfy   35
> With the precious river that runneth from his womb.
> There is none such food, by water nor by land,
> So precious, so glorious, so needful to our intent;
> For it hath dissolved mankind from the bitter bond
> Of the mortal enemy, that venomous serpent,   40
> From the which God preserve you all at the Last Judgment!
> For, sickerly, there shall be a strait examination.
> 'The corn shall be saved, the chaff shall be brent'–
> I beseech you heartily, have this premeditation.[23]

Mercy's speech is interrupted at this point. But before we turn to this interruption, we should point out that, in contrast to the Banns before *Perseverance*, the audience here is imagined as both standing and sitting: 'ye sovereigns that sit and ye brothern that stand right up' (30). In contrast to the Christian democracy that implies a commonality to the hearers ('our Saviour' [34]; 'our intent' [38]; 'the enemy' [40]), Mercy's characterization acknowledges a theatrically apparent division within the audience itself, a division based on the position – and, perhaps, relative ease – of various spectators' bodies during the performance.

This acknowledgment of social divisions within the audience is brought home in a more pressing way when Mercy finds himself interrupted by Mischief, who enters the play saying:

> I beseech you heartily, leave your calcation,   45
> Leave your chaff, leave your corn, leave your dalliation;
> Your wit is little, your head is mickle; ye are full of predication.
> But, sir, I pray you this question to clarify:
> Mish-mash, driff-draff,
> Some was corn and some was chaff.   50

My dame said my name was Raff.
Unshut your lock and take an ha'penny!

In rude but hilarious language, Mischief 'chains' his speech to that of Mercy. The parody is clear; Mischief picks up a heavily Latinized (and literary) vocabulary with its '-ation' rhyme of lines 42 and 44 and deploys similar words to satirical effect: 'calcation', 'dalliation', 'predication' (45–7). What could have seemed sombre and holy just instants before now seems, in the context of Mischief's parody, pompous and hollow. The authority that Mercy has gained through narration of Christ's sacrifice and God's displeasure is called into further question by the irreverent bravura of Mischief's sing-song language with its internal rhymes and playful reduplication.

What we will note as Lyly's turn to the terms 'mingle-mangle' and 'Hodge-podge' to describe the profound heterogeneity of the worlds inside and outside the play (and it seems significant that the former is a phrase that Richard Bernard used as well in his translation of the prologue to *Andria*) can be seen as participating in the same linguistic economy that underwrites Mischief's deliberately confused 'Mish-mash, driff-draff' (49). Implicit within these words is more than the game-loving energy of childhood and of a popular tradition that traditionally drew on the power of folk vocabularies. We can see in such words a profoundly ludic and festive orientation; it is an orientation that resists the more solemn, idealizing claims of Latinity in favour of a more immediately realizable relation to the material world. There is a preference for hybridity, a vicious, lusty, gleeful joy in disturbing tidy demarcations and hierarchies, whether vertical or horizontal. This propensity has implications for the audience of *Mankind*, for, as the action of the play makes clear, they share with the morality's *humanum genus* figure an ambiguity of allegiance when it comes to the authority represented. Such foregrounds itself, in this sequence, in the divisions between an aureate Latin and a playful vernacular: on several occasions *Mankind* forces the audience to participate in what can only be called theatrical sin.

In a move that we see again and again in later plays, the prologue is interrupted by a character from within the play itself. What transition the prologue's liminal thrust generally seeks to accomplish is here dramatized in a clash of two modes of authorization. On one hand we have the clerical *gestus* and homiletic language of Mercy's opening address to the audience. On the other hand the authoritative stance of his biblically sanctioned language and symbolism confronts and is challenged by a different kind of culture, which has its own way of validating dramatic entertainments as sport and game. Thus, Mischief's intrusion is brutally provocative; it gains its momentum through a blatant molestation, even a boisterous harassment; it is marked throughout by an earthy zest, a strictly Anglo-Saxon vernacular, an orally vibrant play with rhyme and alliteration. Provoking, profaning the priest-like habitus of the pious prologue, such inversionary cast of a highly histrionic delivery is authorized by a seasonal occasion of festive release and topsyturvydom. In the midst of a mixed audience of 'sovereigns' and 'brothern' (29), the prologue suddenly issues in an agonistic, thoroughly dramatic exchange largely revealing what the play is all about.

A prologue or opening address that directly flows into such heterological uses of language is not repeated in what remains the best-known of the English moralities, although in its full title *Everyman* (*c.* 1519) echoes the 'mustyr' that the Banns of *The Castle of Perseverance* call: *The Summoning of Everyman*. *Everyman* opens with an authoritative 'Messenger' who acts as a kind of usher (the summoning being accomplished by Death early in the play). This Messenger's prologue anticipates and buffers a lengthy sermon by God – 'God speaketh' is the stage direction – who could not otherwise open this play without violating decorum. His prologue runs as follows:

> I pray you all give your audience
> And hear this matter with reverence,
> By figure a moral play!
> *The Summoning of Everyman* called it is,
> That of our lives and ending shows   5
> How transitory we be all day.
> This matter is wondrous precious,
> But the intent of it is more gracious
> And sweet to bear away.
> The story saith: Man, in the beginning   10
> Look well, and take good heed to the ending,
> Be you never so gay!
> Ye think sin in the beginning full sweet,
> Which in the end causeth the soul to weep,
> When the body lieth in clay.   15
> Here shall you see how Fellowship and Jollity,
> Both Strength, Pleasure, and Beauty
> Will fade from thee as flower in May;
> For ye shall hear how our Heaven King
> Calleth every man to a general reckoning.   20
> Give audience, and hear what he doth say![24]

One could note how this prologue carefully structures its characterizations of playgoers' senses. That is, the Messenger opens by calling for attention, thereby himself 'summoning' an 'audience' (*nomen est omen*), then proceeds to point to the moral to be visualized ('shows' [5]), before, at a half-way point, recalling what should be heard ('The story saith' [10]), touching again on the visual at line 16 ('Here shall you see') before returning to its initial position: 'ye shall hear' (19); 'Calleth' (20); 'Give audience, and hear what he doth say' (21).

We could see this careful patterning of sense faculties and phenomena as the equivalent of an experiential rhyme-scheme in this prologue. If the language of *Mankind*'s prologue involves the authority of a sermon culminating in the proverbially rendered biblical prophecy about the last judgment, *Everyman*, addressing the same sombre issue of 'a general reckoning', sets forth the validity of a show portraying the 'wondrous precious' story of our lives rendered visually or aurally. If the worthy 'matter' of the play (2), verbally contained in a text of unquestioned weight and authority, calls for a reverent response, that response is described, here, as diverse in its experiential basis. On the surface, both *Mankind* and *Everyman* in their prologues offer a representation whose authoritative truth-claim is always already given before the performance begins. While the former's claim is playfully challenged, 'harassed', and scorned even before Mercy's opening speech is finished, the scripted trajectory of such challenge only serves to bolster the pre-inscribed truth claim of scripture, in the widest sense of that word. Scripture has real and potent authority in the world before the play; the actors in these late-medieval moralities can only labour toward a more vulnerable and contingent form of it.

From *Everyman* we turn now to several pre-Shakespearean prologues that explicitly or by implication raise the issue of theatrical authority and its sources. These prologues, in addressing and, partially, embodying the threshold between the world-in-the-play and the playing-in-the-world, serve an enormous variety of cultural interests and functions. Even as the classical and medieval prologues we have examined display a rich array of strategies in relation to authority and authorization, these sixteenth-century prologues make it clear that no general formula explains how thresholds to Elizabethan theatrical performances negotiated cultural differences in the purpose of playing. To demonstrate the variety of socio-cultural interests and perspectives that informed authorization in the pre-Shakespearean English prologue, we will juxtapose two mid-Elizabethan prologues that offer nearly opposite positions, strategies, and preferences. Although each is fairly remote from the Marlovian explosion of cultural energies and divisions (examined here in Chapter 4), they both make claims that will become consequential not only for Marlowe, but also for Peele, Lyly, and, to a certain degree, Shakespeare.

Our first text is a prologue that adheres to a tradition of firmly setting forth the authority invested in the play's text and argument. The prologue to Thomas Lupton's late Tudor moral play *All For Money* (1577), that is, clearly exemplifies the liminal premises on which, in a 98-line summary of moral meaning and doctrine, 'Our Authour' is situated in the framework of a writing fortified by a pious use of classical authority:

> And because that every man of money is so greedy,
> Our Author a pleasant Tragedy with pains hath now made,
> Whereby you may perceive, All thing is for money:
> For *Omnia pecunia effici possunt*, as in Tully's sentence is said.
> In hearing us attentively we crave but your aid,
> Beseeching God, the hearers that thereby shall be touched,
> May rather amend their faults, than therewith be grieved.[25]

An undercurrent of ambivalence may obtain, here, in the relation of 'Our Author' and his 'pains' to the 'greedy' standards of the marketplace. Yet the gesture of legitimation is attached primarily not to the act of writing, but to what is written; not to what is signifying but what is signified. In relation to this inscribed signified – which, like *Everyman* in its prologue's account, requires attentive 'hearing' – the self-legitimating economy of writing, printing, and selling texts is ignored. Similarly, the work taking place in the theatre – the production and reception of the play – does not appear to constitute an independent project, let alone a source of authority. Instead, there is a message that reigns supreme; what thereby is signified can claim to be 'of such force and strength' precisely because, in the welter of worldly change, it is passionately affirmed as both given and immutable: 'Yet heavenly Theology God's word before declared, / Hath been, is now, and ever of such force and strength' (31–2). 'Our Author', then, is autho-rized insofar as he *subscribes to* (both in the sense of 'accepts' and 'writes under') a given transcendental 'word before declared'. The standards of authority residing in the text are doubly pre-inscribed. The sense of their validity is even more pronounced than in those moral plays where, as we have seen with both *Mankind* and *Everyman*, the moral directions of the pro-logue, associated with the opening figure of orthodoxy, are dramatically intercepted by a sinful but lusty and bodily exuberant adversary. This hap-pens not only to Mercy in *Mankind*, but also to the prologue in *Like Will to Like* (1568) and *The Tide Tarrieth No Man* (1576), where the reverent sum-mary of the play's message is either brusquely interrupted or impertinently challenged by the figure of the Vice. As we will suggest in Chapter 4, such vicious impertinence presupposed a particularly strong constellation of per-formative agencies and energies, usually in conjunction with such semi-oral uses of language strongly foregrounded by Mischief's resolutely non-Latin, non-metaphysical, non-symbolic idiom. But wherever the orthodox prologue achieved its authority by subscription to firmly established norms and choices, the authorization of the play was literary in the twofold sense that the author's meaningful writing was grafted upon a scriptural message informed by Christian doctrine.

This was a characteristic stance in the prologues of many Tudor moral plays and interludes, which continued to project unquestionably settled premises of the kind that, as we have seen, had marked the prologue of the pious messenger to *Everyman* earlier in the century. However, such emphasis on prescribed sources of spiritual authority was radically at odds with culturally different uses of liminality, especially such threshold functions as helped bridge the gap between the world-in-the-play and playing in a world where 'every man of money is so greedy'. In particular, the consciousness of liminality was inseparable from authorizing secular purposes of playing in reference to the efficiency of the cultural occasion, its entertainment function, and the degree of audience satisfaction. Here, then, was a different code of legitimation that did not primarily draw on any given, prescribed sources of authority and that was not in aid of validating the truth-claim of representation but, rather, remained basically performance-oriented.

As the prologue to Robert Wilson's *The Three Ladies of London* (*c.* 1581) suggests, the performance-oriented mode of authorization was first of all concerned with the viability of the theatrically produced play. Coming from an actor-playwright who had become a famous leading comedian for his own extemporal mother-wit in the 1570s,[26] the prologue presents the audience with substantial reservations *vis-à-vis* the sheer plenitude of dramatically inscribed representations. One could note how the issue of authority is dissociated both from the author's pride and reputation and, even more completely, from any purely literary discourse in aid of representations of such worthy matter as cosmology, mythology, literary or martial history, the world of romance or pastoral, and even rural realism:

> To sit on honour's seat it is a lofty reach:
> To seek for praise by making brags oft times doth get a breach.
> We list not ride the rolling racks that dims the crystal skies,
> We mean to set no glimmering glance before your courteous eyes:
> We search not Pluto's pensive pit, nor taste of Limbo lake;
> We do not show of warlike flight, as sword and shield to shake:
> We speak not of the powers divine, ne yet of furious sprites;
> We do not seek high hills to climb, nor talk of love's delights.
> We do not here present to you the thresher with his flail,
> Ne do we here present to you the milkmaid with her pail;
> We show not you of country toil, as hedger with his bill;

> We do not bring the husbandman to lop and top with skill:
> We play not here the gardener's part, to plant, to set and sow:
> You marvel, then, what stuff we have to furnish out our show.
> Your patience yet we crave a while, till we have trimm'd our stall;
> Then, young and old, come and behold our wares, and buy them all.
> Then, if our wares shall seem to you well-woven, good and fine,
> We hope we shall your custom have again another time.[27]

Here we have a new, perfectly straightforward, startlingly emphatic rhetoric marked by both forceful modesty and single-minded resolution. It is the language of a prologue authorized, it appears, almost exclusively by material performance requirements. Not surprisingly, its author is an experienced actor, and the prologue – if indeed written before the play's first production (1581) rather than its publication (1584) – must have anticipated the plain and simple stance of the Queen's Men.[28]

But whatever the date of the prologue, it appears situated between the decline of the Interlude tradition and the institutionalization of stages, following the Red Lion in 1567, in such permanent amphitheatres as the Theatre in 1576 and the Curtain in 1577. Although there is, on the part of the prologue, already an invitation for spectators to 'come and behold our wares' (an unlikely gesture, it seems, for an interlude performance in a Tudor hall), it is difficult to discern signs of any presentation that point beyond the Tudor hall-screens. As Richard Southern in his detailed comparison of *The Three Ladies of London* with its sequel, *The Three Lords and Three Ladies of London* (1588) further suggests, only the former has 'a very strong indication that the acting-area was *not* localized' (emphasis in original), while the latter is 'unmistakably devised for public playhouse presentation'.[29] In these years, of course, 'acting companies began to enjoy the use of semipermanent, purpose-built structures for the marketing of dramatic entertainment, staging productions in playhouses that would become regular fixtures in the urban geography of Renaissance London'.[30] It is a new location, an untried venue where the prologue, in stark contrast to the persisting mould of allegorical form, betrays a strange revulsion from the poetics, and of course the authority, of symbolic structure and composition.

Significantly, Wilson's emphasis is neither, as in *All for Money*, on any prescribed mode of legitimating thought, language, and meaning through a given 'word before declared', nor is it, as we shall see in relation to Peele's prologue to *David and Bethsabe* (1593/4), on poesy's 'haughty flight' on the wings of the proud poet's 'muse'. Rather, the installation of authority is associated more modestly and materially with the attempt 'to furnish out our show'. The transaction assumes the imagery of the marketplace and the language of the fair. The play is advertised in terms of its trade value;

its power to please, as G. K. Hunter notes, 'is like that of a stall set up in front of a shop: there is a variety of goods that might attract customers, some one way, some another'.[31] But the principle of exchange-value in the market of cultural goods ultimately helps sanction not simply the quality of 'wares' but also the audience's right to judge them. As Hunter suggests, continuing: 'the decisions [. . .] will always come from the customer, not the author'. That is to say, the spectator is freely authorized to judge; the playwright and, one assumes, the players are content to display theatrical 'wares', that is, the products of their labour. Authority in this theatre, then, is shared with, even ostentatiously surrendered to, those who 'come and behold our wares'. Addressed is not, as in *Everyman*, 'an audience' come with their own ears to 'hear;' the expectation, instead, is for spectators to 'behold' the show or something displayed for them.

As the rhetoric of 'our show' and the imagery of 'our stall' makes clear, author's pen and actor's voice are conjoined in a theatrical craft whose products ('well-woven, good and fine') are offered articles of performance on stages. This anticipates in many ways Lyly's prologue to *Midas* (1589), where, as we shall see, the secular imagery of 'Traffic and travel', together with that of weaving, provides significant metaphors in and for the dramatic enterprise, and where the practice – the craftsmanship – of showing and performing is strongly privileged. But while for Lyly, writing and representation remain crucial for dramatic transaction, for Wilson it is not the eloquence behind the penning of the 'worthiness of the matter itself' that is vital to maintain the 'show'. With an extraordinary degree of consistency, even repetitiveness, therefore, 'the wings' of the Muse are clipped, the 'flight' of 'admired invention' is thwarted, and the celebration of Renaissance fame reduced to 'making brags'.

Yet this prologue consistently relegates to subservience what is represented in terms of its cosmological, mythological, martial, pastoral, or homely truth-claim and meaning. While the full catalogue of relegated representations is of surprising length and consistency, the agency behind this relegation remains very much present in the text. The recurring first person plural, the 'We' imperiously inscribed in the prologue no fewer than 16 times, is Wilson's version of an internal authority stimulating, and circulating among, the different 'ciphers' to this new cultural enterprise. Here, in conjunction with a judging audience, is an agency that amply constitutes whoever and whatever is authorizing this deliberate dismissal of a purely representational (and literary) poetics. This emphatic 'We' includes rather than eclipses the authorial first person singular. Nor can the agency behind this 'We' be exclusively in the nature of a fiction; there is at least one voice speaking, one body performing: that of the prologue. Its voice is an institutionalized one insofar as it validates the play in terms of 'what stuff' is processed as a 'good and fine' contribution to the cultural occasion of its performance.

However, if, in its own turn, this voice is representative in that it represents a body of institutionalized interests, then the line dividing performative (oral, collective) and literary (written, individual) media appears deliberately blurred. The first person plural pronoun strongly but indiscriminately negates a whole catalogue of cultural activities, intellectual and linguistic as well as practical, physical, and theatrical ('We mean to set no glimmering glance . . . / We do not show . . . / We speak not . . . / We do not here present . . . / We show not . . . / We play not . . .'). Potentially, this rich inventory of refusal and displacement could presuppose sources of (hidden) strength or at least singularity of purpose. But then the concluding gesture of advertisement ('Your patience yet we crave a while, till we have trimm'd our stall') sounds so anticlimactic that one must ask whether this catalogue does not conceal a good deal of uncertainty and vulnerability. Could it be that, among other things, these energies of denial betray a thoroughly impromptu stagecraft with no more than a happy-go-lucky concurrence between actor's voice and author's pen?

Whatever the answer to this question, the expulsion of represented forms and meanings is significant precisely because it is connected to, and even spelled out in terms of, an unabashed linking of commercial exchange and cultural communication. The near-conflation of the two may serve as a reminder that, as Jean-Christophe Agnew suggests, the popular theatre of early modern England developed as a theatre in and of the marketplace, at a time when boundaries separating market from other forms of exchange were rapidly dissolving.[32] The prologue rehearses the breakdown of these boundaries with deliberate, even monotonous insistence; in doing so, it indicates a new need for accountability in cultural matters. Behind its overemphatic single-mindedness there may well be an element of bewilderment as to how the imaginary forces in theatrical production and reception can ever match the political economy of the marketplace. Crucial, of course, was how the purely imaginary world of the play could be made compatible with playing in a world (and a theatre) swayed by 'wares' and commerce. The question, in Agnew's words, was 'how or where human acts of representation were to be anchored in the face of such detached and impersonal abstractions as exchange value'.[33]

The prologue to *The Three Ladies of London* gropes for an inclusive institutionalized response to the commodification of the theatre. The mechanism of exchange-value, though, once sufficiently assimilated to a commercially viable cultural institution, must have been conducive to differentiation and division rather than unity. As Shakespeare's Bastard Faulconbridge, a figure of the theatre if ever there was one, has it, 'This sway of motion, this commodity, / Makes it take head from all indifferency' (*King John* [1594–6], 2.1.578–9). In L. A. Beaurline's reading of this passage, commodity, the 'power that inclines or controls' tends to 'force away from' (other editors read 'rush away from') 'indifferency', that is, the state of 'impartiality' or, more to the point, the condition of indifference.[34] As far as this state of 'indifferency' can be read as preceding difference and differentiation, the generously inclusive 'We' of Wilson's prologue must have been at odds with those market forces, that, as we have seen above, could make not only for exclusion, division, and differentiation, but also, and perhaps more strongly, for a new form of inclusion. In this context, the integrative thrust of the 'We' could not effectively cope with things to come – that is, the new sense of self-achievement and intellectual possession that was to emerge among the dramatists of the London public theatre less than a decade after *The Three Ladies of London* was written and performed. It is to the prologues and plays of these more self-consciously innovative dramatists of the late 1580s and 1590s that we now turn.

4 Frivolous jestures versus matter of worth

Christopher Marlowe

We have seen how an actor-author of the 1580s – Robert Wilson – used a prologue to minimize the role of authorship and conveyed misgivings toward certain types of world-picturing representation. Only half a dozen years later, however, such a performance-centred project was to be countered by a strikingly new conception of authorship. Nor was this new conception an outgrowth of what traditional authorship had willingly subscribed to some transcendental 'word before declared'[1] (as in Lupton's phrase) or to some prior authority instilled into 'matter with reverence' (as in the prologue to *Everyman*). In distinction to these, this new concept of writing was prepared to advance accomplishment in authorship as itself a source and site of authority. It was an authority achieved through a power of dramatic representation forceful enough to appropriate, with a text never 'before declared', a major stake in theatrical transactions.

Indeed, Christopher Marlowe's prologue to the first part of *Tamburlaine the Great* (1587) can be read as staking out such a claim, a claim on a self-inscribed authority to lead the later Elizabethan theatre in a new direction. Marlowe moves from both homiletic piety or 'reverence' and performance-oriented and partially pre-symbolic locations of entertainment to a thoroughly secular, more strictly self-contained mode of representation associated with icon and mirror. The poet's new positioning in the theatre is crowned by glorious blank verse, celebrated in the act not simply of discarding the cultural commerce of unlearned hacks and wayward actors but by replacing these with what Ruth Lunney calls the 'rhetoric' of a new 'perspective frame' for his audience.[2] The prologue is of course well known:

> From jigging veins of rhyming mother wits,
> And such conceits as clownage keeps in pay,
> We'll lead you to the stately tent of war,
> Where you shall hear the Scythian Tamburlaine
> Threatening the world with high astounding terms,

And scourging kingdoms with his conquering sword.
View but his picture in this tragic glass,
And then applaud his fortunes as you please.[3]

So familiar has this prologue become, in fact, that we must work hard to hear it anew. Let us reassess the force it must have possessed for its original players and audiences. Only then can we gauge the degree to which his prologue 'is clearly a challenge, almost a manifesto: away with the old, here comes the new (and considerably better)'.[4] Surely this characterization does little to exaggerate the speech's innovative energy and designs; calling the prologue a challenge suggests how it must have struck many early modern playgoers. But putting ourselves in the position of Marlowe's contemporaries – a position from which we could better sense its challenging, even defiant qualities – requires a more nuanced understanding of this prologue's social and theatrical contexts.

As a prelude to discussion of these contexts, it may prove beneficial to note how this prologue relates to our argument about liminality in the previous chapters. One thing that a reader or listener immediately senses about this prologue is its marked ebb-and-flow nature. Beginning with two lines that declare both a time and a practice that his play will supercede, Marlowe in the first two words of his third line ostentatiously announces an ushering, of the audience – and, by the extension of print culture, the reader – into a new mode and topic: 'We'll lead you to the stately tent of war'. We then encounter, in lines 4 through 6, a magniloquent description of what shall transpire alongside that 'stately tent', concluding, in lines 7 and 8, with an acknowledgment of the new exigencies of the commercial theatre. With 'applaud . . . as you please', that is, Marlowe anticipates the ever-increasing appeals to playgoer satisfaction that we see encapsulated in the titles of such plays as *As You Like It* (1599) and *What You Will* (1601). The passage of *Tamburlaine*'s audience over the imaginary threshold of playhouse imagination – 'From . . . to' – finds replication, of course, in the journey of the play's title character, a journey that is both geographical ('Scythian Tamburlaine') and socio-political ('Threatening the world'; 'high'; 'scourging kingdoms').

But was the formal movement this prologue advertises as significant as literary history has maintained? That is, was the old – the 'jigging veins' – 'at once recognizable as the jog-trot fourteeners of the popular drama in the years preceding Marlowe'?[5] This traditional reading may have a point, but Marlowe's challenge does more than advance an admittedly refreshing contrast between the loping regularity of the old metre and the more varied cadence of iambic verse. The metaphor in question ('jigging veins') invokes not the regularity of a controlling disposition but, rather, the unruly temper of popular dance and sport. As a comparison with Wilson's prologue to *The Three Ladies of London* (1581) suggests, Marlowe's thrives on a forthright rendering of cultural difference. It refashions authority in the theatre out of a considerably biased juxtaposition of traditional dance and song with the 'stately' matter to be viewed 'in this tragic glass'. Informed as it is by the authority of Marlowe's own status and education as a university-trained writer, this juxtaposition enables him, on common stages, to circumscribe the rhetoric and impact of a new type of representation.

The play's hero and its setting are inspired by a new source of authority, residing in the 'picture' of a 'world' rendered by the 'high astounding terms' of a poet. Here we have, in Heidegger's well-known phrase, a 'world-picturing' representation. As such it seeks to bridge the gap and remove the difference between the text-appropriating practice of what is representing and the world-appropriating practice which, as in the uses of a 'conquering sword', is represented. Remarkably, the 'high astounding terms' in this prologue are summoned to conquer a scene once dominated by the language of 'rhyming mother wits'. These 'astounding terms' themselves 'force a play;' they are representing, propelling the haughty flight, on energetic wings, of the mighty blank verse used therein. The homology between the presumed meaning of Marlowe's leadership and the rhythm of his language makes for closure of a sort: 'this tragic glass' defines both the 'picture' on stage and the picturing of the painter; the object and the agency of representation entertain a lively and at least partially reciprocal relationship.

In the history of the early modern English prologue such forceful thrust in representational function was unprecedented. In its brevity, the prologue foreshadowed a masculine site, with space for 'Threatening the world', for 'scourging' and 'conquering' it with the help of both the picturing word and the pictured 'sword'. The Renaissance poet derives such authority strictly (and almost menacingly) from values which, not surprisingly, have little patience with the less single-minded world of collective dance and 'rhyming mother wits'. It is on the martial wings of Marlowe's 'muse' that his play is designed to soar above the low-life comedy of earthy clowns and whatever homely authority they possessed.[6] Their dislodgement is effected, paradoxically, with the help of the imagery of the same marketplace to which this 'astounding' eloquence is exposed. For all that, the lofty terms of pure representation are made to look down on the more vulgar order of signs that, being kept 'in pay' by a lowly, semi-literate culture, smack of remuneration. Such careful and even condescending attention to the markers of hierarchy remains in keeping with what we see unfolding in Marlowe's plays themselves. As the action of *Doctor Faustus* (1592) makes clear, Marlowe's fantasy of luxury involves the industry of the study, the arts of reading and writing rather than those at work in a shop. Faustus relies on a written contract which he signs only after exhausting the books of civilized knowledge. His engagement with evil can be read, then, not as the antithesis of 'divinity', but as a perverse extension of a tantalizing drive that marked his humanistic, literary education as the basis of his academic inquiries.[7]

Thus, the propelling force in Marlowe's self-legitimation is twofold, compromising both the book and the mirror, writing and picturing. What in the prologue to *Tamburlaine Part 1* appears striking in its innovation is unlikely to have been part of Marlowe's Latin curriculum. In the words of the famous *doctor universalis*, Alain de Lille, *Omnis mundi creatura / quasi liber et pictura / nobis est in speculum* (all worldly creation, like a book and picture, is ours in a mirror).[8] Even so, it is in recourse to some such traditional terms that Marlowe can proceed to advance a new concept of authority and a new mode of authorization on the strength of his poetically inspired and, it is presumed, self-achieved eloquence. It is, in Bruster's words, the 'personalization' of writing that helped 'to solidify authorship' as an institution which in the first place revolutionized the uses of *liber et pictura*.[9]

Writing in the front rank of change, Marlowe in his prologue as well as in his plays assimilated these changing norms and choices of literacy as, ultimately, a privileged mode of possession itself to be appropriated through 'aspiring minds' (*Tamburlaine*, 2.7.20). The first person plural in line 3 of the prologue scarcely concealed the 'astounding' claim of one who, in Thomas Hobbes's words, 'owneth his words and actions' – that is, an 'AUTHOR'.[10] Such a self-possessed author seemed free to dispense, even through the collective medium of the theatre and its performers, validity from this written store of meaningful language. Marlowe comes close to this position in that, to a highly precarious, still limited extent, his writing celebrates authorial self-achievement.[11] (Ironically, by the time of the play's performance legal ownership of the text may well have passed on to the actors or – if the early venue was that of the 1594/95 revival – to the enterprising builder of the Rose, Philip Henslowe.)

Here, then, in rudimentary, emergent form was a new economy of intellectual ownership in alliance with a new epistemology empowering a poetic language of writing as the dominant agency of knowledge, inspiration, and meaning. On the strength of these conjoined elements, Marlowe's prologue bears witness to a remarkable shift in the paradigm of authorization in the theatre. From the partially anonymous culture of humble clerics, unlearned writers, and common players, the level of legitimation shifts toward (and assumptions of validity are redefined by) a self-confident sense of authorship in full command of the fine arts of rhetoric. Marlowe's language provides the drive and promise of its own configuration for this relocation of authority, thereby superseding Wilson's humbler, more anonymous validation of the 'stuff' and craft of furnishing out a 'show'.

Not without good reason, therefore, did Richard Jones, the nominal printer, assume in his Preface to the Octavo edition of 1590 that these fruits of a literary imagination would have appealed 'To the Gentlemen Readers and others that take pleasure in reading Histories'.[12] We know of course nothing about either the author's design or even perhaps his role in the printing of his texts. But moving easily from stage to page (and cashing in on an unusually successful playhouse production), the printer's hope was that 'the two tragical discourses' would be 'no less acceptable unto you to read after your serious affairs and studies than they have been lately delightful for many of you to see when the same were shewed in London upon stages'. The flow of authority was from text to performance, or – an even more intriguing and consequential circuit – from writing, via printing, to the study, at least for those familiar with 'reading Histories'.

The printed version, as we know, retained the prologue, even though, to judge by Jones's assertion, the text of the play was curtailed. In fact, it may safely be gathered that, by 'purposely' omitting 'some fond and frivolous jestures' which 'were showed upon the stage in their graced deformities' the printer sought through his own medium to boost the appeal and, of course, authority of the dramatic text. As he argued, if these 'jestures' were 'now to be mixtured in print with such matter of worth, it would prove a disgrace to so honourable and stately a history'. No question, then, that the medium of print was so much more compatible not only with what the prologue presented ('the stately tent of war') but with how the world- and war-picturing story was to be rendered (the mighty blank verse itself inscribed in the prologue).

Here, the role of print as a medium was crucial. It served not only to underline the dignity, together with the social status of 'the two tragical discourses;' acknowledging, even enhancing the authority of 'the worthiness of the matter itself', the printer as a matter of course proceeds to delegitimate the nonliterary medium of comic performance. In particular, the juxtaposition of 'so honourable and stately' a worthy matter now in print and the foolish and 'frivolous jestures' reveals an exclusive preference marked by clearly a social as well as a cultural bias. There can be little doubt that the spelling, 'jestures', asks the reader of Jones's preface to think about the connections between a certain type of theatrical *gestures* (in modern spelling) and comic *jests*, as both of them oral and lowly in provenance and delivery.[13]

The printer's position deserves our attention not simply because his prefatory statement in more than one respect reaffirms the paratextual function of the prologue. Even more significant than the support in printed form given to this function is the self-explicating presence of the print medium in the language of one of its outspoken agents. Such self-reflexive utterance of the early modern medium weighs heavily in the scales of what balance between the demands of writing and the exigencies of performance can, for instance, be traced in the Shakespearean prologue. In the opening of *Tamburlaine Part 1* therefore, the post-performance intervention of a representative of the print medium points to that contestation of authority between 'author's pen' and 'actor's voice' which cannot but affect the purpose and direction of the dramatic prologue.

In this connection, it seems helpful to recall a number of recent critical suggestions that may well be said to have redefined some of the premises on which relations between the Elizabethan playhouse and the printing press need to be discussed. Here there is space for only two such reconsiderations. As Richard Dutton has shown in his study of 'The Birth of the Author', there is good reason to call 'into question the common explanation that actors were reluctant to have plays printed which were still successful on stage'.[14] If then there is 'no evidence that the companies were resisting print *per se*' (even though of course they attempted to preclude unauthorized publication), the existence of 'over-length' plays must give us pause to think.[15] If Webster, Beaumont and Fletcher, Shakespeare and of course Jonson all produced over-length plays, the most likely reason is that they did so as 'literary dramatists' (the phrase is that of Lukas Erne), with the expectation of being read.[16] And the greatest number and variety of those so communicated with would certainly become available through 'a print readership'.[17] In other words, the foregrounding of writing, the emphasis on 'high astounding' uses of language in Marlowe's (but also, as we shall see, in Peele's, even in Lyly's) prologues was part of a rhetoric that attracted spectators but also helped in the formation and public recognition of authorship. It did so in the language, almost, of Theseus: for audiences to 'apprehend some joy' in the pleasurable language of 'Fancy's images' is to comprehend 'some bringer of that joy', including the person behind 'the poet's pen' (*A Midsummer Night's Dream* [1596], 5.1.19–20; 15).

Here we do not need to recall Michel Foucault's genealogy of the 'author' as a concept arising out of certain types of individual writing in order to view in a fresh perspective the extraordinary consequences of the 'personalization of print' in late Elizabethan England. The phrase is Bruster's, who has traced evidence from the 1580s and 1590s documenting 'a more intimate connection of person and page'.[18] While the emergent personalization of print affected 'characters, authors, and books', it went hand in hand with a new fame, a new popularity of certain products of the printing press which 'worked to solidify authorship as an essential category for Elizabethan readers and writers'.[19] Although the 'new fluidity' and notoriety in relations between authors and books may have taken some-what longer to reach the collective institution of amphitheatrical stages, by the time of the Wars of the Theatres authorship would already be traced by 'internal rather than external evidence', that is, as the Reverend Matthew Sutcliffe noted in 1595, by 'the phrase and manner of writing'.[20]

Against the foil of these developments it is easy to understand why Richard Jones would go out of his way to eulogize 'the eloquence of the author' and guarantee that his artful rhetoric would not 'be mixtured in print' with performed 'jestures' and 'deformities'. But if the poet-playwright was championed by his printer, this does not mean that Marlowe found himself situated closer to the printshop than to the playhouse. To underline the mutually supportive relations of print and authorship is not of course to argue any state of congeniality between Jones and the poet.

Clearly the printer's humbly remonstrated position is not Marlowe's. True enough, the 1590 edition of *Tamburlaine*, as Fredson Bowers has con-clusively established, bears little if any sign of the playhouse; it was 'a fair copy, whether holograph or scribal', predating playhouse adaptation.[21] Nor would it be possible altogether to isolate the author from theatrical envi-ronment of his day. The line of distinction between, on one hand, a performer-dominated, differential space of liminality and, on the other, the authorially sanctioned, homogeneous space in representation can be mis-leading when conceived as involving mutually exclusive spatial patterns.[22] For one thing, the limen, like any prologue or epilogue, can actually assim-ilate and use the gap between the different types of space that go with 'frivolous jestures' and 'matter of worthiness'.

To illustrate, *Tamburlaine Part 1* presents us with the picture of a relation-ship between playwrights and players that is by far more intriguing and complex than the printer's preface could lead us to assume. Although the mode of its presentation was, admittedly, 'greatly gaped at' (Jones's words), it is clearly not helpful to pit the strong performative of those frivolous jesters against the worthy text of the play as we know it in any exclusively dichotomous manner. Even when the uses of space and language, in fact the sustained dramaturgy in the play, remain strongly indebted to a cul-tural poetics marked by literacy and the art of rhetoric, there is a countervailing movement that has a correlative in the writing itself. In fact, the text advances an author-function that can be described as veritably enthralled by a highly performative use of rhetorical language. In its own way, the peculiar drive and energy of Marlowe's medium gives auditors a specimen piece of extraordinary delivery that is publicly displayed. As Jill Levenson puts it, in a closely argued study of the verbal dynamic of the play, 'Marlowe confronts us with a presentational – instead of a representa-tional work of art'.[23]

Having brought off the coup of his 'mighty line' on common stages, the author managed to infuse his line's verbal zest and energy into powerful action. The usurping gesture is shared between the medium and the meaning of *Tamburlaine*. Thus, in consequence of Tamburlaine's 'vaunts substantial', Theridamas is 'Won with thy words and conquered with thy looks' (1.2.213; 228). The protagonist's invincible strength, in fact, the deepest source of his Renaissance authority, derives from those very 'deserts'

> That *in conceit* bear empires on our spears,
> Affecting *thoughts* coequal with the clouds
>
> (1.2.64–5, emphasis added)

As has been suggested in *Authority and Representation in Early Modern Discourse*, in politically alert types of sixteenth-century writing the traditional signs of nondiscursive, enforceable authority are mightily engaged by an entirely different authority of signs, writings, and reasonings. More specifically, any dogmatic opposition between the authority of political force and the authority of 'a great and thund'ring speech' (*Tamburlaine* 1.1.3) is called into question. Thus in Marlowe's theatre, language and 'swords' – the latter, mere material stage props – can be conflated in the imagery of 'Our swords shall play the orators for us' (1.2.132). Thus, 'empire-bearing spears' serve or even 'play' like a 'conceit' that, on stage, can pierce like the sharpest weapon. Language so used is more than just a medium; it is a tool that *works* on thousands of playgoers.[24] The signifier itself is turned into an object – a daunting one – of display. Or, as Theridamas has it, 'You see, my lord, what working words he hath'. Although it may be said that 'actions top his speech' (2.4.25–6), Tamburlaine's 'high astounding terms' are in fact agents for 'scourging kingdoms', just as 'his conquering sword' is 'Threat'ning the world' inside (and, surely, affecting those outside) the representation itself. One of those affected was his exact contemporary in the drama, for it was an attraction to such 'working words' that led Shakespeare to so vitalize the language of his chronicle plays that they have been called 'the drama of speech acts'.[24]

No matter how arrogant the earlier prologue was in its claim to have taken over, so as to 'lead' the stage to new horizons of representation, the verbal armoury of the protagonist turned the 'worthiness of the matter itself' into an article of spectacular resonance in the playhouse. Thus once the new art of rhetoric and composition was assured of its appeal to multitudes, the authority of signs, and dramatic form itself, became sources of power in the theatrical circulation of cultural energy and awareness. Sharing in the triumph of a huge success, the poet's pen and the actor's voice together attempted an endeavour of the 'highest sort'. Conquest, art, and 'knowledge infinite' came together in an overreaching representation of and for 'aspiring minds':

> For he is gross and like the massy earth
> That moves not upwards, nor by princely deeds
> Doth mean to soar above the highest sort.
>
> (2.7.31–3)

Blurring the boundary lines among the furious pride of the protagonist, the 'soaring' ambition of the playwright, and the desire in the audience for upward mobility, the popular Renaissance theatre achieved a formidable authority in and through such representations.

However, *Tamburlaine the Great* was only a beginning in which – as in Thomas Kyd's *Spanish Tragedy* (1587) – the author's pen guided the actor's voice to a 'thund'ring' display of signifying sound and fury. For the products of the pen fully to goad the voice and body of the actor stipulated a reverse movement whereby the author's pen in actor's voice had to be supplemented by, simultaneously, the actor's voice infusing the writing of the dramatist. In other words, whatever reservations the humanistically educated playwright might have entertained *vis-à-vis* what Robert Greene called 'puppets', vulgar 'grooms', and mere 'antics', the new liaison of writing and performing in the late 1580s and early 1590s, for all its potential of friction and conflict, amounted to more than just a temporizing, makeshift alliance.[25] One can perhaps, with all caution, read a note of consonance in the language of the prologue to *2 Tamburlaine*, when, right at the outset, it is suggested that:

> The general welcomes Tamburlaine received
> When he arrivèd last upon our stage
> Has made our poet pen his second part
>
> (1–3)

Who wrote these significant lines? And in what relationship to playwright, players, and playgoers?

Whether by Marlowe, another theatrical writer, or someone connected to the publisher, the repeated first person plural possessive here ('our stage' is followed by 'our poet') seems to recognize a state of mutual accommodation markedly different from the peremptory prologue to Part 1. Whatever their authorship, these lines hint at an impromptu and somewhat unpredictable circulation of authority in a theatre where the claims of more than one agency of production are acknowledged. The writer sees that theatrical commodities have made a claim on the readers' and audiences' minds:

Where death cuts off the progress of his pomp,
And murderous Fates throws all his triumphs down.
But what became of fair Zenocrate,
And with how many cities' sacrifice
He celebrated her sad funeral,
Himself in presence shall unfold at large.

(4–9)

One could note that the theatrical goods have laid claim to authority, as the prologue itself 'unfold[s] at large' its montage of attractions: 'death', 'Fates', 'triumphs', 'fair Zenocrate', 'cities' sacrifice', 'funeral', 'Himself'. Noticeably absent, it may be argued, is Marlowe's controlling hand; although his rolling polysyllables survive in a number of the lines, this seems mainly imitative, and lacking the transitive quality of his earlier prologue. Thus the possessive 'our stage' and 'our poet' may signal either a verbally reconciled Marlowe or a prologue conceived – by players, printer, or other – in imitation of him.

We of course need to be wary of overemphasizing potential evidence of reconciliation between playwrights and players. But a comparison of *Dido Queen of Carthage* (1586) and a later play like *The Jew of Malta* (1589) can help us pose the question on firmer ground.[26] If, as Tucker Brooke noted years ago, *Dido* provides us with 'an index of the young poet's relationship to the classics and to his profession of poetry' and if, as is almost certainly the case, *Dido* – like *Tamburlaine* – 'was composed, at least for the most part, before he left Cambridge',[27] the issue of authority in both plays differs strikingly from what we have in *The Jew of Malta* and *Doctor Faustus*. As distinct from the latter, these early plays are strongly and perdurably marked by an order of writing that tends to ignore or shy away from the prescribed, rather self-contained world of its own textuality; in neither play is there any sense of a usable threshold between the space *in* representation and the space *for* representation.

As an illustration, *Dido Queen of Carthage* appears significant when – according to the Quarto published by Thomas Woodcocke in 1594 – the play opens from within an enclosed discovery space, with the stage direction, '*Here the curtains draw*'.[28] If, as the title page claims, it was 'played by the Children of her Maiesties Chappell', the use of a consistently projected space in representation may not have encountered too many difficulties in the vicinity of the court. For an example here, let us glance at what was probably the most revealing use of such represented space. When, in a climactic scene, Aeneas announces that 'our travels are at end; / Here will Aeneas build a statelier Troy' – and then proceeds to envision the (purely imaginary) space in which to 'plant our pleasant suburb', the dialogue continues to measure and name:

Achates: What length or breadth shall this brave town contain?
Aeneas: Not past four thousand paces at the most.
Ilioneus: But what shall it be call'd? Troy, as before?
Aeneas: That have I not determin'd with myself.
Cloanthus: Let it be term'd Aenea, by your name.

(5.1.15–20)

Here the space in dramatic representation is verbally ascertained and numerically apportioned. The characters enact a survey of what Garret Sullivan has called 'landscape' in early modern drama: 'a way by which topography is brought into discourse and into knowledge'.[29] The colonizing foundation of 'a statelier Troy' obtains exclusively through the dramatist's text. The representation of this imaginary space culminates in an act of identification by name; in fact, the verbal naming itself is debated over six lines (18–23). In other words, the authority of written language to designate dramatic space, to shape and, actually, to found what then appears 'Carthage new erected town' (26) appears altogether absolute. This dramatic writing can easily authorize a theatrical locale in its 'fairer frame', without having to bother about any threshold, let alone abyss, between the material space for presentation and the imaginary locus in representation. The power of textual representation, with its sheer potential for verbally regulating the spatial order of the scene, is immense; it remains even more remarkable for 'imposing physical (spatial and temporal) limits on a metaphysical signifier (Troy)'. In *Dido*, this strong potential 'to bound off a symbolic Troy'[31] is undiluted; it is certainly not mediated, as in *Henry V* (1599), by any awareness of 'this unworthy scaffold'. The power of the 'poet's pen' reigns supreme as long as it has absolute authority to body forth a purely imaginary site, creating a 'local habitation' by, simply, giving a 'name' to 'airy nothing' (*A Midsummer Night's Dream*, 5.1.15–17).

As with *Tamburlaine*, the uncommon degree of movement ('Backwards and forwards near five thousand leagues' [2: 5.3.144]) finds itself in a strange contrast to the absence of that differentiation, which Shakespeare's chorus to *Henry V* takes for granted, in the theatrical representation of space.[32] This treatment of space to 'break down the barriers of difference' (the phrase is Emily Bartels's) was significant when its impact involved so much more than did any two-dimensional cartography; peopled with characters, crowded with lofty sentiments, undifferentiated space in dramatic action lured spectators on to visions of passion filled with desire and the prospect of infinite riches. And, as Richard Wilson has argued persuasively, the Eastern world teeming with royal treasures that Tamburlaine offers his army conveys through its aggressive imagery 'precisely that from which London importers would generate their wealth', at a time and in 'a culture in which raiding and trading were modes of the same enterprise'.[33]

Such 'indifferency' in the representation of space invites audiences to subsume the vastness of strange lands under coordinates that, to a certain extent, resemble those of a map. The staging invites its viewers to believe that this space is homogeneous enough to be traversed 'Backwards and forwards', no matter how immense an expanse this movement is in pursuit of 'Traffic and travel'. The paradox is that this mirror of the 'whole world' (again, Lyly's term) so pictures its assimilation through language that the effect of the play 'depends on unhesitating acceptance of the verbal picture'.[34] Unlike Shakespeare's *Henry V*, where the difference between the space in the play and the space for playing in the world of Elizabethan London is foregrounded as an area of liminality, the tragic 'glass' of representation in both *Dido Queen of Carthage* and *Tamburlaine the Great* is self-contained and of a piece, not mediated through uses of threshold in the manner we have seen other works display.

It is only when Marlowe in *The Jew of Malta* and *Doctor Faustus* comes to project the space in and for representations as liminal that a new heterogeneity results which in its own way thrives on that 'abuse of distance' (*Henry V*, 2.0.32) that we see in Shakespeare's plays. For example, to give 'a local habitation and a name' in *A Midsummer Night's Dream* is not to homogenize dramatic space but to specify it in all its difference. When Bottom and his players proceed to 'show our simple skill' (5.1.110) they, in their own innocent way, are deeply concerned to bring 'Into this place' (226) a sense of the radical difference between material signifiers ('This loam', this 'lime and rough-cast' [131, 161]) and the symbolic signifieds used to represent imaginary space and action. In Marlowe's plays there is no such playfully ironic preoccupation with the threshold between the material requisites of presentation and their imaginary equivalents in representation; his irony tends to be much less generous and flexible. Nor should we be surprised about the extent of closure in *Dido* when we keep in mind the publicized venue at Court where the author's text was played by the children of the Chapel. In view of a more genteel audience and in the absence of professional players, the dramatist's authority in the text may well have continued to go unchallenged – in contrast to its fate when placed in the hands of adult performers who, once they had access to the text in the public theatre, could adapt it to their own purpose of playing.

What this comparison reveals is how the author's pen can move closer to the stage-as-stage as a site of production, without in the process surrendering its representational reach and rhetorical élan. Such concurrence between two modes of authorization does not achieve the depth of mutual involvement and engagement that, we shall suggest, can be traced in Shakespeare's plays. Even so, there are at least three indications that Marlowe did more than just comply with the conditions and requirements of the common play-house, conditions that – to the Cambridge graduate – could well have appeared as, if not altogether deplorable, institutionally less than desirable. There was, first of all, a readiness to question the closure of representation, to disrupt the self-contained scene and to adulterate the generic convention of tragedy with what critics from Charles Lamb to T. S. Eliot have called 'the mixture of the ludicrous and the terrible' or 'the terribly serious, even savage comic humour'.[35] On a second level, there was a remarkable move to develop further the spectacular element in his early plays and to do so in the direction of a theatricality that was different from what we have in *Dido* or, for that matter, in *Tamburlaine*. Finally (and this brings us back to the beginning of this chapter), in plays like *The Jew of Malta* and *Doctor Faustus*, prologues and choruses were designed so as more strongly to assimilate and turn to account such threshold functions as served both a liminal purpose of playing and, with it, a *gestus* of display through presentation.

We can see all these redirections in *The Jew of Malta*, played in its earliest recorded performance (26 February 1592) by Lord Strange's men. Of course, we do not know the extent to which the Quarto of 1633, in response to a revival of the play a year earlier, reflects the original company's book or promptbook. But while Thomas Heywood, 'the actual entrepreneur for the revival',[36] himself may well have contributed some new material to the existing play, he is unlikely to have deleted or reinvented thoroughly sustained conventions in the text as he found it.

Among these, the 'savage' subtext of comedy, together with the 'terribly serious' cast of the protagonist and, in particular, his massive impervious-ness to closure, are a first case in point. Barabas is continually made to rub against the form of a representation that seeks to homogenize the space and order of the world of the drama. There is an ambidextrous inclination for play when the Jew with one hand, or at least his little finger, wafts signs of awareness or complicity to the audience. But while direct audience con-tact – even in the significant use of rhymed couplets (5.3.119–20; 5.5.50–1) – remains limited, a substratum of apartness, a half-hidden space for con-spiratorial or counterfeiting action runs throughout the play, precluding any effective unity of place therein. This space is invisible and inaudible from within the more hermetic rules of representation to which Barabas's adversaries submit. The Jew's instructions to his daughter to reclaim part of his treasure remain concealed, therefore, even when dovetailed with his interlaced responses to Friar Jacomo (1.2.335–62).[37] Although the quarto's stage directions – 'Whispers to her', together with four 'asides' – seek to absorb the spatial–verbal substratum of the play into a representational framework, this framework remains tenuous. Since there are no 'asides' in

Dido or *Tamburlaine*, these stage directions may of course have been inserted by Heywood when he retouched the play with a more stringent notion of verisimilar representation in mind.[38] The self-contained order of the play is again laid open when Barabas unfolds his scheming plot against Lodowick – without for a moment ceasing to converse with his unwitting victim (2.3.50–96). In other words, even when accompanied with the stratagem of disguise (4.4.31–85), such openings tend to 'forge', in Ithamore's words, 'a counterfeit challenge' (5.1.30) to any consistent, unitary 'glass' of Malta as a self-closed, self-picturing location.

Nor is this differentiation of dramatic space a formal or purely dramatic device. In Malta, among cruel Christians, Barabas is 'a strange thing' (4.4.62), almost an outcast. Like his servant Ithamore, a Turkish slave, the protagonist is alienated from the privileges and exemptions of the dominant classes. This estrangement is in line with his social and moral isolation; it also correlates to the spatial distantiation one sees in the theatrical convention of extended 'asides'. Thus his position apart from and below that of the Maltese knights and merchants is conveyed through a differentiation of theatrical space that correlates to a mode of characterization which reveals Barabas as somehow unenclosed by fortified walls of the city, not subject to communal conventions of unobstructed exchange, speaking, and listening. He inhabits a strange as well as estranged margin in representation, where he can whisper, interject, and interface the speech of others without being 'overheard', except by his daughter and his complicitous servant. Such apartness is sustained enough to stimulate and harbour a continuing series of 'asides' that, taken together, constitute a breach in the unitary mode of the play's spatial and verbal conventions. As Weimann has argued elsewhere, such 'bifold space' revitalizes performance-centred uses of liminality, even perhaps the memory of theatre space marked by norms of simultaneity that blur boundary lines between presentation and representation.[39]

The point here is that the humanistically educated playwright deliberately breaks with the Neo-Aristotelian postulate of classical poetics that asks for unified conventions of time, space, and speech.[40] Thus, the rejection of important tenets in the learned culture of literacy goes hand in hand with new attention to performance-oriented practices and audience expectations. Together, these developments make it possible to produce, onstage, images and actions of strangeness and otherness that purely literary standards of 'meaning' in theatrical representation would scarcely be able to convey. As Barabas urges Abigail, his daughter,

> As good dissemble that thou never mean'st
> As first mean truth, and then dissemble it;

A counterfeit profession is better
Than unseen hypocrisy.

(1.2.290–3)

Here we see that meaning itself is complicated through, ambiguously, a 'counterfeit profession'. The phrase, recently used in the title of Patrick Cheney's study of Marlowe, is an intriguing oxymoron, heavily loaded with pervasive connotations of Marlowe's literary, political, and theatrical careers.[41] But it is surely not too far-fetched also to associate the phrase with the acting profession and to view it in a context of theatricality that, as Stephen Greenblatt has suggested, comes close to 'absolute play'.[42] In *The Jew of Malta*, 'counterfeiting' serves as a metaphor through which to unfold the character's apartness from within. To 'dissemble that thou never mean'st' is a concise description of acting, after all; at the same time, it stands as a stratagem whereby alien formations can embrace their otherness.

And yet, such 'profession' (now in the sense of 'avowal') remains more than a histrionic alternative to 'hypocrisy'. It is a 'cunning' (299) strategy to put representation itself in question, especially its capacity for bringing forth a pictorially conveyed mode of meaning. When Barabas asks Ithamore, his *alter ego* in estrangement, his 'birth, condition, and profession', Ithamore replies, 'my birth is but mean, my name's Ithamore, my profession what you please' (2.3.166–8). Coming, as it does, at the end of the sentence, Ithamore's 'what you please' here seems somewhat diffident; yet we can sense its thoroughly theatrical quality: it is part and parcel of the new industry of playing gestured toward, once again, in the final lines of the prologue to *1 Tamburlaine* ('applaud his fortunes as you please') and, as we have seen, soon to be codified in such titles as *As You Like It* (1599) and *What You Will* (1601). '[W]hat you please'. The recipient of this answer, onstage and offstage, is free to participate in bringing forth meaning in (regard to) *this* 'profession'. Says Ithamore, in a later scene, 'The meaning has a meaning' (4.4.97). Signification in the theatre has an ulterior 'meaning', one that can 'mean truth' through counterfeit.

If, then, there is a 'meaning' beyond representation, the 'counterfeit profession' provides us with food for thought, and in an exemplary manner. Such double-dealing will play upon the playing. As Ithamore, alone onstage, asks the judging audience,

Why, was there ever seen such villainy,
So neatly plotted and so well performed?

(3.3.1–2)

Theatricality is foregrounded when the bifold competence of both the plot-ting author and the performing player is at stake. Here, as in the late medieval Herod and Pilate or in the morality Vice, horror meets with laughter and laughter with horror.[43] Spectacle, once it is both serious and comic, foregrounds its own theatrical 'devise' (*Midas* [1589], Pro. 14). Thus, Ithamore refers to another stratagem – a 'counterfeit challenge' (5.1.29–30) – whereby two suitors of Abigail are 'flatly both beguiled' to kill each other. The cold-blooded, revengeful killing of the suitors recalls a sim-ilar scene, 'neatly plotted' and no less 'well performed', when two friars (Bernardine and Jacomo) are so deceived and compromised by the 'coun-terfeit challenge' of seeming murder that the truly murdering performers – Barabas and Ithamore – can congratulate themselves upon their 'neatly plotted' complot upon the 'two religious caterpillars' (4.1.21):

Ithamore: Fie upon 'em, master, will you turn Christian, when holy friars
turn devils and murder one another?
Barabas: No; for this example I'll remain a Jew.

(4.1.192–94)

Again, the meaning has yet another meaning. The foregrounding of the-atricality is one way to make apparent that other meaning (which also is the meaning of the other). Clearly, the visible, audible double-dealing in meaning culminates here in a reaffirmation that Jewish identity is 'better / Than unseen hypocrisy'. Such absolute play with meaning is purposive; it thrives upon the vicious circle within which the Christian governor of Malta and his knights appropriate Jewish property. Barabas's sarcastic question is much to the point: 'Is theft the ground of your religion?' (1.2.96). But the vicious logic comes full circle when Barabas does no more than paraphrase early modern Christian practice:

It's no sin to deceive a Christian,
For they themselves hold it a principle,
Faith is not to be held with heretics:
But all are heretics that are not Jews.

(2.3.311–14)

Modern editors such as Van Fossen, Bawcutt, and others follow Sir Walter Scott (*The Ancient British Drama*, 1810) and insert 'Aside' as a stage direction, thereby marginalizing an audience address of great weight and reach. But Barabas, even under the show of partially at least conversing with his daughter, 'means truth' and, from this threshold angle, formulates one of the play's crucial concerns. As Emily Bartels has shown, *The Jew of Malta* and Marlowe's plays in general, 'in bringing alien types to centre stage, subversively resist [. . .] the demonization of an other'.[44]

In this project, Marlowe learns from the players. He participates in a theatrical mode of authorizing action clearly unsanctioned by neoclassical precept and authority. Investing into the duplicity of liminal space, the playwright comes close to assimilating a presentational *gestus* of delivery that deliberately addresses an otherwise unspeakable contrariety. This, indeed, is a far cry from the arrogant condescension with which the dramatist's pen sought to obliterate the open space of jigging players in favour of a self-consistent 'glass' of tragic representation. This re-formation of popular Renaissance drama at least in one respect constituted a volte-face: rather than scornfully dismissing 'such conceits as clownage keeps in play', the learned playwright now goes out of his way to turn the part of Ithamore, Turkish slave and servant, into that of a clownish presenter:

> I never knew a man take his death so patiently as this friar; he was ready to leap off ere the halter was about his neck, and when the hang-man had put on his hempen tippet, he made such haste to his prayers, as if he had had another cure to serve. Well, go whither he will [. . .]
>
> (4.2.24–8)

Characteristically, the threshold on which this is delivered finds a correla-tive in the represented limen between life and death; on both levels the boundary between laughing and dying is easily crossed. Although the resonating depth of ambivalence in the Porter's scene in *Macbeth* (1606) easily shows the limits of this particular clownish presenter, Ithamore's bifold uses of theatrical space exemplify a new and newly intensified give and take between playing and writing. To sound the terribly comic bound-ary between presentation and representation in terms of a spatially signifi-cant move between the world of the audience and the absent world in the play is to anticipate, at least in its direction, the two clownish murderers in *Richard III* (1592), the grave-diggers in *Hamlet* (1601), and the 'rural fellow' in *Antony and Cleopatra* (1607). In all these scenes, the uses of space in perfor-mance and the projection of an imaginary theme in representation turn out to be complementary. Dying, the ultimate *rite de passage*, the most consis-tently sanctioned, worthy matter of tragedy, is terrifyingly tinged with laughter. Each of these scenes also features, in the language of anthropol-ogy, a mid-liminal moment saturated with a formidable 'neither-this-nor-that' – a moment in many ways conducive to a 'spontaneous, performative, ludic quality' (Victor Turner's phrase) defying both the pathos of tragedy and the closure in representation.[45]

The spectacular conclusion of the play, when the protagonist's tragic ending resonates with burlesque farce and grotesque machinery, reproduces this duplicity. Barabas, contrariously, is both agent and object of these happenings. Entering 'with a hammer above, very busy' (5.5), he himself is shown as instrumental in the arrangement of the props, with 'cords', 'hinges', 'the cranes and pulleys' (5.5.1–2) all ready for employment. Having set up his 'dainty gallery' of horror, Barabas, alone on stage, directly addressing the audience, does 'mean truth':

> Why, is not this
> A kingly kind of trade, to purchase towns
> By treachery, and sell 'em by deceit?
> Now tell me, worldlings, underneath the sun
> If greater falsehood ever has been done.
>
> (47–51)

The rhymed couplet underlines the play's final opening where, from outside the logic of the character's representation, treachery is at last called 'treachery' and deceit is named 'deceit'. He who is at work here presents, rather than represents, treacherous skill galore. A hellish machinery is displayed gloatingly, in its making, before it swallows its own producer and agent. In other words, the play's ending sees a horrible–laughable interface between stagecraft and representation. Perfect contrariety results when the protagonist serves as both presenting producer and represented victim of his own machinations. Straddling the threshold between the plotter and the plotted, Barabas finally blurs the boundary line between the world of the play and playing in the world of the London theatre.

There is no epilogue to *The Jew of Malta*. The play's ending reveals a circuit of authority accommodating diverse forces of production; this final piece of theatricality in its own way returns to what is adumbrated in the opening prologue to the play. An imaginative and rhetorical *tour de force*, the significance of this prologue to *The Jew of Malta* is difficult to overestimate. Ludger Brinker has argued that, with the exception of 'Rumour' in the second part of Shakespeare's *Henry IV*, it is the 'most fully dramatically realized prologue . . . in Elizabethan tragedy'.[46] Brinker praises the intensive dramatization of this prologue, the manner in which it incorporates the dramatic tension of the play that will follow, and speaks of a 'figural plasticity' absent in English prologues before this play.[47] The prologue to *The Jew of Malta* is indeed unique in that its medium is a reinvented agent of unspeakable thought in secret alliance with the protagonist.

Even more shocking, 'Machevil', as he opens the play, is not a devilish figure of the past. To the contrary, reversing the trajectory of the morality play, Marlowe has Machevil's 'soul' blasphemously resurrected:

Albeit the world think Machevil is dead,
Yet was his soul but flown beyond the Alps;
And now the Guise is dead is come from France,
To view this land and frolic with his friends.
To some perhaps my name is odious,
But such as love me guard me from their tongues;
And let them know that I am Machevil,
And weigh not men, and therefore not men's words.
Admired I am of those that hate me most:
Though some speak openly against my books,
Yet they will read me . . .

(1–11)

Marlowe sets out this prologue's authority with a distinctly literary note. The speaker is an author whose 'name', albeit controversial, is very much alive. The 'I' of Machevil finds its true (re)incarnation in 'my book'. Those who 'know' the name, who have heard its fame or notoriety, need only read his texts. But if the prologue's 'personal pronouns appear as signs of textual identity',[48] this identity, even in the language of its pronouns, is marked by the liminal difference between who is showing and who is shown. When we look closely at the prologue's opening, the speaker's persona appears duplicitous; his imaginary identity comes and goes in the course of the speech itself. Introduced as third person singular ('Machevil . . . his soul'), this personage is embodied by the prologue only after the initial act of illeism (that is, reference to oneself in the third person) has led to an act of identification between the 'I' of the speaker and the 'soul' / the 'books' of Machevil. But the 'I' is unstable; the mask of Machevil sits lightly on the head of the presenting prologue. Thus, concluding the impersonation yields to the voice of the prologue returning to his liminal task:

I crave but this, grace him [the Jew] as he deserves,
And let him not be entertained the worse
Because he favours me.

(33–5)

The prologue, in fact, both presents Machevil *and* represents him; the speaker introduces the play and, in this introduction, plays a role.

But as this role is redefined on the threshold of the play that is about to begin, the 'identity' of the performed Florentine writer collapses into the language (and the function) of the London performer whose task is not 'To read a lecture here in Britany, / But to present the tragedy of a Jew (28–30).

The prologue therefore exemplifies in miniature the doubleness in function that marks Barabas himself. The prologue is and is not a representation. His bifold authority derives from both the imaginary role that he plays and the actual function that he serves. So to straddle the gulf between the world of Renaissance *histoire* and the *discours* of theatrical production in the world of the London playhouse underlines the overwhelming impact of authorship; through a strategy of 'neither-this-nor-that', even the predominance of authorial authority is momentarily kept at bay.

Thus when finally this bifold projection is seen in the play at large, there is no doubt that the representation of Machevil looms much larger than the act of presentation enacted by the prologue. The figuration is first and foremost that of a political writer. And yet, behind this figure of authorship, the presenter of the prologue – speaking on a mere scaffold – comes 'not in confidence' of authorship. As the prologue proceeds, there is a lapse of assurance in the ability of writing and, even more so, of representation to remain on the precarious stage of worldly 'Might' and 'strong-built' power:

> Might first made kings, and laws were then most sure
> When like the Draco's they were writ in blood.
> Hence comes it that a strong-built citadel
> Commands much more than letters can import.[49]

At issue is the vulnerability of early modern authority itself. To read 'import' (23), in this connection, in the sense of 'to obtain, win a victory' is to conceive of the authority of letters as, in Bawcutt's words, unable to 'command obedience like a fortress'.[50] But since the speaker of the prologue, through his persona, has theatricalized the threshold to the imaginary world of the play even while foregrounding it, his use of 'letters' may well carry a more immediate, self-reflexive connotation: writing confronts the 'citadel' of 'Might', the site of power itself. What this 'Might' commands is 'much more than' can be conveyed in writing. The representation of authority has its limits; but what cultural authority derives from the act of representation itself, from the assumed validity of signs, meanings, and reasonings is even more vulnerable. The 'laws' are not 'then most sure' when written in ink, which is, as *Doctor Faustus* and other of Marlowe's plays show us, thinner than blood. Rather, what is at stake is something greater than written representations. A 'strong-built citadel' has more power than signs or 'letters can import'. Thus speaks a Renaissance voice that obdurately resists the anticipations (and illusions) of Enlightenment, a voice closer to Nietzsche than Rousseau.[51]

5 Kingly harp and iron pen in the playhouse

George Peele

If we set aside the mischievous prologue of Rumour before *2 Henry IV* (1598), it seems clear that the 'figural plasticity' we have seen in the prologue to *The Jew of Malta* (1589) left little trace on prologues of the 1590s. This lack of widespread resonance is perhaps surprising, on first glance, for Marlowe's works are central to the dramatic canon we know. Added to this is the fact that Machevil makes a bold statement on the transgressive potential of representation in the early modern playhouse. So daring and extensive are its implications that we could call *The Jew of Malta*'s prologue a performance of performance itself – a distillation of what Tamburlaine dubbed the 'quintessence' of a thing (*1 Tamburlaine* [1587], 5.2.102). How, then, should we explain its apparent singularity?

To begin with, the lack of immediate sequels may come from its very daring. Such may be owing, that is, to the avant-garde liberties that Machevil takes, liberties that would be more at home in the 'angry Satyr-days' of the late 1590s and early 1600s than in *The Jew of Malta*'s own moment of origin a decade or so earlier.[1] This prologue's lack of resonance may also have derived from Marlowe's imposing example. Although Marlowe's fellow writers engaged with his texts, frequently responding to them and sometimes even parodying them, his works – perhaps more than those of any other writer of his time – proved in the end incapable of being assimilated to others' compositional practices. Marlowe was, in short, more admired than successfully emulated. For all its romance, the portrait of Marlowe as an isolated overreacher not unlike his central characters – but signally unlike the majority of his contemporaries – helps us understand what James Shapiro describes as the near eclipse of Marlowe's literary presence and reputation by the middle of the seventeenth century.[2]

We can see that the stunning innovations of that prologue did not generally inform the playwriting of his contemporaries or successors when examining the prologue to George Peele's *David and Bethsabe* (1593/94):

Of Israel's sweetest singer now I sing,
Of holy style and happy victories,
Whose Muse was dipt in that inspiring dew,
Arch-angels 'stilled from breath of Jove,
Decking her temples with glorious flowers,   5
Heavens rain'd on tops of Sion and Mount Sinai.
Upon the bosom of his ivory Lute
The Cherubins and Angels laid their breasts,
And when his consecrated fingers strook
The golden wires of his ravishing harp,   10
He gave alarum to the host of heaven,
That wing'd with lightning, break the clouds and cast
Their crystal armour, at his conquering feet.
Of this sweet Poet Jove's Musician,
And of his beauteous son I prease to sing.   15
Then help, divine Adonai to conduct,
Upon the wings of my well tempered verse,
The hearers' minds above the towers of Heaven,
And guide them so in thrice haughty flight,
Their mounting feather scorch not with fire,   20
That none can temper but thy holy hand:
To thee for succour flies my feeble muse,
And at thy feet her iron Pen doth use.[3]

Here the dissociation of the written text from the agents and site of its performance is carried a good deal further than, for example, in *Doctor Faustus*
(1592). The players are resolutely ignored, the 'actor's voice' (as distinct
from his role) is silenced, his body invisible except for the sudden action
performed by the speaker of the prologue after line 23 – an action that
may be seen as announcing and effecting a metamorphosis to that very
speaker: 'He draws a curtain, and discovers Bethsabe with her maid
bathing over a spring' (3: 193). But this move, which, among other things,
foregrounds the materiality of the booth or pavilion,[4] refrains from otherwise processing or articulating any nonsymbolic articles projecting a
'swelling scene' (*Henry V* [1599], Pro. 4). The dramatist's refusal to concede
to the public stage any authority in excess of his own poetic medium of
authorization appears to dominate the utterance at large. Yet, again, the
assumed autonomy of his text and the imaginary world *in* this text is at
least partially suspended in the juxtaposition between David's 'ivory lute'
and Peele's own 'iron Pen'.

Because this latter image – that is, that of the 'iron Pen' – is so striking,
and because it will be used as a heuristic in the following analysis, we

should pause for a moment to establish not only its source, but – and this is of course related – its significance for Peele's contemporaries. The image of an iron pen occurs twice in the Bible as translated in the sixteenth century; it appears in the books of Job and Jeremiah. In the former, this image arises during Job's reproof of his friends – here provided in the Geneva translation: 'Oh that my words were now written! oh that they were written even in a book, / *And* graven with an iron pen in lead, or in stone for ever!' (19: 23–4). In Jeremiah the image opens the seventeenth chapter: 'The sin of Judah is written with a pen of iron, *and* with the point of a diamond, *and* graven upon the table of their heart, and upon the horns of your altars.'[5]

In both instances the 'iron pen' represents, of course, not merely a durable and forceful writing instrument, but an instrument whose force attaches itself to its products, rendering them durable ('in stone for ever') and even indelible through their inward impact ('even in a book, / *And* graven;' 'with the point of a diamond, *and* graven upon the table of their heart'). The eternizing topos would accompany this image in John Fletcher's and Nathan Field's *Four Plays, or Moral Representations, in One* (1613) when the Duke wishes for a lasting mode of signification:

> A pen of iron, and a lease of brass,
> to keep this Story to eternity:
> and a Promethean wit. O sacred Love,
> nor chance, nor death can thy firm truth remove.[6]

Like Fletcher's and Field's Duke, Peele's prologue makes recourse to sacred rhetoric that draws equally upon classical mythology and Judeo-Christian resources. Where Peele, for instance, invokes both 'Jove' and 'Adonai' in a three-line sequence (14–16), and follows up mention of 'Cherubins and Angels' (8) with a reference to Icarus (20–1), he borrows the image of an 'iron pen' from the Hebrew bible and lends it to his 'feeble muse' in a gesture that anticipates the powerful hybridity of Milton's oeuvre.

To be sure, the represented divinity of David, the inspired 'sweet Poet Jove's Musician' (14), contrasts with the 'feeble muse' of Peele the playwright. Yet it also links the dramatist's writing to the same divine sources of poetry and power. Thus, although Peele's prologue, as A. R. Braunmuller notes, 'personalizes the play and advances himself and his poetic task', its 'movement of ascent and descent' projects a significant and altogether representative perspective on both the writing and the meaning of the play at large.[7] Complementing the respective positionings of the juxtaposed sources of inspiration ('divine Adonai' and 'iron Pen'), this movement, interlaced with Christian and pagan Renaissance attributes, prevents the prologue from becoming a purely authorial medium affiliated with 'the wings' of the dramatist's own poetic ambition. Rather, by linking the author's 'feeble muse' to the conditions under which a playwright's writing for the public stage is predicated on the use of an 'iron Pen', the equation between the poet's eloquence and his 'matter of worthiness' is significantly impaired. Between them stands – in contingent, constraining circumstances – the theatre in an iron age, as an 'iron' commercial medium of dramatic composition. In circumstances such as these, the authority of the poet, even when sanctioned by his muse, is enfeebled.

We should note that this reading of the 'iron' medium of the commercial theatre complicates, even adulterates the Biblical meaning of the topos examined in the preceding pages. A doubly encoded topos, the 'iron Pen' asks its audience to confront the latent tensions between these two readings, between the attractiveness of a golden age and the material realities of the commodity form of dramatic performance. Acknowledging such odds, the prologue persists in its dual function of bearing witness to the poet's own inspiration *and* introducing semi-divine 'matter of worthiness'. This twofold function constitutes a significant departure that at least partially echoes the intricate emplotment of a dual authority, deriving from the union, in David, of singer and ruler, poet and king. We will remember that Sidney gave important place, in his *Apology*, to the poetic works of the 'holy David' dramatized here by Peele.[8] Hence, Peele's 'iron Pen' may well have been overwhelmed by the celebration and, of course, confusion of the two most vibrant agencies in a Renaissance dream 'Of Power [. . .] and omnipotence' (*Doctor Faustus*, 1.1.54). Between them, these supreme locations of authority in poesy and politics beckon 'The hearers' minds' (characteristically, not the spectators' visions) to follow the 'holy style *and* happy victories' (2; emphasis added) of the poet-king. As in *Tamburlaine*, the power of language and the heroics of conquest reinforce each other. In the writing of the play both the represented 'kingly Harp' and the representing 'iron Pen' engage one another in their respective upward/downward trajectories. Soaring 'Upon the wings of [his] well tempered verse', the dramatist, in the words of Solomon, the future seer-king, is enthralled to gaze 'on the burning wings / Of zeal divine' (ll. 1766–7).

At the same time, the prologue reflects Peele's own sense of his high reputation, which by 1594 was well established as (according to Nashe) that of 'the Atlas of Poetrie, and *primus verborum artifex*'.[9] With this lofty vocation before him, Peele could pride himself on literary 'endeavours of art' that overshadowed all other cultural sources of legitimation and, as a matter of course, must have fortified his position as *verborum artifex* in the theatre. It was no mean project, therefore, to turn the prologue into the poet's mouthpiece, and thereby use the Elizabethan playhouse to appeal to the 'golden wires of [David's] ravishing Harp' (10). Peele's lyrical genius, his own 'ravishing' notes of 'Lute' (8) and 'harp' (20), together with 'Shalms', 'Cymbals', and 'Pipes' (699), aimed at verbally heightened world-picturing representations that, through their 'worthiness', induced empathy on the part of the spectator and fame on the part of writer.

Accordingly, in this prologue, the voice that sings and the voice that is sung tend to be conflated in an act of representational closure that captures the minds and hearts of audiences. Such a capture of the audience helps support the writer's 'iron Pen' just as much as this pen – for all its enfeebling, prosaic circumstances – is captivated and inspired by 'Israel's sweetest singer'. Hence Peele could hope both to make a living of a sort in the theatre and to pride himself on the peculiar 'pleasance' of a writing grounded in the musically attuned union, figured in David, of sweetness and power, markedly different from the swelling, imperious force of Marlowe's stirring blank verse. Peele's poetic power derives not, as elsewhere, from a 'conquering sword' conveyed by 'high astounding terms', but from a 'well-tempered verse' (17) interiorized and located in 'the bosom of his ivory lute' (7). Thus, the speech of the chorus, the language of the poet, and 'David's kingly Harp' (582) are made to conjoin in a wondrous 'scene individable' (*Hamlet* [1601], 2.2.399).

But for a moment only, as the closure of the prologue's speech coincides with an opening of the booth whose spectacularly non-verbal interior strangely jars with the prologue's last words. Peele's personalized instrument of poetic excellence falls back on an epic invocation of divinity, as his own 'feeble Muse' sings of a singer whose greater inspiration 'was dipt in that inspiring dew / Arch-angels 'stilled from the breath of Jove'. Peele invokes as poetic inspiration the imaginary representation which the player, discovered on stage, has corporeally brought forth: 'To thee for succour flies my feeble Muse, / And at thy feet her iron Pen doth use'.

At the feet of his own poetic, sensuous and elevating figuration, the playwright's feebler muse 'her iron Pen doth use'. As distinct from the effortless, dual authority in the royal use of an 'ivory Lute', the 'iron Pen' of the playwright is hard put to cope with the realities of an unembellished institution of popular entertainment. Peele's use of a traditional invocation of the Muse in terms of sacred rhetoric and his expressions of self-doubt *vis-à-vis* his own prosaic surroundings call attention to the complicity through which, on common stages, the 'matter of worthiness' is exposed. Thus, the very representation by which Peele hopes to body forth poetic inspiration is too impure to be divine, especially if the workings of the 'ivory Lute' are themselves merely the products of the works of the theatre's tire-man and Peele's own 'iron Pen'. In a manner radically different from Marlowe's *Tamburlaine*, the self-enclosed moment of unity and continuity between the

'Muse' represented and the 'Pen' representing turns out to be extremely vulnerable.

Peele's prologue is significant in that it runs counter to and effectively contradicts any tidy or linear order in the theatre's process of socio-cultural differentiation. As distinct from Wilson's mode of opening the play, the prologue to *David and Bethsabe* on the surface of things seems to mark a resolute shift from player's to author's theatre. However, even in the admittedly limited context of Peele's own writings, such shift cannot be considered as representative, let alone as the dramatist's last word. If anything, Peele's choice reflected an Oxford education able to choose among multiple and highly unconventional options in the authorization of dramatic discourse. For the author of *The Arraignment of Paris* (1581) it must have been tempting to vindicate the reputation of *primus verborum artifex* and to reactivate such modes of authorization as were reminiscent of the epic-style invocation of a classical muse.[10] Throughout the play Peele appears anxious to pursue the poet's project, if necessary against the contingencies of production in the public theatre. When, for instance, the Chorus reenters (1577–88), his subject is 'this story', that is to say, the Old Testament narrative which 'lends us other store, / To make a third discourse of David's life' (1584 ff.). Even when the 'I' of the poet, grammatically at least, here gives way to a plurality of agents, the 'discourse' in question is authorized in terms of its biblical source and epic subject-matter rather than its theatrical transaction, its public reception and effect. With his own interests even more split between pastoralism and patriotism, Peele here as elsewhere was drawn to diverse cultural practices of a mingle-mangle sort. In response to a veritable gallimaufry of choices, his versatility must have served as a congenial means of somehow reconciling with one another, at least in cultural matters, a middle-class background, an Oxford education, and the exigencies of an emerging market for cultural goods.[11]

With these as yet unfiltered items in the household of an aspiring ambition, Peele was free to strike an innovative note in *The Old Wives Tale* (1590). In particular, he was able to narrow and thereby assimilate the liminal site between the representation of textual matter and its social occasion. He achieved this by turning liminality itself into a strategic space for the authorization of 'this thrice haughty flight' (*David and Bethsabe*, Pro. 19). In at least partially straddling the threshold between the craft of theatrical production and the act of composing the imaginative matter that was represented, both the prologue to *David and Bethsabe* and the induction to *The Old Wives Tale* have one thing in common: in their liminal functions, they prepared for, and actually thrived on, the gap between dramatic representations and the public site of their actual presentation. Like many Elizabethan epilogues, the prologue and the induction served an obvious need to address the heterogeneity of the theatrical occasion and, where possible, to conduct participants across the thresholds in question. But this passage implicated more than one order of authority and authorization; the cultural practice that helped usher various parties across the threshold was not contingent upon an act of writing. Rather, to cope with such passage and to launch the play materially on the boards of the platform stage required a more practical kind of assimilation. It was an assimilation of the represented matter to the actual cultural and commercial purposes *behind* the writing and performing of the text that informed theatrical production.

With respect to such a threshold, the radically different matter of *The Old Wives Tale* allowed for an even bolder departure, in the form of an induction that projected a persona distinctly remote from any cultural location and stratification of authorial status. As opposed to the classically shaped convention of an inspiring muse, this persona – identified with the woman's voice behind the story – could adopt both an oblique and a highly immediate, even immanent relationship to the play at large. Here, the represented world of fantastic folklore was effectively prepared for by, literally, being 'produced' by an entirely unlettered agency of narration and presentation.[12]

The peculiar opening of *The Old Wives Tale* is of interest here because it contradicts any strong claim concerning the trend toward an author's theatre in the early 1590s. On the contrary, the play reveals the astonishing degree to which the recuperation of the authority of the author through 'David's kingly Harp' could, to all intents and purposes, be complemented by an altogether different regime of dramatic authorization. Although *The Old Wives Tale* boasts no 'muse', feeble or otherwise, it offers plenty of orally transmitted folklore. Here, the dramatic assimilation of a preliterate storytelling culture to the author's written representations appears deliberately to forego the academic arts of rhetoric and composition. Insofar as this perception is deceptive, the relation between the two cultures can be summed up best by saying that it is marked by affirmative uses of difference in a floating nexus of mutual engagements.

For, far from being structured by any rigidly upheld boundary between learned and popular, *The Old Wives Tale* is knit from their mutual engagements. These engagements do not here empower the university graduate to 'lead' the audience away from orally transmitted products of 'rhyming mother-wits' (*1 Tamburlaine*, Pro. 1). On the contrary, the play unfolds the story-telling jumble of semi-oral lore against the foil of both adaptations from printed vernacular romances and entirely hybrid uses of the classical *miles gloriosus* and related braggart motifs. In this thoroughly mixed cultural scenario, the learned hankering after English equivalents of classical diction and metre is effectively exposed to ridicule. As Mary Ellen Lamb has shown, the play so 'devalues learned culture' that its incessant calls 'for discipline and manliness' are ridiculed as 'meaningless noise' and eventually relegated 'to an ultimately laughable form of "play"'.[13] *The Old Wives Tale* thus challenges the authority of the schoolroom, where young males were encouraged to internalize the denigration of old wives' tales as unwelcome memories 'of the degraded and feminized subculture of childhood'.[14]

Drawing upon a bounteous harvest of folklore motifs, *The Old Wives Tale* recomposes them, as Patricia Binnie notes, into a dreamlike and 'unique, rich and strange blending of moods and episodes', a remarkable galli-maufry processed, last not least, as Frank Hook observes, 'by coloration of the courtly masque'.[15] For all that, Peele's artfully artless transformation remains moored to the spirit of seasonal festivity where songs of sowing and mowing set the scene, for example, for Celanta to comb 'ears of Corn . . . in her lap' (170). Employing more than 90 folklore themes, motifs, and figurations,[16] Peele's 'well tempered' adaptations nonetheless refrain from imposing any learned neoclassical regime of order and unity on the elusive matter of this play. Even where the language of the stage directions consistently betrays the writing of the professional playwright, rather than a theatrical hand, Peele's approach to his folklore material remains, in Hook's phrase, 'completely naive' (340). There is a simplicity in the presentation that has no ironic overtones and no artful code of ambiguous meanings. But there is no artlessness; it is only that the presence of Peele's art and his elite background do not here draw attention to themselves. Rather, there is the attempt through this induction to project the homespun site of narrative presentation and direction into the fanciful matter of dramatic representation itself. The result is quaint, but it precludes any self-conscious irony in the construction of what otherwise would amount to a hopelessly garbled sequence of dramatic images and actions. Of course, this jumbled mix is not uncharacteristic of Peele. As John Wilson points out, 'One often notices when reading Peele . . . that he simply tries too hard to get everything in . . . . Such a mélange has led some critics to complain (I think justly) that one gets the sense they are viewing pageants or a slide show rather than plays'.[17]

Whatever the source of this jumbled composition in *The Old Wives Tale*, the play finds itself in astonishing consonance not with humanist doctrine, but with a storytelling pattern in gamesome response to the question, 'Come, what do we to pass away the time?' (6–7). Next to a 'game at Trumpe or Ruffe', Madge, the 'old wife', invites her visitors 'to drive away the time with an old wives' winter's tale' (95–6). What is most unassuming, and yet sophisticated, in the dramatization of this tale is the fact that its dramatic form resonates with the gesture and direction of the relaxed story-telling style of Madge herself.[18] Whether the resulting *confusion* (stressing, with this word, connotations of blending ['con-fusion'] as well as disorder) subtly reflects any deliberately intended design seems a conjectural matter. Much more remarkable is the shift by which the author's authority, surrendering the 'anchor-hold' of a highly literate education, comes to reconstitute itself not against, but in and through the act of an elusive but for all that peremptory use of 'mother wit' in narration:

Madge: Once upon a time, there was a king, or a lord, or a duke, that
            had a fair daughter, the fairest that ever was [. . .] and he sent all
            his men to seek out his daughter and he sent so long, that he
            sent all his men out of his land.
Frolic: Who drest his dinner, then?
Madge: Nay, either hear my tale, or kiss my tail.

                                                                (130–49)

The pun behind Madge's wordplay was well known to Shakespeare, of course, and points in its obscenity to a rock-bottom plane of reciprocity between grasping the (spoken) word and touching a signifying part of the body. If anywhere, mother wit resides in how the 'either . . . or' between the told romance and the untold depth of corporeal indifference does not constitute alternatives but, rather, mutually sustained gestures of assonance. Madge could not care less whether the fairest of daughters had a 'king, or a lord, or a duke' for father. What irrelevance, then, to inquire into the identity of the person preparing his meals. The teller of the tale refuses to particularize or explain; the object of her narration and the metaphor of her remonstrance are made to connect on the level where the romantic discourse of the tale and the vulgarity of the teller's own language clash in a purely homonymic relationship. Madge's narration abounds in forgetfulness about ordered sequence, elevated agents, and gendered identities: 'O Lord, I quite forgot! [. . .] O, I forgot! she (he, I would say) turned a proper young man to a bear in the night' (142; 149–151). Causality, particularity, individuality do not matter: the wittiness in the telling and the worthiness in what is told are (deliberately, one would assume) at loggerheads.

This is of course no prologue in the classical sense, but an aperture through which, intermittently, Madge is authorized to assume the roles of chorus, presenter, and director of the performed play (cf. 246–9; 255–6; 530–3; 540–3; 920–4). It is no doubt part of the design that such an instance of a popular story-telling culture should remain visible and audible even in the process of being transformed, via the induction, into what comes close to being a self-legitimating agency in the theatre. Along these lines, Peele's use of the induction emphasizes the strength of the links between story-telling and dramatization. The framework, as Hook notes, 'is unique in the way the play within the play develops out of the surrounding story. This is the only play in which characters act out a tale begun as a narrative in the framework' (3: 21).

To say this is not to deny that, in Peele's case, the move across the threshold from epic presentation to dramatic representation is a somewhat vulnerable operation. The concomitant incoherence in *The Old Wives Tale*, the haphazard sequence of events, the precarious relations of epic/dramatic personages – all point to what Harold Jenkins calls a 'parsimony of treatment'.[19] Moving in a direction opposite to that of the prologue to *David and Bethsabe*, Peele discretely refrains from such rhetorical endeavours of art as could foreground an elaborate type of writing.[20] Such writing would ill consort with either the gossamer of a fantastically woven act of story-telling or the cryptic, sturdy, charm-like mother-wit of 'Booby the Clowne' (identical with Corebus-Clown), who is given to semi-nonsensical exclamations such as it be no great deal for him 'running through a little lightning and thunder, and riddle me riddle me what's this' (275–6).

As the foregrounding of authorial authority in *David and Bethsabe* and its displacement in *The Old Wives Tale* suggests, there was in the early 1590s no unalterable, or, for that matter, representative position in the authorization of stage plays. Rather, the circuit of cultural authorities in the opening of stage plays, far from being closed to either learned or popular impulses, continued to be sustained by what, in the following chapter, will be discussed as the socio-cultural 'mingle-mangle' of the Elizabethan period. In line with this circumstantial situation in the world of the Elizabethan settlement – to which Shakespeare owed so much – there were of course other significant factors that for a University graduate could preclude any abrupt break with traditional modes of authorization in Tudor England. Complementing the larger contours of a veritable 'Hodge-podge' (again, Lyly's term) among classes and institutions, many male agents and products of a sixteenth-century humanist education must have been marked by a hybrid cultural conscience. While social stratification, despite considerable mobility, remained ineradicably strong, its cultural counterpart was never really congruent with the lines of class division. On the contrary there was a marked degree of interdependence, mainly, but by no means exclusively, derived from upper-class participation in the culture of the unlettered.[21]

As a result, many of those who – thanks to grammar schools and university – could read and write Latin were, in Peter Burke's phrase, 'amphibious, bi-cultural, and also bilingual'. Such 'amphibious' proficiency for crossing cultural boundaries was not of course taught in the university or grammar school curriculum. Rather, it ultimately derived from childhood experiences that educated male members of the upper-class, according to

Burke, largely owed to 'peasant nurses who sang them ballads and told them folktales' as well as to ongoing contact with 'their mothers, sisters, wives and daughters'.[22] The sources of an immediate and lasting contact with the culture of the unlettered flowed from an environment that was much closer to the nursery than to the schoolroom. As Mary Ellen Lamb has shown in her path-breaking studies on the subject, this environment was of profound consequence to Sidney and Spenser.[23]

In Peele's case, such 'bi-cultural' grounding of a dramatist's imagination is obviously of considerable importance when the radically differing cultural moorings of *David and Bethsabe* and *The Old Wives Tale* are to be accounted for. While the former play ends on a manly note of 'princely chivalry' (1882), recuperating 'royal rule' (1862), 'when elsewhere stern war shall sound his trump' (1887), the latter concludes with an invitation for a shared, homely 'breakfast', with 'a piece of bread and cheese' (927). Peele, having grown up in more than one culture, could have it both ways; in one play acclaiming the manly dream of conquest, art and royalty ('Take but your Lute, and make the mountains dance', [1648]); in the other, celebrating the comfortable, soothing warmth of nature and the natural woman's abundant physicality and hospitality, welcoming straying youths with a tale and 'a pudding of my own making' (58–9).

For all the differences between them, however, both plays have at least one element in common: in both there are, preceding the dramatic representation proper, significant traces of a presentational performance practice. Again, these show great variety: the fragmenting narrative presentation of *The Old Wives Tale* strongly contrasts with the brief personal union of the prologue and presenter in *David and Bathsabe*. But when both are seen in conjunction with the elaborately presentational *The Battle of Alcazar* (1589), the relationship between presentation and representation deserves to be considered more closely.

In *The Battle of Alcazar*, this relationship, to begin with, is marked by much greater variety in the respective uses of theatrical space and authority. Part of the reason is that the presentational element is enhanced by a number of significant links among prologue, chorus, and dumb show, which together achieve an unprecedented density. Relating directly to spectators, the play's Presenter fulfills a coordinating function that, from the audience's point of view, makes him, rather than any of the represented monarchs, appear 'the chief character in the play'.[24]

> Sit you and see this true and tragic war,
> A modern matter full of blood and ruth.

(49–50)

The speaker of these lines does not serve to represent a character in the plot; instead, he presents the process of emplotment itself, the space of collision, the motivation for revenge. If anything, he is in alliance with, even instrumental in terms of, the surviving 'Plott' of the play that – as ingeniously reconstructed by David Bradley – served as a 'call-sheet' and 'skeleton key by which the actors' parts can be fitted together in rehearsal'.[25] As such, the Presenter provides an important link between the authorial version of the text and its stage revision that, with the help of the 'plotter' or stage reviser, was produced during rehearsals, possibly, as Bradley suggests, in the absence of the 'Book' that of course had to be submitted to the Office of the Revels. This subjection of the 'Book' of the play to censorship by the Master of the Revels presupposed a textual fixity that the corresponding 'Plott' denied.

As distinct from the 'plotter', the Presenter – even while he could take the resulting instability of authorial authority for granted – could go considerably further, not least owing to his actual stage presence. Allocating theatrical space, directing and thereby interpreting each of the four dumb-shows, the Presenter emerges, at least partially, on the threshold between extra-dramatic and dramatically contained agencies, an instance of what elsewhere we have called a 'bifold' type of theatrical authority. He ushers the audience, poses as an observant but also rather sweeping eye-witness; he acts throughout as the showman in charge of summaries and scene changes; and, last but not least, helps tie up the various ends and locales of the action.

One might note the stirring energy and rhythm of a speech following the stage direction, 'Enter the presenter and speaks', which, incidentally, gives some taste of his masterful ability to display with his own presence the unfolding of such 'matter of worth' as culminates in another project 'to cross the swelling seas':

> Lo thus into the lake of Wound and gore,
> The brave courageous king of Portugal
> Hath drencht himself, and now prepares amain
> With sails and oars to cross the swelling seas,
> With men and ships, courage and cannon shot . . .
>
> (737–41)

Whether Shakespeare remembered, in his own use of a 'swelling scene' (*Henry V*, Pro. 4), the strength of the assonance in Peele's own 'swelling seas' (740), the presentational force in the language of the University wit (one could note the strongly performative 'thus' and 'now' [737, 739]) clearly anticipates Shakespeare's way to 'digest / Th'abuse of distance' in the Chorus to *Henry V* (2.0.31–2).

In Peele's theatre, then, there first emerged a chorus-function that went far beyond the cogitating, debating, discriminating, rhetorically informed (and of course exhorting) chorus as it existed from Seneca to *Gorboduc* (1562). No matter how emotional, ethically evaluative, or carefully didactic such a chorus might be, the neo-classical precedent remained remote from the performed action on which it commented from a distance. One might take as representative of this remoteness the prologue to George Buchanan's tragedy *Jephthes* (*c.* 1540–3). The prologue of this text bitterly relates the plot to come, yet never engages with audience or actors, and never touches on the playing space or the materiality of performance. As distinct from such neo-classical uses of the chorus, in Peele's play we have an influx of performative energy and showmanship that was less present in plays marked by humanist learning and literacy. Flowing from Peele's 'iron Pen', the space for liminality is deliberately foregrounded through the institution of a chorus-like mediation between the world of the audience and the world of representation. Thereby, the circulation of authority in the play's representation is redefined. Rather than simply remaining subject to the play's worthy matter, the Presenter can match the representation of power by a power of (re)presentation all its own. Part of this strength derives from the extraordinary degree to which Peele's Presenter is verbally and materially engaged in the theatre's production process – far more fully, as we will see, than the chorus to *Henry V.*

While the author's muse virtually absents itself from the drive and rhythm of this productive (and directional) enterprise, the presenter has the stage for himself and carries all before him. In what comes close to an extra-dramatic function, his performance is instrumental in timing and, possibly, marshalling in due order the appearance of such spectacular non-verbal figurations as 'Nemesis above', 'three Furies bringing in the scales', 'three devils. Then [. . .] three ghosts' (746/747). Similarly, upon the conclusion of Act 3, the same agency follows up with a thoroughly presentational *gestus* of guidance: 'Now hardened is this hapless heathen prince, / And strengthened by the arms of Portugal' (978–9). The demonstrative gesture behind 'this . . . prince' creates precision and helps audiences to follow the show. Even as it does so, it preserves the kind of distance that prevents spectators from complete identification with what here is confirmed as a staged, rather than life-like, figuration. Thus, empathy is strictly controlled when the theatrical apparatus itself takes over, in direct address, to foreground the gamesome quality of dramatic representation itself: 'Now listen, lordings, now begins the game, / Sebastian's tragedy in this tragic war' (327–8).

As in the narrative components of *The Old Wives Tale*, the unique and entirely innovative network of presentation in *The Battle of Alcazar* tends to acknowledge the medium itself. By and through this medium, the dramatically composed text is being processed as a theatrical event marked by 'bloodcurdling violence and splendid pageantry'.[26] Whatever literary sources – Seneca, and closer to home, Marlowe and Kyd – Peele may have tapped here, they were not appropriated so as to bolster the author's own authority. Rather, the sustained uses of presentation took on a nearly eyewitness authority of their own. They underlined the theatrical requirements of staging a highly involved historical-tragical-biographical matter bristling with contemporary politics and anti-Spanish sentiment. Not so remote from these requirements, the expectation of spectators ennobled as 'lordings' is amply acknowledged in the attempt to outline, clarify and compress, for their understanding, an entirely rambling and distracting source material. There can be little doubt that, as Braunmuller argues, the structuring medium of the presenter is indebted to civic shows and Peele's experience in writing them.[27] On public stages, his use of it is significant as a sustained acknowledgment of the theatre's own authority. It was an authority to fashion and control such means and devices as mediate between symbolic representations and their nonsymbolic functions in aid of audiences.

On the threshold between these two cultural formations – on the one hand elite, lettered, educated, representational, and, on the other, popular, oral, presentational, performative – performance practice in the Elizabethan theatre could serve a double-bind type of function. Although the author textually devises the performed presentation, its provenance is that of a cultural institution attracting socially mixed audiences, expectations, and conventions. *The Battle of Alcazar* was a far cry from the aristocratic and pastoral beginnings of Peele's career as a dramatist, and worlds remote from his poetic exercises in such celebrations of nobility as the verses dedicated to the Earl of Northumberland. *The Arraignment of Paris*, as Louis Montrose has shown, was 'a cultural manifestation of the Elizabethan court; the Court itself provides the code in which Peele entertains it'.[28] The public stages, as Peele's later plays witness, did not provide any one given code or ideology; instead, they offered the dramatist, the player, and the spectator alike multiple discourses and, for the dramatist, a host of options ranging from the representation of Biblical matter and contemporary politics to home-spun stories of country folk. The theatre's medium, the stage itself, provided the space and the measure for authorizing diverse types of discursive practice

Without too much anticipating our reading of Shakespeare's prologue and chorus to *Henry V*, we would suggest that the presentational thrust in

Peele's play can best be viewed in perspective by relating it to the uses of the prologue in and after *Romeo and Juliet* (1596). What the liminal space in the opening to Shakespeare's early tragedy witnesses (more so than does the chorus to Act 2, the only one preserved in this play) is the evocation of a diverse but fairly integrated ensemble of productive and receptive forces in the theatre – a joint endeavour that has no equivalent either in the voice of the presenter or the writing of the 'iron Pen'. Still, for all the differences between them, Peele's plays pursue a network of legitimation strategies which, in Shakespeare's *Romeo and Juliet* – but also in the prologue and chorus to *Henry V* – are either intertwined or artfully collapsed in aid of the cultural occasion itself. In Shakespeare's tragedy, the project so launched is circular in the sense that the prologue moves from a poetically heightened précis to the actual terms of its theatrical production:

> Two households, both alike in dignity,
> In fair Verona, where we lay our scene,
> From ancient grudge break to new mutiny,
> Where civil blood makes civil hands unclean.
> From forth the fatal loins of these two foes   5
> A pair of star-cross'd lovers take their life;
> Whose misadventur'ed piteous overthrows
> Doth with their death bury their parents' strife.
> The fearful passage of their death-mark'd love,
> And the continuance of their parents' rage,   10
> Which, but their children's end, nought could remove,
> Is now the two hours' traffic of our stage;
> The which if you with patient ears attend,
> What here shall miss, our toil shall strive to mend.

There is a considerable amount of give and take among the institutional-ized sources of legitimation in Shakespeare's theatre. The ensemble quality, as inscribed in this prologue, allows for both accountability and empower-ment; such can be projected so as to establish an opening, in Edward Said's terms, with its own 'rules of pertinence'.[29] But in contrast to Said's suggestion, the agencies behind both the writing and the performing are not 'free' beyond the terms of their proto-contractual relationships. In par-ticular, the prologue's function on the threshold of an actually addressed entertainment opens with the collective pledge (inscribed in the first person plural) to provide a pleasurable transaction for a story with local habitation 'In fair Verona'. In submitting to the need for naming 'our scene', the poet's 'iron Pen' participates in the effort to 'strive' to satisfy the market-controlled, paid-for-terms of the implicit contract with the audience.

Yet, participating in relations of theatrical production does not mute the playwright's not-so 'feeble muse'. The outline of the matter itself is poetically rendered 'Upon the wings of well tempered verse'. The prologue takes the form of a sonnet, the first quatrain introducing the family feud, the second the 'pair of star-cross'd lovers'. But then the final sestet wrests a conclusion from the Petrarchan form that thematically transgresses its generic boundaries through a turn from poetic representation to (trans)active presentation. Although the prologue is at pains poetically to integrate the threshold occasion, his implicit acknowledgement of its 'contrarious' components is, momentarily, an analogy of Peele's descent from 'kingly Harp' to 'iron Pen'. Again, Renaissance poetic form sustains a process of authorization that is of the theatre though not finally contained by it.

Beginning as a strictly thematic paraphrase, the well-wrought form of *Romeo and Juliet*'s prologue helps discipline what could otherwise be a sprawling plot summary; and, by forewarning unsuspecting spectators, it positively controls the grievous sense of irredeemable loss in youth and beauty through the play's tragic ending. Thus the poet's presence in the theatre is that of the poetic form of the prologue itself. As such it remains unobtrusively assured: his author-function entirely submits to the theme, the purpose, the occasion, and yet cannot be overlooked by those who 'with patient ears attend'. But on the crest of the sonnet's movement, the sestet transfigures the lyrical pathos of the 'star-cross'd lovers' into the institutionalized space of its cultural reception. The transition comes precisely half-way through the sestet; whereas the first three lines summarize the preceding quatrains, the following line, with great ease, swiftly turns lofty poetry into theatrical practice: the 'passage' of this excellent and most lamentable story is 'traffic of our stage'. The representation of 'ancient grudge' and 'death-mark'd love' is inseparable from 'traffic', the business of transaction, a word derived either from Latin 'transficare', (that is, 'transfacere') or from Arabic 'tarrafaqa', 'to seek profit' (*OED*). In contrast to Jonson's 'detheatricalization of theatre',[30] this is a theatricalization of writing. The poetic potential of the sonnet form energizes the business performed on 'this unworthy scaffold' (*Henry V*, Pro. 10). The writing deliberately surrenders the absent, represented pathos of foreshortened tragedy to present the 'traffic' sustaining the theatrical production itself.

The writer's authority, it appears, is self-assured and strong (drawing on the prestige of the Petrarchan form and theme in the mid-1590s), but it is not unlimited. 'What here shall miss . . .' – the prologue's concession, coming as it does in the concluding line, seems significant: in T. J. B. Spencer's paraphrase, 'what may seem to you to be inadequate' in the spoken text of the play, 'our toil shall strive to mend'.[31] The prologue's first person plural possessive belongs to the actors (of which the prologue declares himself one). Their work, their 'toil' while the play is on, can have a shaping impact on its success – an impact over and beyond the author's function. Our players, the prologue suggests, are prepared to improve what the story of the play, the 'two hours' traffic', leaves to be desired, provided that 'you with patient ears attend'.

The emphasis, then, is not exclusively on the writing or on the dramatic composition as the tragic mirror. Authority here flows both ways: contact and interaction among writing and playing (and viewing) is taken for granted. Relations between text and performance are, like those between actors and spectators, reciprocal. While the prologue's rehearsal of the play's 'fearful passage' culminates in the paradox of 'death-marked love', the 'tragic glass' (Marlowe's phrase) is, with a sleight of hand, turned around to mirror a stage performance as another 'passage', one steered by the work of the theatrical company as a whole. Within fewer than a dozen lines, the time and place represented ('Two households, both alike in dignity / In fair Verona . . .') are metamorphosed into the time and place of the presenting ('the two hours' traffic of our stage'). This metamorphosis is all the more remarkable for the number 'two' carried over, as though the imaginary antagonism has an equivalent of sorts in the actual, measurable temporality of the playhouse and playing. And indeed, it may not be fortuitous that the much-limited duration of the performance is mentioned here: the prologue's sonnet culminates in an attempt to realign the absent authority of what is textually and imaginatively *represented* with the actual work, the unsparing 'toil' in the fleeting present (and in the future) of those who are doing the *representing*.

That the Folio text omits the prologue to *Romeo and Juliet* (even though it otherwise follows the third Quarto of 1609, which contains the prologue *in toto*) suggests that the collective mandate of the chorus may not be quite as benign and unified as the artfully balanced threshold between the world in the text and its 'traffic' (or transaction) on 'our stage' seems to indicate. The play, in a passage found only in the first Quarto (printed 1597), contains a reference to a 'without-book prologue, faintly spoke' (1.4.7). Although there is clearly nothing impromptu about the play's own prologue, there was beginning to prevail, in 1590s London, a feeling that any such extemporal, self-authorized voicing of the play's opening consorted poorly with the more self-contained space for representation in tragedies.

Earlier in this study we saw that the dramatic prologue was said to have become old-fashioned by the end of the century. This may well have been a result of its problematic relation to the poetics (and the politics) of representation in the drama itself. When Shakespeare returns to a prologue or chorus in his later plays, for instance – in *Pericles* (1608), *The Winter's Tale*

(1610), and in *Henry VIII* (1613) – the effect is distinctly that of an old convention, as when Gower, 'an old man' (*Pericles*, 13), sets out 'To sing a song that old was sung' (1). Nevertheless, there is a sense of permanence in change, and of change in seeming permanence, when the chorus, 'in the name of Time', presents matters of 'swift passage' (*The Winter's Tale*; 4.0.3; 5). Indeed, Time, the chorus, pledges both to 'pass / The same I am' *and* 'To use my wings' (4). Providing authorization of contingency in change itself, this chorus is powerful on two levels: his is an agency both in the wilting of things past (and their representation) and in what, in the time of the performance, is doing the presenting and the planting of 'what is now receiv'd'.

> [. . .] since it is in my pow'r
> To o'erthrow law, and in one self-born hour
> To plant and o'erwhelm custom. Let me pass
> The same I am, ere ancient'st order was
> Or what is now receiv'd.
>
> (7–11)

Thus, the chorus, representing eternal motion, is himself a presenter who cannot be subsumed under the purely imaginary representation of an old tale. The presentation of this 'tale' can 'make stale / The glistering of this present' (13–14), which is not the time represented, but that of the performance.

While the convention of the chorus with its temporal narrative can be felt to be time-bound as well as time-honoured, it nevertheless can still be used, as in *Henry VIII*, as an index of representational meaning, a breviary of 'things now / That bear a weighty and a serious brow, / Sad, high, and working, full of state and woe' (*Henry VIII*, 1–3). Accordingly, the prologue, as an ushering agent of liminality is far indeed from being fixed or static. Fittingly, it can serve as both a seismograph of cultural change and itself a changeful vessel of theatrical convention. Thus, in the late history it is appropriately consigned the task of (re)presenting what in 'truth' is rendered in the play. This mandate appears the more emphatic when the speaker, in line with the alternative title *All is True*, seeks to intercept several kinds of spectators' expectations by assuring the 'believing' audience that they 'May here find truth, too' (9) and, finally, by pledging the company's own efforts as a guarantee:

> Our own brains and the opinion that we bring
> To make that only true we now intend.
>
> (20–1)

As of this late date, the prologue as purveyor of 'our chosen truth' (18) retains the commission to mediate between symbolic representations and the nonsymbolic act of their reception in the playhouse. But now he does so by resigning the task that was associated with Peele's Presenter, of helping to fashion, control, and inform the production process itself. What his presentational agenda finally amounts to is an endeavour to transfer the truth-claim from its epistemological setting to one of verisimilitude:

> Think ye see
> The very persons of our noble story
> As they were living.
>
> (25–7)

The prologue to *Henry VIII*, then, whether it is Shakespeare's, Fletcher's, or a product of collaboration, provides us with a crucial instance that points beyond the mutual accommodation of author's pen and actor's voice in the prologue to *Romeo and Juliet*, or even, for that matter, *Troilus and Cressida* (1602). In the late history play, the space for liminality in the prologue is marked by a self-consciously upheld but troublesome balance between culturally dated uses of theatrical representation and the all-too deliberate, three times reiterated truth-claim of a dramatically self-contained mode of representation. No longer may relations between text and institution be rehearsed as of old.

6 From hodge-podge to scene individable

John Lyly

As may be apparent from our examination of Marlowe's 'tragic glass' and Peele's 'iron Pen', the friction between the representation of textual meaning and performance practice on the Elizabethan stage had a history of its own. Much neglected by critics, its history was marked by fits and starts rather than by any linear pattern of development. This history witnessed its first climax in the alliance of common players and humanistically educated poets in the formative period of London's popular theatre in the 1580s. In contrast, no comparable antagonism marked the relations between writing and showing in the near-contemporary indoor theatre of the boys of the chapel. In the case of John Lyly, arguably Shakespeare's most important predecessor, the division of interests between dramatist and actors found scarcely any articulation. Here, for better or worse, the unfolding uses of dramatic representation were not entangled with (and did not have to be secured against) any encroachment by 'jigging veins of rhyming mother-wits'. In these circumstances, Lyly must have felt free to use the opening of *Midas* (1589) for launching a remarkable précis on the new art of Renaissance representation – the more so because it anticipated and combined the Hobbesian politico-juridical notion of a contractual type of representative action and what Heidegger defined in modern epistemology as the setting forth of a masterful world-picture 'in relation to oneself' or one's emerging national culture.[1]

Lyly was master of a boy's choir and writer of their plays. His prologue to *Midas* on dramatic representation deserves further attention as one of the most revealing negotiations of authority in theatrical transactions before Shakespeare's *Henry V* (1599). In both prologues, although for different reasons, there is a kind of truce between text and institution, in fact an attempt to establish a workable balance between them. Lyly's prologue brings the expectations of the audience, the work of the actors, and the composition of the dramatist together in an audacious 'Hodge-podge' fashion as much a 'mingle-mangle' as the 'world' and the 'matter' to be represented. As a result, text and institution, like playing and watching, are subsumed under a workable order that relocates the site of its authority amidst relations of production and reception. Even more remarkably, the prologue makes these representative on two levels: epistemologically, as insightful images or structures mirroring one another; and, socially, in the sense that one stands for or finds itself in the same situation as the other. The epistemology and politics of this ordering are such that the dramatic text and its theatrical performance mutually reinforce one another. Thus conjoined, the production effort is strong enough to overrule even classical authority. The new model forcefully embraces both the gaps and the links between what represents and what is represented (and received). In fact, these gaps and links are constitutive of a new poetics of representation in the Elizabethan theatre.

Despite its traditional elements, Lyly's was an innovative project for a 'scene individable' (*Hamlet* [1601], 2.2.401) on which the contingent world of history could be represented and the representations themselves historicized in a poetics of reference and reception. Here, the issue of authority in the legitimation of theatrical discourse is negotiated in terms of the changing disposition of the agents, the objects, and the aims of representation itself. There is a sense that the theatre, in direct response to audience demand, serves a legitimate cultural function and, in doing precisely that, is bound to represent and to signify. The issue of authority is inextricably linked with the complex positioning of a theatrical poetics that charts the theatre as an institution which both represents and is representative. The prologue to *Midas* is as follows:

> Gentlemen, so nice is the world, that for apparel there is no fashion, for Music no instrument, for diet no delicate, for plays no invention, but breedeth satiety before noon, and contempt before night.
>
> Come to the Tailor, he is gone to the Painters, to learn how more cunning may lurk in the fashion, than can be expressed in the making. Ask the Musicians, they will say their heads ache with devising notes beyond Ela. Enquire at the Ordinaries, there must be sallets for the Italian; picktooths for the Spaniard; pots for the German; porridge for the Englishman. At our exercises, Soldiers call for Tragedies, their object is blood: Courtiers for Comedies, their subject is love; Countrymen for Pastorals, Shepherds are their Saints. Traffic and travel hath woven the nature of all Nations into ours, and made this land like Arras, full of devise, which was Broad-cloth, full of workmanship. Time hath confounded our minds, our minds the matter; but all cometh to this pass, that what heretofore hath been served in several

dishes for a feast, is now minced in a charger for a Gallimaufry. If we present a mingle-mangle, our fault is to be excused, because the whole world is become an Hodge-podge.

We are jealous of your judgments, because you are wise; of our own performance, because we are unperfect; of our Author's device, because he is idle. Only this doth encourage us, that presenting our studies before Gentlemen, though they receive an inward mislike, we shall not be hissed with an open disgrace.[2]

The prologue's culinary metaphor begins early, with 'sallets', 'picktooths', 'pots', and 'porridge', and continues with 'dishes for a feast', 'minced in a charger', and 'Gallimaufry'. Thus does the usher figure we have seen in other plays locate the institution of the playhouse *vis-à-vis* an ordinary (a tavern or eating-house) offering up its fare to a diverse clientele. While not directly assuming the role of waiter or table-attendant, the prologue identifies the cultural and social valences of the theatre by means of a strongly grounded sense of 'unperfect' service.

This serving prologue's allusion to the world of 'Traffic and travel', linked to 'all Nations', is suggestive. His implication is that the space for representation is large enough to reconstitute itself, and to do so in reference to a more broadly national and mobile society. This refashioning, in turn, allows for much greater latitude in the uses of signs and genres. In and through these strategies of representation, Lyly multiplies the efficacy of a coherent world-picture by setting out (in Heidegger's sense of *Vor-stel-lung*) the picture before and in relation to an agency. This turning of the world into a picture of a representation answers a need for self-orientation and control in the face of a bewildering rate of change. By the time of Lyly's prologue, the traditional, limited repertoire of choices in moral allegory or in the Tudor interlude had been superseded by more experimental norms of writing, reading, and understanding.

More than anything, the world-picturing thrust of this prologue resides in its suggestion that what is represented in the play can be related to changing constellations of reference outside the theatre, as these affect 'our exercises' and 'our minds'. But again the first person possessive plural, which points to the representing agents, is an inclusive one to which the whole theatre, including but not limited to the poet, is eligible. This encompassing text, groping toward a new cultural stock-taking, demonstrates how the conflation of the picturing and the delegating, of the imaginative and the social registers of representation, has become the keynote and criterion of writing for theatrical productions. But this keynote, as soon as performance is acknowledged as authorizing more than purely textual meaning, is doubly encoded: it participates in what Susan

Wells calls the 'typical' as well as the 'indeterminable' registers of representation.[3] The performer, just like the playwright, is, in Jacques Derrida's phrase, 'not only someone who has representations, who represents himself, but also someone who himself represents something or someone'.[4]

This is one reason why the referents and addressees in the prologue's use of signs appear so interactive: in acknowledging the expectations of the soldiers, courtiers, and countrymen in the audience, the dramatist is prepared at least to justify his own writing as a response to their differing modes of self-projection. Lyly's prologue goes further than other types of contemporary discourse in relating the act of authorization itself to communicative realities in the uses of language, realities in this case that involve audience response and expectation. The situatedness of these grounds of legitimation collides somewhat regretfully with traditional (classical) norms of authorship. Thus, the representation of 'a mingle-mangle' is sanctioned by its reference to the expectations of its audience, even though Lyly continues to deplore any generic deviation from what his editor, R. W. Bond, described as 'the regulating check and control of classical taste' (2: 248). To the dramatist this deviation appears unprecedented in being so deeply implicated in time, place, and circumstance. Despite Lyly's own courtly aspirations, the new uses of representation, which Lyly projects almost reluctantly, are referred not to any given order of discourse – not even to one particular location such as the court – but to 'the whole world', precisely because it itself 'is become an Hodge-podge'.

Lyly scarcely conceals the improvised quality of this authorization: such improvisation seems linked to a comparable agency in the novel ability of this writing to point to its own situatedness. The demands (and unexplored possibilities) of the communicative process themselves appear to privilege a new kind of authority in representation that can best address this situatedness. In the prologue's acknowledgment of a mixed audience, the 'Soldiers', 'Courtiers', and 'Countrymen' are of course nothing but signs, and as such far from having any compelling social referent. Even so (and just because they themselves are part of a heavily stylized representation), the signification cannot be read in isolation from the deliberate reference to what Jonson would later call, in the prologue to *Every Man out of His Humour* (1599), 'the disposition of those times' – as such times affected the dominant groups in Lyly's private theatre.

Lyly's prologue correlates peculiarly what is representing 'at our exercises' and what is represented as its product. Such correspondence serves a mimetic desire for socio-cultural identification. In other words, the audience is depicted as desiring to see its symbolic equivalent on stage, but the audience itself has more than one social identity; in response to this composite desire, various projected social positions receive their cultural and symbolic correlatives. Their 'call for' a representative space of fictional equivalence is responded to in dramatic forms and images transcending the text of the prologue. Here the prologue represents a larger, self-propelled use of discursive space; this use remains inseparable from the projected image of a mixed audience demand for unprecedented self-articulation. For Lyly with his humanist background, the continuity between these signs and their identifying, self-acknowledging meanings predominates. But although such continuity must not be underrated, it does not preclude elements of contradiction and discontinuity, and the new norms of representation must somehow cope with them if they are to be at all efficacious. 'Soldiers', 'Courtiers', and 'Countrymen' are signs that serve a twofold function: they represent, and are represented by, theatrical 'object[s]' and 'subject[s]'. The prologue links these social representatives and their cultural represented. The new authority of these post-allegorical representations is amply recognized in the language of the prologue, who draws on symbolic uses of 'blood', 'love', and 'Shepherds'. The notion of language as a self-authorized vehicle of symbolic equivalences is central to this acknowledgement of thematic preferences among theatre audiences. What the prologue himself conveys is, more than anything, the energizing interplay, in his own text and in the theatre, between the representing and the represented, but also, and simultaneously, between showing and writing.

'Soldiers', 'Courtiers', and 'Countrymen' point to a more complex and by no means univocal signified on the level of what they stand for; in the playhouse where the prologue is speaking, it is the mixed audience. But they also point to some symbolic level not in the cultural institution but in the writing of the play. Hence, in a more symbolic register, 'blood' is called for as an 'object' of tragedy (and a cultural correlative of soldiers); 'love' as a 'subject' of comedy (corresponding to courtiers); and 'Shepherds' are claimed as the protagonists of pastoral (related to countrymen). Taken together, these significations artfully enclose both institution and text, but they also serve to suggest a new kind of heterogeneity in the social uses of representation. The note of bewilderment, then, from the point of view of the writing, seems perfectly understandable. It is precisely because authority has ceased to be available as given in the culture of any one class or ideology that the new poetics of the theatre is forced to cope with the incongruity of these differing angles of expectation: 'If we present a mingle-mangle, our fault is to be excused'. In this situation, to grope for new foundations of authority in representation is not to ignore but to face and spell out the collision of diverse socio-cultural interests. It is out of this collision that the figure of 'Gallimaufry' and a new accommodation of difference in representation emerges.

As the prologue appeals to various social positions among spectators and proceeds to sanction the representations they themselves call for on the stage, the world of the audience and the forms of drama are made to interact in an unprecedented fashion: the element of social mobility among the spectators and the 'mingle-mangle' among dramatic forms and genres are playfully (and of course quite schematically) intertwined. For all this, the new perspective on tragicomedy reveals a generic self-consciousness comparable only to that of Italian tragicomic theory. But in Lyly's text, neither the language of tragedy or comedy (or indeed, pastoral) appears sufficiently privileged by itself to represent dramatic significations of 'the whole world', 'all nations', even 'this land'. What the prologue envisages is a more encompassing dramatic language that leaves behind traditional generic distinctions.

Nor is the search for this broader space in theatrical discourse limited to the language of the prologue; more importantly, the play *Midas* irresistibly moves to confront the antagonism, articulated stridently in pro-English and anti-Spanish terms, between rival nations. Hence, the traditional moral disquisition on the allegory of ambition, lust, and cruelty cannot satisfy when its object is Midas/Phillip who, representing the hostile forces of Phrygia, foolishly attempts to conquer Lesbos/England. But here the uses of allegorical signs fail adequately to address the contingencies of early modern European history; this failure is especially marked when the larger subject-matter ('this land', 'all nations', 'the whole world') is made to squat uncomfortably on the familiar rungs of an allegorical debate where the curse of the ass's ears is fitted into a moral parable of military power, national pride, and self-deception.

Faced, then, with a crisis both in the authority of neoclassical poetics and the validity of allegorical form, the problem for Lyly was one of appropriating, in terms of representational strategy, a larger and more contingent correlation of sign and matter. For all intents and purposes, the uses of moral debate – of such great significance in what Joel Altman called 'the Tudor play of mind'[5] – could not contain an untidy world of 'Traffic and travel'. The neat projection of allegorical order proved outdated, or at least unable to cope with a huge and quite unpredictable proliferation of signs and meanings. The problem for Lyly was to redefine the imaginative uses of what he believed to be truthful knowledge and to do so through his awareness of a new social function of (self-)referentiality in the theatre. The result was that, astonishingly, 'confusion' itself could inform representation. Henceforth contingency and mobility themselves had to inspire the representational project so as to break up any tidy, preordained set of correspondences between signs and meanings.

For writers before the sixteenth century, allegory was a mode of discourse in which thematic interests predominated over mimetic interest, where the structure of meaning was more predictable than in postallegorical writings.[6] But Ariosto, Pulci, Spenser, and other Renaissance poets had already discovered that fixed meanings, unambiguous contrasts, and clear moral options were at odds with early modern mutability. As Lyly in his theatre gradually surrendered the dramatic tradition of allegorical personification, he must have felt both the continuing impact and the limitations of traditional moral and rhetorical exercises.[7] Once the universalizing chain of being and the transcendental figure of cosmological correspondences ceased to be of much help in the business of dramatic signification, the structuring principle of 'unification around debate' was gradually perforated. Now a much less stringent form of composition (described by G. K. Hunter as 'harmonious variety'[8]) offered its own welcome alternatives. But even these, as Peter Saccio has suggested, did not sufficiently allow for the more complex mimetic mode by which the static 'situationalism' of the 1580s was discarded in favour of a more temporal kind of dramaturgy – one that brought forth 'an unfolding narrative plot' capable of engrossing the spectator.[9]

The prologue to *Midas* must therefore be seen as participating in and promoting the transition to a temporally structured form, even when this form, in the playtext itself, was grafted upon a partially sustained frame of allegorical meaning and moral debate.[10] The resulting inconsistencies, far from being conclusive evidence of a revision, at least in part reflected the difficult strategy of what Saccio has called 'projecting allegorical meaning in a narrative drama'.[11] Small wonder, then, that this prologue, despite its remarkable foray toward a new and distinctly early modern poetics of representation, cannot suppress memories of paratactic catalogues and recollections of a tripartite order of things, which, revealingly, are spread out in a non-hierarchical, horizontal array rather than a vertical one ('Come to the Tailor . . . Ask the Musicians . . . Enquire at the Ordinaries . . .'). But this residue of a premodern state of affairs was consistently transmuted into a theatrical presentation that served as a vehicle of conflicting interests, a site of social delegation, an opening for diverse cultural tastes and pursuits. The difficulty involved in this transmutation, however, was not simply a verbal one, but had to do with mustering sufficient authority for more encompassing and less circumscribed uses of theatrical (re)presentation. These changeful standards of the diversity of 'invention' in dramatic composition are hinted at, again, in a horizontal rather than a vertical order, and embedded in a welter of cultural changes involving fashion, music, and cuisine. The prologue, fully aware of the interrelation of the variegated modes of cultural consumption, situated the theatre in a contingent world that must have been exhilarating as well as troublesome once –

in the playhouse – it had to be coped with in terms of neoclassical doctrine. What for Lyly the humanist dramatist was bewildering about a notion of the theatre as a site of shifting and mingle-mangle practices was not only such practices' heterogeneous form and representative functions, but the complex way the former was to dovetail with the latter. Just as the uses of representational form had become less static, representative functions – the norms of representativeness itself – were also conceived as unpreordained and mobile. They were contingent in the sense that relations between those who represent on stage and those who (in the prologue) were represented in their calls for cultural identity follow no unambiguous, fixed formula. On one hand, members of the audience call for representative forms and images of their own social particularity; on the other, these heavily stylized spectators are themselves representatives. They represent something or someone outside the theatre: their social (un)conscious asserts itself after it is no longer shrouded in the universalizing garb of 'Mankind' or *humanum genus*.

Instead, the overall links (and gaps) between representational form and representative function clearly are in motion. In the prologue, their kinetic energy is stronger than any generic boundary, any pure form of identity and demarcation. If there is any one socio-historical correlative for such force, the prologue is anxious to give it a local habitation and a name; thus, they are specified in terms of the mobility and heterogeneity of social interests that 'this land' will yield through 'Traffic and travel'. From here, the prologue irresistibly proceeds to a global picture in which the representation of 'the whole world' implicates a symbolic form or topography 'like Arras, full of devise'. The pattern in the new tapestry of representation is manifold; it cannot be uniform or univocal when the devising faculties themselves are imbued with heterogeneous experiences that transcend the structure of hierarchy and isolation characterizing the previously rigid framework of the various estates and professions. Here, ultimately, is both the liberating force of 'mingle-mangle' composition, and the nascent use of a masterful 'world picture' that through representation helps appropriate a highly contingent, mobile set of circumstances.

Thus, in this new departure in poetics, the grounds of authority and the contexts of history have, as it were, formed an unprecedented alliance. In Lyly's prologue, an element of contingency appears inseparable from this new authority, and not only in terms of what is represented as 'the matter' of drama: 'Time hath confounded our minds, our minds the matter'. The confusion thus works both ways: the 'minds' behind the signifying activity, the uses of language itself, are affected by 'Time' and by what is to be represented, as these times go. But the mingle-mangle 'matter' which the prologue presents, the product of representation itself, is in its turn affected, and confounded, by the author-function in the writing – a writing fully aware of the opaque forcefulness of 'Time' in the act of representation itself.

The voices of historicity inscribed in Lyly's text make themselves felt in both the metaphorical language and the cultural topography that the prologue uses, not to mention the synonymous variations of 'Hodge-podge' and 'Gallimaufry'. Dislodging the authority of immutable rules within the neoclassical tradition, Lyly harkens back to the language of Euphuism which, even in a faint echo, appears fantastically unsettling, as well as revealing. For at the point of this confusion, where 'minds' and 'matter' are 'confounded' by 'Time' itself, the neat order of triads and catalogues breaks down, making room for something more deeply unsettling and incommensurate. Here is the point where, as we have suggested, integration and division collide. If anything, the language of both kitchen and manufacture conveys the paradox that 'mingle-mangle' synthesis and new forms of socio-cultural differentiation mutually condition one another. It was a paradox by which, for a few precious years, the Elizabethan theatre brought forth an unprecedented spectrum of both difference and inclusiveness in dramatic representation. Along these lines, if 'Traffic' must be read (following the *OED*) as semantically involving 'the transportation of merchandise for the purpose of trade; hence, trade between distant or distinct communities;' similarly, 'travel' (still resonating with French *travail*) can be understood as connoting 'the outcome, product, or result of toil or labour'. But both trade and labour, in bringing together diverse and hitherto isolated goods, lands, people, and activities, establish a new order of stratifying uses of property and commodity.

These social correlatives of Lyly's language betray a historical awareness the more impressive for having been so neatly adapted to the metaphorical texture of the imagery of 'weaving', the foremost industry of the time. While the new order of weaving hitherto alien things 'into ours' helps appropriate and integrate a world of products and relations, it also and simultaneously brings forth 'satiety', 'fashion', new 'devise', and a diversity and division of labour. The innovative pattern, richly tapestried with newly accessible signs of diverse tastes, tools, and practices, reveals that bewildering surplus of the signifier which by far exceeds the discursive possibilities of the morality and interlude traditions. The resulting fullness of 'devise' and 'workmanship' goes to inform the imagery Lyly calls on: both the kitchen and the loom conjure metaphors that are representative *of* the times and are made to represent something *in* their time. The new authority behind the metaphoric use of such *sermo humilis* is doubly potent because this imagery serves to sustain both an object of and an agency in the project of representation. The appeal, sustaining the link between the two, is to the contingent world of work, travel, and consumption, to communication, circulation, exchange, and trade. With this circulatory energy set free, the correlation made by the readers and spectators between what this pictorial language shows and what the picture in the language does releases a new type of 'imaginary puissance' in the theatre.

The newly mobile conjuncture between representational form and representative function anticipates what in Gayatri Spivak's terms is the joining of 'portrait' and 'proxy'.[12] This conjunction goes hand in hand with a language of unlimited social interaction that has an important correlative outside the theatre. Social historians ever since the days of A. L. Rowse and J. B. Black have amply documented this state of affairs; there is as little doubt about the 'mobility of social classes' or even the 'babylonian confusion' of social relations in late Tudor England as there is, in the more recent terminology of Peter Burke, Keith Wrightson, Roger Chartier, and others, about differentiation and withdrawal as a process of European dimensions.[13] The Elizabethan stage could take this confusion for its platform, in the sense that the livelier intercourse between 'minds' and 'matter' seemed to be contiguous to a distinctly modern type of knowledge and epistemology. There was an uncanny interplay, even complicity, between the manifold confusion in the 'matter' of historiography and a complementary fullness in the working of the mirror. Representation, and especially closure between 'portrait' and 'proxy', must have helped cope with the confounding challenges of a new mode of poetic knowledge. In terms of cultural history, it was at this moment of rapid change and transition that a sense of contingency in social history and the emergence of post-lineage, contractual relations first appeared to complement and even stipulate one another. It was then that, as in Lyly's prologue, a sense of the interdependence of variegated forms of cultural and social change emerged and that the impact on the theatre of unheard-of mobility and distant trade could first be articulated as a moment in and for poetics.

What the prologue to *Midas* seems to suggest, then, is a linkage between the availability in the theatre of some highly contingent (and confusing) 'matter' and the advent of unprecedented aims and modes of representation. These new representational strategies by no means limited the sign to what Michel Foucault has called its sixteenth-century functions of resemblance and repetition, by which, in its various forms of *convenientia, aemulatio,* analogy and so forth, the principle of similitude maintained the world in its unity and identity. Nor did the new profusion of signifying activities anticipate its classical phase in that these became a 'determinate form in our consciousness'.[14] On the contrary, there emerged a heightened capacity of the new representation for simultaneously relating to a diversity of referents (in Foucault's terminology, 'indication') *and* manifesting its own new aperture and motion in its form or (again Foucault's term) 'appearance'. This capability opened up unprecedented space for both the perception of difference and its accommodation and socialization in world-picturing form. There was, on one hand, a greater sense of the hardness and self-sufficiency of circumstances and, on the other, an increased space for the theatre's self-assertion and for the self-projection of its own institutionalized workings. For these, the language of manufacture and the kitchen served only too well.

Lyly's prologue pointed the way to a largely unformulated source of authority, inseparable from what 'devise', through the theatre's own 'workmanship', could be brought forth in production. Releasing its performative energies in the playhouse, Elizabethan representation could serve as both 'indication' and 'appearance'. The contingent world of 'Traffic and travel' had entered the theatre itself. Here was exchange, circulation, intercourse, and, most important, the disavowal of difference between the sense of the world in its hardness 'out there' and its engagement on the stage. Similarly, the newly opened space for product and process, allowing for the display of both the result and the effort 'to bring forth / So great an object' (*Henry V*, Pro. 10–11) was visible for all who cared to see (and pay for) it. As the authority of humanist poetics diminished, it was this strenuous modern intercourse between mind and matter, the cause of intellectual appropriation itself, which, more than anything else, helped validate the new departure in representational form and energy.

Lyly's prologue to *Midas* marked the advent of cultural practices on the Elizabethan stage that led to far-reaching complications within the circulation of authority in theatrical representations. Against the authority of current generic conventions, from neoclassical drama to popular farce, the various forms of both written and performed representation were now no longer exclusively 'served in several dishes;' instead, they were rapidly becoming so 'minced' – and so interdependent – that in the country's metropolis the result was a dramatic discourse excluding neither the farcical nor the learned, neither the comic language of *sermo humilis* nor the 'high astounding terms' of tragedy. The Elizabethan theatre had 'the best actors in the world, either for tragedy, comedy, history, pastoral, pastoral-comical, historical-pastoral, tragical-historical, tragical-comical-historical-pastoral, scene individable, or poem unlimited' (*Hamlet*, 2.2.95 ff.). Shakespeare's 'swelling scene' (*Henry V*, Pro. 4) had so engaged a mingle-mangle world, that the order of 'Gallimaufry' was represented as well as representing: it was an order informing both an emerging world picture and the process of theatrical production. Here, maturing in the 1590s, was a cultural institution which claimed, in Lyly's words, 'the whole world' for its province and endeavoured to embrace a range of appropriations no smaller than 'the great globe itself' (*The Tempest* [1611] 4.1.153).

Lyly, as a recent critic argues, may have provided Shakespeare with 'his leading model'.[15] What for the later dramatist was most exemplary in this model was a practically unsanctioned strategy of 'minced' representation, 'full of devise' in a divided or at least 'distracted globe' – which phrase in *Hamlet* (1.5.97) in its turn resounds with a 'confounded' sense of boundaries between memory and matter, inside and outside the theatre. Toward the end of his career in the theatre Lyly was still groping for what Shakespeare was about to achieve: an abiding linkage between the theatre's puissance in the appropriation of the world and its cultural identity as a 'mingle-mangle' institution of its own, with its own 'global' metaphor. As Louis Montrose suggests, 'theatrical power' in Shakespeare's playhouse 'lay precisely in the combination of representational resources that enabled it to enact and to epitomize the *theatrum mundi* metaphor', that is, 'in the doubly mimetic capacity' to serve 'as a representation of, and provocation to' performative action.[16] By the logic of this link the theatre was safely transgressing the old decorous rules of exclusion; meanwhile, the capacity of the 'charger' had become copious enough almost to take for granted the 'Hodge-podge' of myth and politics, the variegated 'Arras' of courtly fashion, the 'workman-ship' of commercial profit, 'high astounding' rhetoric, and the humbler language of the tavern. And, perhaps most remarkably, this capacity found its legitimation not in reference to any existing, let alone authoritatively sanctioned, poetics, but through the institutionalized form and purpose of theatrical communication itself – through criteria such as audience demand, desire and pleasure, as pregnant with the 'disposition of those times'.

Both Shakespeare and Lyly, for all the gulf between them, were con-cerned with broadening areas of concurrence and difference between mind and matter – 'matter' in the sense of both 'material stuff' and (traditional) *matière* in plot and story. This, incidentally, implicated a new awareness of relations between writing and performance and of the need for assimilating possible tensions between them in the theatrical transaction itself. For instance, Lyly's own stance, in more than one sense, anticipates Shake-speare's as that of a 'bending author' – 'bending' in the sense of 'prone', 'tractable' (with its root meaning of 'yielding', 'restrainable'). The strange mixture of boldness and modesty of the prologue to *Midas* is echoed in the language of Shakespeare's prologue to *Henry V*, which both brandishes and apologizes for the theatre's new departure in self-fashioned authorization. But whereas Shakespeare's chorus effectively assists in the projection of a concurrence of writing and performance – even while regretfully emphasiz-ing its necessary 'imperfections' (*Henry V*, Pro. 23) – these contradictions in Lyly, while addressed in the prologue, remain awkwardly visible in the rest of the play. It is above all in sounding the new space for representation and in interrelating its social and epistemological dimensions that Lyly contributes to the project on stages 'to bring forth / So great an object' (*Henry V*, Pro. 10–11).

However, neither the bewilderment in the language of Lyly's prologue nor the surprising modesty of Shakespeare's chorus can conceal the impromptu manner in which each dramatist's gestures of legitimation make common cause with the rather aimless direction of spatial, cultural, and social mobility. The chorus to Act 2 offers to 'digest / Th'abuse of distance, force a play' (31–2). In the structure of *Henry V*, mobility itself is there to 'force' or contrive the impromptu solution, to cope with what is unforeseen or with what has never been done before. Here as elsewhere, Shakespeare's is a 'swift scene', (3. 0. 1–3) whose kinetic energy derives from more than just the need to fill an empty stage with 'two hours' traffic'.

Appropriation in the Renaissance, as Stephen Greenblatt reminds us, presupposed 'improvisation' – that is, 'the ability both to capitalize on the unforeseen and to transform given materials into one's own scenario'. Such 'opportunistic grasp of that which seems fixed and established'[17] is at least partially what links Lyly's rather static situational dramaturgy to Shakespeare's 'swelling scene'. In contrast to Sidney's neoclassical demand for a unified representational space ('the stage should always represent one place') and for tragedy to be 'tied to the laws of *Poesie* and not of *History*',[18] the assimilation of 'distance' in time and space by the new dramaturgy to a scene 'in motion' was a vital representational strategy in the early modern public theatre. Here, the practically felt (and apologetically spelled out) need for what Sidney dismissed as a 'a kind of contrariety' in representation appeared to collide with and undermine the authority of neoclassical poetics.[19] 'For the law of writ and the liberty', the City players were 'the only men' (*Hamlet* 2.2.401). They indeed disposed of a liberty (an authority) to forego the 'law of writ' together with its classical heritage. What to them was disposable was not simply a given body of writings but the assumption that writing *per se* could be considered law even before it was read or used in performance. In the theatre there was no room for any installation of authority that preceded the actual performance and reception of the text. Traditional modes of literary authority, those given before the writing or the reading (or even the performance) of the text, had to be discarded. To dismiss any poetic authority 'before declared' was one of the most vital requirements of a living theatre whose expanding horizon of representation actually seemed to thrive on this crisis of poetic precept in humanist doctrine. Neoclassical order was therefore superseded by a new, thoroughly opportunistic regime of 'forcing' representations beyond their generic and temporal boundaries.

However, in this project there was a difference, incalculable in its consequences, between plays on common stages and Lyly's chapel boys. In the public theatre, there was a far more intricate and forceful ability for representation to 'digest / Th'abuse of distance' in both a spatial and a social sense of the word. In Shakespeare's theatre, the 'swift scene', its unfixed, 'swelling' potential, and finally its inherent propensity for 'bifold authority' was deeply associated with a circulation of authority in which both performers and a wide variety of spectators participated. They did so on a level that was crucial for the diversification of such representational strategies as fully responded to highly different and partially divisive uses of theatrical space. This space itself was marked by a capacity for 'motion of no less celerity / Than that of thought' (*Henry V*, 3. Chorus 2–3), in that it allowed for a rapid shifting in the respective locations of authority. 'Bifold authority' obtained, by which the representation of power (the dominant 'matter of worthiness') could strategically be intercepted, complemented but also enhanced through the power of performance.

We can turn here to the more fundamental and altogether conspicuous circumstances under which 'bifold authority' was as a matter of course linked to highly performative uses of theatre space. Existing on one hand under the shadow of the city's protests, restrictions, and repressive gestures and, on the other, under the gracious canopy of royal and aristocratic benevolence, the theatre was thrown back upon its own resources in coming to terms with the underlying clash of these differing authorities. Such resilience was possible in part because the public playhouses enjoyed a unique place in the cultural landscape of Elizabethan London; they were located in the Liberties, the area just beyond the city walls, perhaps the most licentious and unruly, as well as juridically the least defined, of sites – situated in the very teeth of the contradictions between city, court, and county. The very location of public stages may have embodied unresolved conflicts among diverse sources of political, economic, and juridical power in early modern England. The Liberties, as Steven Mullaney has shown, were 'ambivalent zones of transition between one realm of authority and another', an 'ambiguous realm, a borderland whose legal parameters and privileges were open-ended and equivocally defined'.[20] Resonant with long-standing traditions of ritual sport and pastime, this area of temporary release and distraction could be appropriated by such social groups as remained in touch with a traditional culture marked by strongly performative uses of voice and body.

No doubt these locations tended to privilege arts of display that presupposed, as we have suggested, not so much the representational uses of symbolically encoded signs but the physical presence and demonstration of skills, feats, and virtuosity in all kinds of achievements. In the neighbourhood of minstrels, puppeteers, rope-dancers, tumblers, acrobats, contortionists, mountebanks, bear-wards, jugglers, and ballad-mongers, common players must have continued to cherish a style of performance generated out of, or in response to, a communicative situation involving playful contest, gamesome challenge, repartee, and mother-wit. The cultural topography of Bankside and Finsbury Fields, in which strong memories of Tarlton and Kemp must have lingered, was obviously rather remote from the world of Lyly's chapel boys. And although after Paul Griffiths' study of *Youth and Authority* in early modern England we cannot continue to envision the schools of these boy actors as temples of unsexed innocence, and modest obedience,[21] the uses of performance in Lyly's private theatre must have differed greatly from the unlicenced pleasure and commingling traffic in an area no longer 'contained by the customary antitheses of rule or misrule, order or disorder, everyday and holiday'.[22] The commercially funded, secular, professional enterprise of the public theatre inevitably tended to go much further toward a mingle-mangle of textualized 'matter of worthiness' and the highly performative 'jestures' of frivolous voices and bodies. While 'heretofore' eloquent writing and robustious bodies had been 'served in several dishes for a feast', they were 'now minced in a charger for a Gallimaufry'. Shakespeare, who – using a congenial metaphor – was prepared to 'digest th' abuse' of (neoclassical) rules in his theatre, was not very particular about mincing his own 'dishes'. Here we only need to recall the early history of Shakespeare's career as playwright, when his writerly authority was notoriously challenged by Robert Greene, largely though not exclusively on the grounds of his hodge-podge capacity for assimilating 'several dishes' in the theatrical 'feast':

> Yes, trust them not: for there is an upstart Crow, beautified with our feathers, that with *his Tigers heart wrapt in a Player's hide*, supposes he is as well able to bombast out a blank verse as the best of you: and being an absolute *Johannes factotum*, is in his own conceit the only Shake-scene in the country. O that I might entreat your rare wits to be employed in more profitable course: & let those Apes imitate your past excellence, and never more acquaint them with your admired inventions . . . for it is pity men of such rare wits, should be subject to the pleasure of such rude grooms.[23]

Greene disapproved of Shakespeare's appropriation of the academically privileged 'rare wits' of university-trained playwrights: shocking to think that the 'past excellence' and 'admired inventions' of an Oxford or Cambridge education could now be competed with by 'an absolute *Johannes factotum*'! The undertone of insecurity and threatened privilege is transparent, and the shifting ground of authorial function is revealed when the authority of class and education needs to be summoned against an association with 'those Antics' – mere players from the country – when one of them thought himself capable of 'bombast[ing] out a blank verse' like 'the best of you'. What Greene most abhors (next to being 'forsaken') is to accept a conflation of hitherto separate activities as sufficient to guarantee public success in the theatre. Thus the phrase '*Johannes factotum*' (a 'Jack-of-all-trades'), which the *OED* defines as 'a would-be universal genius' or 'one who meddles with everything', is revealing: behind it lies the unexpressed anxiety that the academically sanctioned authority of possessing 'rare wits' and of being in command of the fine arts is being challenged by something more broadly viable than a purely literary education. Here Greene seems to defend himself against the impurity of a different inspiration for writing that must have appeared contaminated by its greater proximity to so unliterary and unlearned an institution as the common stage.

To make the composition of blank verse coextensive with its reproduction on the stage – and, worse still, with its impersonation by common actors – appeared scandalous to Robert Greene. In voicing his disappointment, Greene not only emphasized the social distance between poets and players; he reconfirmed the gulf between the more lowly and robustious culture of voices and bodies associated with 'the jigging veins of rhyming mother-wits' and those endeavours of art that culminated in 'the admiring inventions' of the humanistically educated 'rare wits', in the eloquence of those 'high-astounding terms' that Marlowe might justly take pride in. Since Shakespeare was not a university-trained writer and since, factotum-like, he combined acting with writing for the common stage, in his early years he may well have appeared to Greene as the ungentle epitome of one 'indecorous' enough to annul the genteel distance between mother-wits and rare ones. For a mere upstart actor to have snatched the right for himself 'to bombast out a blank verse as the best of you' was to exploit to the full the recent cultural points of interaction between proliferating discourse and social mobility. As Walter Cohen has convincingly argued, the public theatre 'was a composite formation in which disparate modes [of production] coexisted and intertwined',[24] and, we might add, in which cultural hybrids and theatrical factota thrived.

Shakespeare's early success in the theatre as a 'Jack-of-all-trades' appeared to threaten the ambitious (if precarious) stand of the *literati* on their privilege, if not dominance, of writing. Crucially, his career began in circumstances which preceded the Jacobean assumption 'that drama had to defend itself from irrelevant producers, bad actors, and stupid audiences'.[25] Even as he pursued the arts of dramatic writing to an unprecedented peak of literary excellence, he retained the sense of immediacy where the performed text continued to be generated out of, or in response to, a cultural occasion for which the audience was constitutive. As a dramatist he combined the traditional perspective of a culturally integrated author-function with a new and differentiated notion of dramatic art as a specifically representational, 'unlimited' and composite practice. This traditional perspective more and more tended to come into conflict with what Robert Knapp has called the 'real newness in Shakespeare', that is to say the growing assumption 'that a play should pretend not to be implicated in the "non-literary"'.[26] But while Shakespeare continued to contradict this assumption, from his earliest work to *The Tempest* he continued to draw on sources of authority in the theatre that preceded as well as those that participated in the early modern differentiation among cultural practices. This half-way position in the Elizabethan theatre was to prove a unique source of strength, particularly in assimilating and revitalizing, in the playhouse, what continued to remain viable of the mingle-mangle culture of the times. Thus, Shakespeare was especially fortunate to absorb and turn to account a commingling juncture of openings when 'Time hath confounded our minds, our minds the matter'.

Authority in the Elizabethan playhouse, then, was not unified, conclusive, or given prior to a performance; it needed to be validated by the audience and was implicated in the effect of and response to the theatrical production itself. In other words, the theatrical uses of authority were remarkably open-ended; far from being prescribed or given by one specific tradition, they were pragmatically decided upon in the composite manner of unlimited representation itself. They were linked to a multiplicity of divergent social and cultural functions by which a persistent confounding of 'minds' and 'matter' could be rehearsed in the very 'form and pressure' (*Hamlet*, 3.2.24) of their theatrical performance.

For Shakespeare, actor and 'Jack-of-all-trades', to launch upon a career in the dramatic art of composition was, from the very outset, to be exposed to the complex and potentially divisive circulation of authority in the theatre. It involved an experience and a point of view from which it must have appeared desirable to confront both the gaps and the links between the poetics of representation and the craft of performance in the theatre. Such an experience somehow had to embrace and to reconcile with one another the literary representation of fictive meaning and the actual circumstances of performing practice. Even in attempting to view (as Hamlet was to do in his advice to the players) fictional representation and corporeal performance as two sides of the same coin, the dramatist must nonetheless have felt that they were far from identical. For one thing, he would have observed how the textualized fiction of dramatic dialogue was simultaneously exposed to, realized by, and adapted to the order of performance.

Even more important, an actor (or otherwise engaged factotum) in the theatre must have perceived that in the Elizabethan playhouse the order of performance was again and again bound to invoke the disorder of contemporary existence. No doubt the gap between the literary text of representation and theatrical agents of performance could be suspended by an exceptional degree of concurrence and complementarity, so much so that Lyly's 'Hodge-podge' could become what Polonius refers to as a 'scene individable'. But for someone like Shakespeare who came to stage-playing young, beginning his career as a veritable 'upstart', this artful medium of fictional representations was undeniably a site of real work and profit, an existential location of human effort and chaos, a source of postscriptural memory, forgetfulness, and desire.

7   *Henry V* and the signs of power

William Shakespeare

From Lyly's 'Gallimaufry' before *Midas* (1589), we turn now to what remains the best-known prologue of the early modern theatre: that to Shakespeare's *Henry V* (1599). This prologue retains its status partly because it encapsulates so thoroughly a dense variety of issues related to the early modern theatre itself – in particular, the theatre's desire for legitimation. Along with its choruses and epilogue, the prologue to *Henry V* constitutes a salient figure of presentation and liminality and addresses concerns of legitimation.[1] In particular, these parts of *Henry V* seek to authorize, justify, and accommodate the text of history in the theatre of 'playing holiday' (*1 Henry IV* [1597], 1.2.204) but also, and even more consequentially, to legitimate the common stage as a public medium of historical understanding regardless of its imperfect iconography. To say this (and to suggest that such a project was beset by profound strains) is not to deny the multiplicity of other functions belonging to the chorus. As it begs the audience's 'humble patience . . . / Gently to hear, kindly to judge, our play' (Pro. 33–4), the chorus helps to insure success, applause, response, and communication on behalf of the drama in performance. But whatever other functions the chorus serves, its project draws on, and invests in, a liminal position between the world in the play and playing in the world of Elizabethan London. As vehicles of display, mediation, and legitimation, the speeches of the chorus straddle the threshold between the presentation *of* the play and the representation *in* the play.

The chorus as usher and presenter, mediating between text and institution, has considerable authority on several levels. The ravishing, even 'coercive',[2] in Andrew Gurr's phrase, use of iambic language and the golden throatings of a 'Muse of fire' work to captivate, entrance, and carry away the spectator. But then the eloquent speaker also achieves a fair degree of independence, even the liberty, to counterbalance the play in action. Great partiality characterizes his (re)presentation; the chorus selects from, re-emphasizes, misreads, even partially obliterates the text of the play.

The resulting discrepancy between what the play does and what the chorus says it does raises questions that vitally concern the relation of text and institution. It is clearly not sufficient to view this relation in representational terms only – that is, as to whether (and if so to what degree) the chorus faithfully reflects or indeed re-invents the play itself. But if, as an expositor, the chorus remains extremely unreliable, we need to confront the fact that the exposition itself seems to be plagued by redundancies, irrelevancies, and a heavy dose of ideology. Nor can we at this late date account for the obvious gap between presentational efficacy and representational inaccuracy by renewed recourse to doubt 'that the choruses and the play were written by the same hand'.[3] Clearly a gap exists. The perception of this gap has become more and more significant; this is especially the case in light of growing scepticism that 'the actual purpose' of prologue, choruses, and epilogue was 'to sound a patriotic note in exaltation of the heroic king', so as to 'link the five acts together'.[4]

Over the past decades, *Henry V*'s prologue and chorus have been reread an astonishing number of times. It was against the view of the chorus as a unifying patriotic force in the play that, with growing force from the late 1970s, diverse counterproposals have been put forward. It has been asked, for instance, whether the 'unexamined and questionable premise: that the chorus is the very voice of the public playhouse' need not be scrapped in favour of the entirely different conclusion that 'the Chorus is symptomatic of court performance'[5] in the Royal Cockpit. On another level, 'the pomp and glory of which the Chorus speaks' have been taken to serve a complementary function in that they 'represent one extreme of the spectrum of ideas on patriotism, as Pistol represents the other extreme'.[6] From the point of view of its generic affiliation, the chorus with its appeal to 'a Muse' is viewed as the epic voice that envisions 'a golden world true to the imagination' while 'the action of the play, more often than not, presents the brazen truth of history'.[7]

These readings have important implications for the issue of early modern authority, especially in generically divergent discourses. But there is a limit to which any generic or ideological juxtaposition (let alone opposition) between chorus and playtext can go. No doubt it is possible and, indeed, helpful to read the chorus as the antipodal voice of an 'official historiographer' whose 'orthodox legend' of events clashes with and is engaged by the representation of 'the real historical movement' with a view to establishing 'discrepancy' between the two as a 'strategy for reception'.[8] However, as long as we fail to address the strange symbiosis of historiography and theatricality in the chorus, we shall miss a countervailing flow of authorizations in and through the presenter, a flow that profoundly complicates the picture. For while the chorus flaunts his ideologically charged bias at spectators, he also (and at the same time) appeals to them to sanction an entirely different type of history. Out of the ambivalence of his liminal position, in fact, his 'tone tells us that he's sorry but proud, and proud of being sorry'.[9]

Such ambivalence ultimately participates in and promotes the newly interactive, confusing formula of historiography we saw outlined in Lyly's *Midas*: 'Time hath confounded our minds, our minds the matter' – especially the matter of history as divided between its political and its cultural legends.[10] For the chorus, even in rehearsing the grand narrative of English conquest, does so through his performance, which is part of an unsanctioned cultural production. If anywhere Shakespeare's theatre continues to excel at what, in Jean Alter's definition of the 'performant function', is a display of virtuosity, a feat in exquisitely skilled delivery, it is in the strong performative associated with the chorus.[11] As Michael Goldman has poignantly noted, his speeches serve as 'display arias for the commanding actor; they stimulate us to share his noticeable effort, to be aware of the glory and labor involved in making authoritative sounds' until there is, together with 'the sensation of stupendous energies at work', a sense of his delivery even as 'a remarkable athletic exercise'.[12]

It is not true, then, that in *Henry V* we have 'a Chorus who contrives to get, really, *everything* wrong'. As an epistemological issue, the question of getting it 'right' or 'wrong' provides us with a somewhat inadequate perspective – unless, of course, we proceed to an ironic reading of 'the Chorus's apologies' and 'inconsistencies' as 'saying . . . not how the theatre has failed, but how it has triumphed'. In fact, as one critic has noted, such features say nothing simply; they 'force us to *think*, not perhaps always comfortably [. . .] about what it is that being a hero actually means'.[13]

However, these 'contradictions' must not be seen to be in the nature of a 'dichotomy' (Antony Hammond's term) but as putting both sides of the proposition in question. If the patriotic fervour of the prologue were altogether irreconcilable with the language of the play at large, it would surely be impossible to demonstrate – as Goldman and Lawrence Danson have persuasively done – a surprising number of correlations between chorus and king in the play.[14] And vice versa: if the play in itself can be read as a disruptive text, it seems equally desirable to reread prologue, chorus, and epilogue as *rupturing* the unity of time and place, the stability of signs and their meanings, as well as received positions in historiography and politics. But, again, to do so in terms of a purely ideological critique is less than fully helpful; rather, a more yielding approach to the chorus is one that, in Joel Altman's phrase, would – without foregoing this critique – engage 'the play's power in terms of its crafted interaction with the needs of its players and its first audiences'.[15]

In the present context, such reading would seek to explore the relationship of play and prologue in terms of a circulation of authority that is obstructed by, and yet traverses, the boundary line between the worthy matter of heroic action and the 'unworthy' concerns of getting the play across. In this view, the chorus itself, rather than being pitted against the events in the play, will appear to serve a double, even perhaps a double-dealing, function, As Graham Holderness has noted, the 'relationship between the 'heroic' and the 'ironical' dimensions of the play is not in any balance or synthesis of incongruous truths; [. . .] The Choruses are there to foreground the *artificiality* of the dramatic event, placing a barrier between action and audience'.[16]

Again, the doubleness, not to say contrariety, in the functions of the chorus finds an equivalent in the play itself, especially in what Annabel Patterson has called 'the play's unstable representational field'.[17] Such instability begins with the playtext; it appears most striking, in fact, when we take into consideration the large area of difference between the Folio and the Quarto versions of the play. By omitting the prologue, chorus, and epilogue, the Quarto eliminates the play's vulnerable self-(re)presentation of its thresholds as well as the idealizing voice of epic stylization. It does so, however, without obliterating the language of *sermo humilis*, including those parts of the play in which characters like Pistol or soldiers like Bates and Williams figure prominently. Gary Taylor, to whose *Three Studies in the Text of 'Henry V'* all commentary on the two versions of the play is heavily indebted, had first suggested 'that virtually every major change in the Quarto is the logical and clear consequence of an adaptation presupposing a reduced cast'. Even when casting exigencies cannot exclusively account for changes that may reflect larger, cultural motivations, 'we must always be conscious of possible theatrical motives' behind such omissions.[18] As an illustration, such motives almost certainly guided the most notorious of Q's interpolations, where, at the end of 4.6, the insertion of Pistol's final words to his French captive, 'Couple gorge', culminates in the horror and laughter and, presumably, the murderous bravado of a sacrificial act, involving both the life of the prisoner and the loss, to its captor, of ransom as a vital means of existence and subsistence.[19]

At the same time, the publication of the Quarto (between 4 and 14 August 1600), coming well after Essex had returned from Ireland in the autumn of 1599, must have been under formidable pressure to preempt (at least as prophecy) the highly ambivalent claim of the chorus that 'the general of our gracious Empress' was, 'from Ireland coming, / Bringing rebellion broached on his sword' (5.0.30; 31–2). Since, in these months, merely to praise Essex could result in imprisonment, it was, as Patterson has shown, 'hardly surprising that the published quarto text of the play makes this interpretation unreadable by erasing it'.[20] Whatever else must have induced the omission of the complete chorus from the Quarto, this circumstance by itself attests to how contingency would enlarge the range of explanatory factors to such a degree that one holistic model appears incapable of patterning the Quarto/Folio relationship in any satisfactory manner.[21]

If, then, as in the case of the prologue to *Romeo and Juliet* (1596), the textual history of the prologue would seem to indicate hidden tensions in the act of authorization itself, it is perhaps not fortuitous that the note of authority seems palpably impaired by a humble, even apologetic, tone:

> But pardon, gentles all,
> The flat unraised spirits that hath dar'd
> On this unworthy scaffold to bring forth
> So great an object. Can this cockpit hold
> The vasty fields of France? Or may we cram
> Within this wooden O the very casques
> That did affright the air at Agincourt?
>
> (Pro. 8–14)

The prologue asserts the difficult liberty of writing and performing the intractable matter of pre-Tudor history. Here we have a masterful account – in fact, an embodiment – of 'Traffic and travel' among international claims and possessions, one that confidently assures us, in a revealing phrase, that it will dispense with neoclassical authority: 'we'll digest / Th'abuse of distance; force a play' (2.0.31–2). The unity of place in particular is broken up, but this fragmentation is authorized on the grounds that it helps, in Alexander Schmidt's definition of 'force', 'bring about or effect by constraint or violence' a representation.[22] The culinary metaphor, recalling the prologue to *Midas*, suggests the ineluctable absorption of basic, material needs. Thus, the need to 'force a play' implicates the uses of physical space, in particular the spatial assimilation, in the performed play, of 'distance'. The question is not, primarily, how to represent a movement across the political geography of England and France; rather, what needs to be tackled and 'digest[ed]' is, we suggest, a forceful relationship between the representation of the (wide open) imaginary space in the story and the (severely limited) material space on the platform stage. The 'contrarious' challenge of performance on this platform is to match the difference between the demands and limits of the cultural occasion in 'this cockpit' and the representation of 'the vasty fields of France'.

Between these locations, then, 'distance' is positively used as well as abused. Once the authority of classical poetics was dislodged (or 'abused'), a 'swelling' proliferation of forceful signs and potent meanings was called for. Hence, the chorus appealed to a sense of 'motion of no less celerity / Than that of thought' (3.0.2–3): 'imaginary puissance' (Pro. 25) was to come 'with winged heels' from 'here and there, jumping o'er times' (Pro. 29). Such expansive thrust of signification united the written text and the practice of performance itself, with plenty of 'celerity' from 'here and there' bridging the cultural and physical gap between the eloquent representation of distant places and a mere scaffold. And yet 'this unworthy scaffold' (Pro. 10) was one on which a matter of past 'worthiness' – to recall the terms of Marlowe's printer Richard Jones – now had to be performed in the presence of mixed audiences. What better way to map out the difference between them than on a spatial plane marked by 'distance'? Thus, to 'force a play' was to cope with and make compatible two levels of 'motion': one on the plane of what, in the discourse of history, was represented between the imagined *loci* of London, Southampton, and France; the other on the platform stage, as that platform was, to the extent of its abilities, to mobilize the kinetic energies, the 'puissance', of performers and spectators inside 'this wooden O' (Pro. 13).

The element of contrariety between these two planes was as obvious as it must have seemed ineradicable. Here the culinary metaphor is crucial to the implication that the resulting disparity had to be swallowed. To 'digest' these diverse uses of 'distance', required an awareness of two basic levels or locations of authority. It was of course paramount to have 'the scene . . . transported' (2.0.34–5) from the Globe in London; but it was equally important, with 'no less celerity', for players and spectators to traverse the field between present actors and their absent dramatic identities. Such agility would have been impossible without the bifold capacity of Shakespeare's theatre to project *and* dissolve the scene, to associate *and* to rupture theatrical signs and their meanings, to digest both the use and 'abuse' of distance, to usher various groups across thresholds.

The 'unworthy scaffold' appears to have harboured a highly complex scene that did not provide a unified space for representation. If this was so, the use of prologue and chorus in *Henry V* may well be understood as a singular attempt to demarcate and interrelate divisive locations of time, place, and authority in the Shakespearean theatre. To grapple with so 'worthy' and 'so great a project' on an 'unworthy scaffold', to relate both sides through their difference and still to coordinate them, required an unprecedented density of symbolizing and signifying practices. It was no easy matter to abuse the neoclassical postulate, and thus digest the unsanctioned space for contrariety that marked the 'distance' and disparity between here and there, between now and then, between players and their roles. The attempt to meet this task demanded what Bernard Beckerman called 'a new theatrical endeavor'.[23] Whatever else the prologue stood for, it articulated a new awareness of the difference that inhabited the uses of space on the platform stage.

Most noteworthy in this articulation is that the discourse of imperial historiography appears so devastatingly triumphant that, on the surface, the contemporary uses of theatrical place are substantially reduced. Residual functions of the *platea*-dimension are either minimized or reappropriated with a view to stimulating the celebration of national unity and popular royalty. There is a fanfare note in the trumpet of the chorus, as in the iambic language that opens Act 2: 'Now all the youth of England are on fire, / . . . and honour's thought / Reigns solely in the breast of every man' (2.0.1; 3–4). And yet, in the most stirring speech of them all, when the chorus to Act 4 articulates the patriotic fervour of 'brothers, friends, and countrymen' (34), the tensions between 'the swelling scene' and 'this unworthy scaffold' remain quite unresolved and culminate unexpectedly in these lines:

> And so our scene must to the battle fly;
> Where – O for pity! – we shall much disgrace
> With four or five most vile and ragged foils
> (Right ill dispos'd, in brawl ridiculous)
> The name of Agincourt. Yet sit and see,
> Minding true things by what their mock'ries be.
>
> (4.0.48–53)

The swift, rousing flight to the scene of 'battle' is arrested, as if in mid-air, by a liminal relapse on the part of the chorus. It is unpersuasive to account for the resulting anticlimax by saying that it is to preclude spectators' disappointment over the scenes to follow. What appears more promising here is to trace a positive function in the prologue's uses of the space of liminality. If there is in Shakespeare's theatre any such thing as freedom of the threshold, then this site is used, in Ruth Lunney's phrase, to provide a 'perspective frame', even a 'framing rhetoric' whereby to intercept the jubilant memories of 'Agincourt'.[24] One could say that these memories of their genuine celebration are suspended in an unambiguous sense of self-resembled place and property in the Elizabethan public playhouse. The chorus, at the height of its liminal powers, serves as a down-to-earth reminder of the actual 'betwixt-and-between' of the agents of representation. The ferocious weapons of victory are theatrically transcribed into 'four or five most vile and ragged foils'; the glorious battle itself is rhetorically framed as a 'brawl ridiculous'.

A peculiar way indeed to 'digest / Th'abuse of distance'. It tells us that the signs of the signs of glory can indeed 'disgrace' the discourse of historiography, especially when a mixed and somewhat licentious audience is, in no uncertain terms, urged to assist. At this point, the 'imaginary forces' of 'mean and gentle all' become an unpredictable element in the production of theatrical meaning. To tell such a varied audience, "tis *your* thoughts that now must deck our kings' (Pro. 28; emphasis added) expands the margin of indeterminacy in interpretation and expresses considerable confidence in, even bestows authority on, the signifying capacities of ordinary people. Rarely does the Elizabethan stage acknowledge its audience as 'so great' an authority. Here the chorus in liminal proximity to the audience authorizes spectatorship as a privileged instance of signification in the theatre.

Emphasis on the many 'imperfections' of the platform stage may therefore serve a bold and strategic rather than an exclusively humble design. This emphasis must have engaged an audience who, 'Minding true things by what their mock'ries be', would have been stimulated to assimilate 'Th'abuse of distance' between them. Spectators, it seems, had their share in bringing forth and sustaining the element of contrariety between 'so great a project' and its treatment in a mere 'cockpit'. There is little doubt that the audience's participation in this ensemble occasion becomes especially important when the chorus is about to rehearse (not to say resurrect) a festive sense of English patriotism and glory, with some daring resonance of Essex preparing to return from his Irish expedition. While this celebration of revitalized national unity was, in the critical days of the autumn of 1599, already invoked in the teeth of its immanent destruction (with the Hayward/Essex crisis positively hastening this process), the twilight of the Elizabethan Settlement might still have favoured an unambiguous reading of 'our gracious Empress' receiving from her 'general' 'rebellion broached on his sword' (4.0.30–2).[25] Was there, in this situation, room enough in which to continue to hope for an inclusive perspective on the social uses of drama rather than one riven by divisions of class and education? In this context, the image of the theatre as 'cockpit' serving 'mean and gentle all' is revealing; the language of popular sport and pastime attests to the uses of cultural licence, associated with both the location and the agencies of the theatre, to bridge social distance in shared play.

Although, then, the alleged 'imperfections' of the scaffold stage continue to be introduced on a note of exceeding modesty, the strategy behind the chorus's delivery has an element of ambivalence. The prologue does seem to denigrate almost everything theatrical; it is excessively apologetic about what is doing the representing in 'this wooden O', while at the same time acknowledging the overwhelming authority of what is being represented. The note of humility seems strongest where the site and the signs of the theatre are made to appear 'unworthy' of what is to be fully signified, as when the question is asked, 'Can this cockpit hold / The vasty fields of

France?' What is apologized for is, apparently, the imperfectly achieved continuity on the almost bare platform stage between theatrical signs and historiographical meaning. But, again, at this juncture the note of humility, the entire stance of modesty and apology, clash with that early, infectious sense of self-assurance spurred on, in the opening words of the prologue, by appeal to the dramatic powers of 'invention' to serve and inspire 'the swelling scene:'

> O for a Muse of fire, that would ascend
> The brightest heaven of invention!
> A kingdom for a stage, princes to act,
> And monarchs to behold the swelling scene!
> Then should the warlike Harry, like himself,
> Assume the port of Mars, and at his heels
> (Leash'd in, like hounds) should famine, sword, and fire
> Crouch for employment.
>
> (1–8)

The opening line, invoking the classical instance of a 'Muse', deserves our particular attention, for it was obviously written in reference to or anticipation of the enormity of the challenge that the sprawling matter of history posed for authorship. The phrase may safely be read as seeking to inspire, of course, yet it also authorizes such poetic powers as inform the dramatist's craft, including his specially singled-out capacities for 'invention'. The message conveyed in these lines has a force, an urgency, which is far from being affected by the topos of humility that in due course will reduce the idea of authorship to the image of a 'rough and all-unable pen' (Epi. 1). Having said as much, we can proceed to underline a truly astonishing move which must come as a surprise when what the dramatist appeals to is a hybrid 'muse' for an inspiration 'individable', for a work 'unlimited'. The classically sanctioned pathos of the invocation in the first two lines unnoticeably gives way to spelling out the basic needs of a performing theatre. As we learn the very next moment, the true project is to transform the 'stage', to 'act' leading roles, to expand the 'scene' (3–4). Thus, Shakespeare's authorial position in this prologue is worlds remote from presuming either to lead the audience to new horizons of sensation and insight (Marlowe's claim) or to 'sing' in the first person singular 'Upon the wings of my well tempered verse' (Peele's project). Nor does Shakespeare's prologue aspire to Lyly's gaze on the turbulent presence of the world in the theatre (and the theatre in the world).

In Shakespeare's London career, this prologue comes almost mid-way, at the turn of the century. Fully to appreciate the complexity in the overlapping

angles of authorization demands more than looking back at authorial positions in the late sixteenth-century prologues we have examined so far. For a
broader foil to Shakespeare's position, it seems justified to throw a comparative glance at the uses of authorial authority in early seventeenth-century
prologues, particularly those written by Ben Jonson. In conjunction with the
work of Timothy Murray, Richard Dutton, Joseph Loewenstein and others,
we can trace a remarkable shift in early Stuart prologues. In an exceptional
and yet largely exemplary fashion, the uses of liminal discourse explode but
also, if the phrase passes muster, implode in Ben Jonson's plays. They
explode in the form of several inductions (even though few of these achieve
the sophisticated quality of Beaumont's induction to *The Knight of the Burning
Pestle* [1607]); but they also implode in that the writer of the prologue collapses the range and dynamic of what the prologue says and stands for into
an authorial self-explication.

One of its dominant strains is perhaps best anticipated in Lorenzo
Junior's words in the 1598 version of *Every Man in His Humour* concerning
'The state of poetry' as 'most true divine', with 'invention' as a 'Sacred' gift
of a 'true poet' (5.3.316ff.; 322; 342). Of course, some such perspective on
poetry is also at work in the prologue to *Cynthia's Revels* (1600) as it literally
establishes an enlightened space in which 'The lights of judgment's throne'
find 'this [. . .] their sphere' (3–4). From such judicious, elevated position
'Our doubtful author' speaks: 'In this alone, his Muse her sweetness hath'
(9). From her throne, she 'cast those piercing rays / Round as a crown'
(17–18). If such claim for a highly (and exclusively) poetic authority feels
free to articulate itself in the imagery of royalty, the true weight and measure of 'poesy' in the theatre is quite remote from the ordinary business of
performance, especially when the poetry 'affords / Words, above action;
matter above words' (20).

While the high-flown pathos of this rhetoric may be viewed as at least
partially deflated in the preceding Induction, Jonson's prologues, with the
exception of those in his later plays, tend to surrender the public space for
liminal action to a privileged site of authorial self-vindication. Take only the
somewhat notorious 'armed Prologue' to *Poetaster* (1601) where 'our author'
(15) is centrally (and stubbornly) introduced 'As one that knows the strength
of his own Muse' (24). Even here, it seems, poetic genius is as dominant as it
is unique: the inspiration itself is appropriated and as such owned, but never
shared, by the dramatist. It is a controlled situation of presumed possession
in the theatre, from which even Jonson's mature plays are not free. Thus,
the opening to *Volpone* (1606) with its refreshing couplets is usurped by 'our
poet' (5) in order to defend himself against the 'envy' of those 'whose throats'
exclaim 'hoarsely' false stories about the gall and the painstaking pace of its
author. Similarly, the prologue to *The Alchemist* (1610) is designed first and

foremost to do 'To the author justice' (4) and to offer proof and reason that 'This pen / Did never aim to grieve, but better men' (11–12).

To be sure, a new awareness of the need for introducing subject matter, theme, and occasion marks the prologues to *Bartholomew Fair* (1614), dedicated 'to the King's Majesty', *The Devil is an Ass* (1616), as well as his last great play, *The Staple of News* (1626). But even here Jonson remains incorrigible when what really matters is the one medium, which is language; and when, therefore, among spectators the capacity is paramount 'to hear, not see a play'.

> For your own sakes, not his, he bade me say,
> Would you were come to hear, not see a play,
> Though we his actors must provide for those
> Who are our guests here, in the way of shows,
> The maker hath not so; he'd have you wise,
> Much rather by your ears, than by your eyes.
>
> (Pro. 1–6)

It is difficult to exaggerate the difference between the early Jonson (or Marston, for that matter) and Shakespeare. The most memorable pun in the prologue to *Henry V* (to which we shall return in a moment) leads to an articulation of that sense of corporate bonding which made it possible for the prologue to be to double business bound. No reason, then, in this 'wooden O' for a poet's pen to play down performer's voice and body:

> O, pardon! since a crooked figure may
> Attest in little place a million,
> And let us, ciphers to this great accompt,
> On your imaginary forces work.
>
> (Pro. 15–18)

Remarkably, the question is not one of 'bifold authority'. What the cooperation in the playhouse among all the springs of 'imaginary puissance' aims at is, ultimately, to work on 'imaginary forces' in the pit and in the galleries. The corporate sense of being 'ciphers' to a great account, is to pool and thereby multiply a *comptum*, a reckoning, which as in modern English 'account' is both the cause as well as the narrative, the great story *and* the profit, the calculation in monetary terms. Again, the represented and the representing complement and thereby enhance one another. Realism and a sense of bonding go together. If anywhere, we here have that 'ensemblist-ensemblizing dimension of social representing/saying' which Cornelius Castoriadis has provocatively defined.[26]

Against this background, Shakespearean and Jonsonian uses of 'invention' and 'Muse' in their respective prologues must be differentiated greatly. Shakespeare's is a 'Muse' that can impart 'imaginary puissance' to the scene itself, to the account and the action of assimilating, absorbing, authorizing 'princes' thereon 'to act'. It can, without much fuss, locate a 'kingdom' in the narrow and unspectacular space of an 'unworthy scaffold'. Rather than reinforcing the traditional interpolation between *locus* and *platea*, the positioning of royalty on common stages collapses, to a degree, the difference between elevated, self-contained locality and open platform space. It is one way of securing the expansive force of localizing and visualizing the stage in the interaction of its differing sites and effects. Such force informs 'the swelling scene' – that is, the unfixed, performative thrust of drama in production. It is a 'scene' with the capacity for both 'crescendo' and 'decrescendo' of locale, involving a movement of 'swelling', like waves, in ebb and flow, bringing forth and dissolving a local habitation and name. It is possible to feel in this ebb and flow an acknowledgement of the liminal movement we have seen associated with prologues during this period. In any case, such 'motion' in the uses of theatrical space is inseparable from a cultural semiotics marked by a new kind of 'traffic' and contingency, an exorbitant kinetic energy in relations of signifiers and signifieds[27] – in short, the movable, audible, visible extension in the use of signs, symbols, and localities in rapid succession and interaction.

Once in command of forceful significations over the breadth of the platform space, the 'swelling scene' has plenty of authority to represent for the audience *and* on stage 'mean and gentle all', ordinary soldiers as well as 'princes' – even, in fact, a plurality of relations in a 'kingdom'. This is how the role of the king is projected for and through performance: 'Then should the warlike Harry, like himself, / Assume the port of Mars'. As Holderness has shown, 'the king is characterised as an *actor* rather than a monarch: the drama displays his capacity to masquerade and perform, his ability to generate acclamation and excitement in the *theatrical* context. The *playing* is very obviously *play*'.[28] Thus, the swelling force of this scene can stir up emotion, inflate a mere masquerade to the rank of a deity. But then the represented image of the king is shown in its histrionic making: it is so recast that the actor, in addition to filling the role of Harry, is visualized as assuming simultaneously the bearing of Mars. The unfixing, expanding thrust of 'the swelling scene' makes the king himself 'ascend / The brightest heaven' of theatricality. 'In such a theatre-state', as Stephen Greenblatt notes, 'there would be no social distinction between the king and the spectator, the performer and the audience; all would be royal, and the role of the performer would be to transform an actor into a king and a king into a god'.[29]

When the space of kingdoms and the title of a prince can so freely be appropriated on the scaffold stage, the self-representation of the theatre in the language of the chorus cannot itself be dissociated from an unfixing, swelling quality in the relations of text and institution. In mediating the two, the chorus fulfills a dramatic role which is not that of either the writer or the performer. In particular, his thickly performed account of inter-actions between the discourse of history and the uses of the scaffold stage is strangely unreliable and even to a degree confusing. Whatever areas of fruitful interdependence existed between writing and stagecraft, between the allegedly 'rough and all-unable pen' and the spatial and semiotic potential of the platform stage, are minimized rather than articulated. The festival occasion had plenty of room for fanfare, but no space in which to set out anything like the full range of the contradictory spectrum between cooperation and friction.

We have seen astonishing incongruity between what the representing chorus says the play is about and what is actually represented in the text of the play. In this ambivalence, the chorus to *Henry V* found itself in that tra-dition of unreliability already remarkably developed by Marlowe, whose chorus in *Doctor Faustus* (1592), as we have seen, has recently been described as articulating a language of 'half-truths, false leads, tricks and imprecise statements', a language in which 'words bristle dangerously with an ironic charge'.[30] Except for his intense concern with two differing types of authority in theatrical representation, Shakespeare, then, followed an already established convention of complex openings to performance. Along these lines it would be possible, even within the language of the chorus himself, to trace an ambidextrously handled difference in the uses of the prologue and those of the epilogue counterpointing, in Marjorie Garber's words, 'a prediction of the future and a memory of the past – the future in history, the past in the theatre'.[31] But perhaps the duplicity of functions associated with the chorus can best be discussed in terms of a remarkable strategy of interpolation whereby the signs of power are mediated and potentially challenged by the puissance of dramatic signification itself. Such puissance can be traced not simply in the use of the play metaphor, but wherever in the language of the chorus the *topos* of humility is turned into the swelling thrust of unforeseen strength in its own signifying practice.

The self-referential figure foregrounding the playhouse's sense of theatri-cality is most revealing where – along the lines of Lyly's prologue – its own cultural semiotics are representing as well as represented. At this point, the language of popular sport and pastime is significantly intercepted when the site of game and entertaining struggle called a 'cockpit' is subjected to another extension of movable signs and symbols. Thus, the harmless enough miniature shape of 'this wooden O' is tossed into another figuration of wordplay revealing 'this cockpit', with its 'unworthy scaffold', for what, in this text, it actually is: 'a crooked figure [which] may / Attest in little place a million' (15–16). The theatre, modestly inscribed in the figure of an O, is a mere nought. While this reiterates the strategic *topos* of unworthiness, at the same time this naughty figure so expands the meaning of a sign that the value of a nought swells it to 'a million'. Even so, the scaffold stage, like the number nought, is a *crooked* figure, and not to be trusted; as the Elizabethan polymath John Baret noted in his four-language dictionary, the *Alvearie*, under *A Brief Instruction of Arythmetike* (1580), the 'cipher' or the number zero 'is no Significative figure of it self, but maketh the other figures wherewith it is joined, to increase more in value by their place'.[32]

This definition almost uncannily suggests the 'swelling' force of signs and icons on the platform stage, which, without their localizing thrust, is just an open *place*, 'no Significative figure of it self'. While 'this wooden O', the unsanctioned 'cockpit', does retain a potential of non-symbolic space in the nature of a *platea*, such a non-representational site, like a naught, is a 'crooked figure;' it possesses a remarkable duplicity through its very adaptability to 'other figures wherewith it is joined'. For these are made 'to increase more in value by their place' – a 'place' that has all the space and quality of a cultural occasion with the platform at its centre. Hence, the representation of the theatre as 'a crooked figure' is one which has a unique *authority* of its own; it can (as the etymology of the Latin *auctor* and *auctoritas* suggests) *augment* 'other figures wherewith it is joined'. In other words, 'this wooden O' can enlarge, 'bring forth' (Pro. 10) by signifying something in conjunction with other things, but it is nothing by itself. The scaffold stage, by itself empty, is capable of a 'swelling scene'.

Seen in this 'double dealing' function, the prologue negotiates its own version of the clash, in the theatre, between authorities representing and authorities represented. To read this clash merely in terms of a fixed difference between an 'unworthy' platform and the overbearing weight of historiographical 'worthiness' clearly distorts the purpose of the prologue. Rather, its opening function has to do with how and on what grounds a representing medium like 'this unworthy scaffold' can presume to engage 'so great an object' already represented in contemporary discourse. For this, the crooked figurations in the prologue's own language point the way. To say that warlike Harry 'Assume[s] the port of Mars', only to have 'famine, sword, and fire' follow at his heels is 'by outward signs to shewe' him 'otherwise' than in his previous representation in the Tudor myth of history – even though, as we have come to learn, Elizabethan historiography had its moments of previously unsuspected frankness and forthrightness.[33] But as opposed to its treatment in the historical discourse of the time, in the drama the authority of royalty is not simply given, but has to be achieved through actions and contestation. It is through performed action that – even before authority is ultimately settled – the playhouse calls for (and helps constitute for others) some 'imaginary puissance' (Pro. 25). As the context of the phrase suggests, 'puissance' conflates the representation of powerful forces with its reception by an audience: the object of performance and the response to it are brought together. Thus, 'imaginary puissance' is located within and without theatrical representations; it is inseparable from a responsive audience whose own 'imaginary forces' are mobilized. They are invited to assist and thereby share in the authority, the validity, the impact of what is performing – but only on the condition that they are prepared to help assimilate, through their responses, the order of that which is represented.

The 'swelling scene' refers to both the forceful performance and the powerful effect of what is represented and received. Such again underlines this twofold connection of, on one hand, the world of the play, and, on the other, the playing and watching in the world of the Elizabethan theatre. It is a connection inscribed not only in 'imaginary puissance' but in similar phrases informed by the 'bifold' and 'brief' nature of 'authority' in Shakespeare's theatre. The use of 'The Globe' itself was a 'crooked figure' by which the world was collapsed in a cockpit but the cockpit made potent enough to 'Attest in little place' the 'vasty fields' of early modern Europe. Throughout the prologue, other pregnant signs appear to balance (and contest) the forces represented and those representing. The duplicity inherent in the clash of two paronomastic meanings is analogous to the bifold nature of theatrical legitimation. The same could be said of, for example (taking just the text of the prologue), the playful use of 'port' denoting 'part', but also implying 'bearing' (as in the word 'comportment'). Even more specifically, 'imaginary forces' signifies 'powers of imagination' but may simultaneously be read as playing on the sense of 'unreal armies'. In their twofold meaning these words submit to 'bifold authority' of a sort, authorizing both the fictional, absent *histoire*, and the really available *discours* as ongoing practice. By seeming to refer to history, to the represented, imaginary object on stage, they also invoke the present, institutional agencies in the theatre, the irreducible expenditure of physical and intellectual energies in the performing of and responding to a life show.

However, the awareness of duplicity went hand in hand with a perception that the staged quality of this double-dealing language was most appropriate to authorize, even to apologize for, the alleged 'imperfections' (Pro. 23) of the scaffold stage. It is because these 'imperfections' are established so emphatically that the audience is enjoined to supply 'thoughts that now must deck our kings' (Pro. 28). This demand for the audience to 'deck' royalty points to the need for an act of cooperation; such an act sanctions a medium of perception hitherto unauthorized in the popular theatre. As Edward Berry reminds us, the early modern meaning of 'deck' suggests assistance in the imaginary recreation of an epic world of golden resolutions.[34] But the point, of course, is that the forces of the epic imagination are throughout made to clash and mingle with the brazen meanings of an 'iron Pen' brought forth on wooden boards supporting plebeian players. In other words, whatever the hallowed origins of the Muse, once its 'imaginary puissance' is appropriated on common stages, the assimilation there of its authorizing powers is bound to fetch rewards and gains totally unknown to the political economy of the epic.

Thus, the unleashing of a need for 'imaginary forces' to grapple with the representation of histories can be accounted for neither in terms of an epic heightening and depiction of things as they should be nor as a premature anticipation of aesthetic/Romantic liberation of the poetic vision. Rather, the chorus's repeated recourse to 'imaginary forces' points to the cultural potential of transformative energies, here recruited to serve both audience response and authorial ascent to 'The brightest heaven of invention'. Once representations in the early modern period ceased to subscribe to the order of similitude (erroneously claimed by Foucault to dominate the period's cultural episteme),[35] the imaginary achieved an unprecedented role in important areas of discursive practice. In particular, there was an enormous proliferation in the uses of imagery and related forms of picture-making. This involved, as Christopher Braider has shown, scarcely explored links between an inflation of verbal imagery and the early modern extolling of painting to 'the flower of every art'.[36] At the same time, this implicated an explosion of interpretative activities, especially where, in the wake of Reformation, 'interpretation promised emancipation'[37] and, paradoxically, emancipation itself included surrendering of divine sources of inspiration in favour of 'the authority of the imagination'.[38]

Although the authorization of the imaginary in its cultural and political context was largely anticipated by Francis Bacon, editors of Shakespeare's texts and historians of his theatre have been slow to acknowledge the implications of Shakespeare's uses of the imaginary. In *Henry V*, the authorization of 'imaginary forces', the summons even to 'deck' royalty is deliberately tied to 'mean and gentle all'. Even more unambiguously, the dramatist may well have had illiterate spectators in mind when he made the chorus pledge 'to those that have not read the story' that he would 'prompt them' (5. 0. 1–2). There is no more perfect illustration of what alarmed Stephen Gardiner about 'the loose disputation' of players, printers, and preachers that threatened 'the anchor-hold of authority'. Positively speaking, here was in action a new medium, usurping the 'authority of public instruction', abducting what was supposed to rest in the hands of 'Ecclesiastical Ministers, and temporal Magistrates'.[39]

What resulted was a public intervention in the order of the represented. Today we can only speculate on how much interaction there was between the strong performative of players and the emphatic licence for spectators to interpret. At the end of the play, the epilogue hints at what Sir Henry Wotton in his letter to Sir Edmund Bacon had to say about those 'many extraordinary circumstances of Pomp and Majesty' in the production of *Henry VIII* (1613): these representations were 'sufficient in truth within a while to make greatness very familiar, if not ridiculous'.[40] While almost certainly such representation aimed at no deliberate 'mock'ries', familiarity with greatness cannot be shrugged off as entirely unconnected with the spatial limitations (enabling superb theatricality) of Shakespeare's stage. But while these, again, are acknowledged in seeming modesty, their 'imperfections' are held to *confine* the representations of 'mighty men'. This, then, is what performance space on the 'unworthy scaffold' can do to the mighty and the glorious: 'In little room confining mighty men, / Mangling by starts the full course of their glory' (Epi. 3–4). Here the representation of 'might' and 'glory' is viewed as in collision with the alleged ineptitude of the scaffold stage. Authority figures in historiographical discourse are at least indirectly affected, if not (in the wider meaning of 'mangling') positively spoiled, disfigured, mutilated. The chorus, in humbly attempting to explain such treatment, by implication projects the 'little room' as one where the position of high office, the *locus* of glorious action, 'the course' of warlike deeds, are bound to be redefined or even thwarted by theatrical place and action. Suddenly, an unsuspected source of strength emerges out of 'this unworthy scaffold', on which the representation of political power can literally be confined, if not mangled, by the imperfect, but for all that forceful, power of theatrical performances. Here, finally, is another level on which the common stage could, on its own terms, 'digest / Th'abuse of distance'. As far as such distance was constitutive of a space for cultural difference, that space was also one of challenge, interception, and mediation. The worthy signs of 'Pomp and Majesty', of 'mighty men' and their 'glory' were mediated and at least partially intercepted on the site of their performance, through 'imaginary puissance' on the part of players and spectators.

This reading of *Henry V* must remain, of course, somewhat provisional as long as the text of the chorus is not carefully related to what the play itself docs, or does not do, to the collision of authority in the world of the theatre and authority in the discourse of history. This is not the place to pursue such a reading of the play at large; but let us in conclusion at least suggest that the ambivalent humility in the language of the chorus has a figural correlative in the language of the play that strangely echoes what Erich Auerbach calls the *sermo humilis* in the midst of heroic matter.[41] If

anywhere the authority of royalty, might, and glory is momentarily challenged, such challenge is performed, face to face with the king and yet
remote from the *locus* of privilege, in a language unauthorized in the discourse of history. It is a grim *sermo humilis* in the voice of a common soldier,
a discourse literally lowly, that presents the king with 'a black matter',
'when all those legs, and arms, and heads, chopp'd off in a battle, shall join
together at the latter day and cry all, "We died at such a place"' (4.1.45;
135–8).

Disguised in the manner of Germanicus in Tacitus's *Annals* (translated in
1598), King Henry confronts his soldiers. When he does so, Henry hears, as
Geoffrey Bullough notes, something 'very different from the conventional
praise in Tacitus;' in contrast to the Roman historian, 'Shakespeare takes us
below the surface glitter'.[42] The bifold allocation of performed plays of history was such that it opened up an untrodden social space, a space virtually
inaccessible to discursive practice from Tacitus to Holinshed and beyond.
Thus, it is precisely among the stage-centred mingle-mangle of 'worthy'
and 'unworthy' authorities that a character like the ordinary soldier
Michael Williams can make his appearance. For him to consider the 'heavy
reckoning' of the soldiers' lives and 'their children rawly left' (135; 141) – a
'reckoning' that will lay upon the king if 'the cause be not good' (4.1.134–5)
– is sharply to invoke from below the issue of authority. Such language
would have connotations in the Elizabethan present. This is how, in this
swelling scene, a cry for legitimating those 'that die in a battle' (142) must
have transgressed the traditional political groundings of authority.

At the same time, the scene foregrounds a sentiment, even empathy,
associated with a *locus* of such true feeling as 'passeth show'. And yet the
occasion is dark, the scene an irreverent place in the camp, the main character theatrically concealed in disguise. *Vis-à-vis* this occasion, *locus* and *platea*
are brought together in a kind of complicity that makes it possible to foreground all sorts and conditions of 'abuse', including that of suspending the
'distance' between king and commoner. Contrariety is writ large across this
stage, but it remains somehow capable of containing different levels, discourses, perspectives, a true 'scene individable, or poem unlimited'. As the
disguised king attempts to authorize his foreign policy, pleading 'his cause
being just and his quarrel honorable' (4.1.127–8), the honest soldier
Williams has the curt reply: 'That's more than we know' (129). His answer
illustrates a political version of 'bifold authority', transposing the issue into
the text of representation itself. It does so in a scene where the customary
locus of royalty is concealed and at least partially collapsed into a site reminiscent of an open, public *platea* inhabited by late sixteenth-century spectators.

Afterword

Examining the early modern dramatic prologue as text, actor, and performance, we have traced its popularity and variety over an era that witnessed the rise of the commercial playhouses in England. A brief literary and cultural history of the prologue was followed here by suggestions concerning the prologue's relation to the playgoing experience itself. We argued that the early modern prologue typically worked to facilitate a theatrical rite of passage. This rite of passage often involved a double movement across a representational threshold. That is, even as the audience was ushered, by the prologue, over this representational threshold and into the playworld proper, there transpired a similar movement by the actors and the playworld characters they represented across this threshold and into the dynamic, participatory arena of the world of the playhouse. The prologue therefore helped bridge, where it did not temporarily erase, the gap between the world in the play and playing in the world. This 'bifold' movement occurred at the crucial and liminal inauguration of the theatrical performance, and replicated in many ways those very divisions within the uses of authority in the theatre upon which many early modern prologues came to focus.

It has been our contention that one can see the early modern theatre's emerging self-consciousness in its deployment of prologues that were frequently reflexive and – given the resources and patterns for prologic address available to dramatists of the time – invariably creative in their collocation of play, playhouse, players, and the worlds inside and outside the theatre building. This self-consciousness, we have maintained, makes dramatic prologues extremely valuable for the pursuit of not only literary history and the history of performance, but cultural history as well. To the extent that the playhouses of Shakespeare's time had an important perspective on English society – and, perhaps especially, on its busy centre of trade and government – the prologues to plays enacted in these venues have a great deal to tell us about issues of representation, performance, and authority in early modern England.

We noted in the first chapter to this study the ironic timing of the prologue to *Henry V* (1599): Shakespeare wrote what remains the most admired instance of the genre at precisely the moment during his lifetime that the dramatic prologue appears to have experienced its greatest disfavour. To be sure, the 'moment' of the early modern dramatic prologue bears discussion, and for more than its relation to literary fashion. The prologue to *Henry V* displays the form's ability to offer insights on the various resources behind dramatic productions and habits of reception in the commercial playhouses. But at the same time, such insight already stipulates a lively type of participation: the chorus declares a shared need to brace 'our swift scene' hither and thither. To participate in and understand a 'motion of no less celerity' (3.0.1–2) asked for imaginary agility in coping with the prologue's twofold, liminal movement. Celerity in crossing imaginary thresholds was of course a requisite part of the playgoing experience in the commercial theatre and the playing venues it influenced. As such, this imaginative responsiveness was fully in keeping with the changeful modes of life, especially in the nation's capital, that accompanied the rise of modern, postfeudal relations. Prologues encapsulated images of these new relations, which included the offering of plays in a cultural marketplace where success or failure was much more than a matter of prestige.

If early modern dramatic prologues remained centrally concerned with passages across and through a liminal space, they were written and performed at what was itself a transitional moment in the history of the nation and its theatrical culture. We can locate these prologues, that is, at a historical threshold that witnessed the intensification of various energies associated with modernity. It is not too much to see in the reflexive self-probing of the dramatic prologue – from Marlowe's Machevil in *The Jew of Malta* (1589) and Shakespeare's cynical Rumour before *2 Henry IV* (1598) through Ben Jonson's commercially inflected beginning to *Bartholomew Fair* (1614) – some awareness of the social transformations that would characterize the transition toward an imminent modernity. This transition, of course, was much more clearly exemplified in the strivings of such resonant figures as Bacon, Harvey, Hobbes, and Descartes. But when we recall the figures of Machevil, Rumour, and the contract-reading Scrivener introducing plays of this period, the relation of the prologue to historical change and its enunciation becomes difficult to deny.

The dramatic prologues we have examined can be seen as negotiating divisions between and within not only such agents and entities as players and playgoers, text and spoken word, and the present and impending moments of dramatic performance, but also between the English past and future. Indeed, there persisted (and such was evoked in prologues) a pre-purtian, pre-commercial sentiment on stage and in the yard. The paradox was that old and new existed in mutual dependence. The impact of commerce, print, and social mobility resulted in and allowed for that 'motion' of a 'swift scene' which inspired prologues with a communicative inclusiveness enfigured by a traditional stance of 'gentles all'.

Increasingly, the energy of the dramatic prologue emanated from and centred upon the novel relations and ambitions of the commercial playhouse. As institutional reckoning, the prologue gives us a version of what it was possible to think and say about theatrical performances, and about those who produced and consumed those performances, in the playhouses of early modern London. For all their significance, of course, prologues were not alone in providing such information. And we would be remiss were we to conclude our argument without confirming, once again, the prologue's own boundary-crossing relationships with other dramatic forms and events. When the prologue to *Henry V* asks to be admitted as a chorus to that play (Pro. 32), he retains his complex standpoint on the play's action; with only a brief nod toward changing hats, he takes his own sense of liminality into the midst of the play's production and reveals the protean business of threshold-crossing to be essential to Shakespeare's theatre.

In just such a way do the elements of self-awareness we have located in the prologue occupy other moments in plays as well, especially when these moments inaugurate and comment meaningfully on action to follow. From Shakespeare's plays alone one could adduce a number of instances and episodes that parallel the functions we have ascribed to the dramatic prologue. To the central character's prologue-like beginning in *Richard III* (1592), and Time's appearance in *The Winter's Tale* (1610), for example, one could add – to mention only these – the framing dialogue between Philo and Demetrius in *Antony and Cleopatra* (1607) and the Porter scene in *Macbeth* (1606), where, it is worth pointing out, the (repeated) three knocks upon the door uncannily mime the three trumpet blasts that typically preceded the formal prologue itself. In each of these instances the audience is ushered across a threshold to another place within the larger theatrical representation. Like Time's liminal functioning in *The Winter's Tale*, for instance, but reversing that figure's generic directions, *Macbeth*'s Porter literally ushers the audience, and the play's characters, across a comedically tinged threshold into the horrifying tragedy of his play's final acts.

We are proposing, that is, that any insights this study has generated about plays, playing, and playgoing in early modern England – to gather a host of issues under the most convenient headings – be recognized not only as present to the prologues we have examined, but as insights characteristically applicable to moments and forms of liminal address that patterned themselves after prologic speech – even, of course, as such prologic speech drew from them. Here we are thinking of such varied cultural and literary forms as preface epistles, addresses to the reader, commendatory poems, invocations, playbills, vendor's speech, and gossip. Each of these forms and activities contributed to the shape of various dramatic prologues. Thus along with them the early modern dramatic prologue can be seen as 'equipment for beginning': a conventional but supple literary form that not only inaugurated dramatic performances, ushering audiences and players alike across the threshold of representation, but simultaneously lent itself to posing – and, sometimes, answering – a new institution's most profound questions about its diverse roles in the business of writing and staging plays, and, importantly, how its audiences could come to understand and enjoy these plays in the course of their performance.

Notes

Preface

1 Cornelius Castoriadis, *The Imaginary Institution of Society*, trans. Kathleen Blamey, Cambridge, MA: MIT Press, 1998, 238.
2 Bertolt Brecht, *Brecht on Theatre*, trans. John Willet, New York: Hill & Wang, 1964, 22, 37.

1 The Elizabethan prologue: text, actor, performance

1 Alan Dessen, *Elizabethan Stage Conventions and Modern Interpreters*, Cambridge: Cambridge University Press, 1984, 11. Our debts to Dessen and to other historians of theatre and performance in early modern England can be chronicled only insufficiently here and in the pages that follow. We would mention in particular the great deal we owe to the work of Melissa Aaron, John Astington, David Bradley, S. P. Cerasano, Andrew Gurr, William Ingram, Rosalyn Knutson, David Mann, John Orrell, J. A. B. Somerset, Tiffany Stern, and William Tydeman, among many others. In conjunction with the work of these theatre historians, any sustained study of the prologue must acknowledge its debt to the foundational work on Shakespearean dramaturgy that revealed the uses of open, presentational form, a form which predisposed the institution of prologues and epilogues. See, in this connection, not only the work of S. L. Bethell and J. L. Styan, but such specifically focused studies as, among others, Barbara A. Mowat's *The Dramaturgy of Shakespeare's Romances*, Athens: University of Georgia Press, 1976, and Meredith Anne Skura's *Shakespeare the Actor and the Purposes of Playing*, Chicago: University of Chicago Press, 1993.
2 Alan Dessen, *Recovering Shakespeare's Theatrical Vocabulary*, Cambridge: Cambridge University Press, 1995, 2–3.
3 Formal study of the prologue in early modern English drama appears early on in G. S. Bower, *A Study of the Prologue and Epilogue in English Literature from Shakespeare to Dryden*, London: Kegan Paul, Trench and Co., 1884. A remark of Bower's anticipates our sense of the prologue's richness for those interested in history, culture, and the theatre: 'Of all the manifold shapes which the literature of our country has at different times assumed, none has furnished a greater quantity of illustrative matter for the use of the historian in so small a compass as the Prologue, with its twin brother, the Epilogue' (1). Bower's work was notably advanced by the research of Autrey Nell Wiley in various publications, among

them 'Female Prologues and Epilogues in English Plays', *PMLA: Publications of the Modern Language Association of America* 48 (1933): 1060–79, and her collection *Rare Prologues and Epilogues, 1642–1700*, London: George Allen and Unwin Ltd, 1940. We have also benefited greatly from the dissertation of James William Gousseff, 'The Staging of Prologues in Tudor and Stuart Plays', Dissertation: Theatre – Northwestern University, June 1962, UMI 63–1290: 580–1, from which this chapter draws for some of its information about the staging of early modern prologues. We should point out, however, that we depart from Gousseff's conclusions about some particulars of the performance tradition. Other relevant studies of the prologue in early modern England include Ernst T. Sehrt, *Der Dramatische Auftakt in der elisabethanischen Tragödie*, Gottingen: Vandenhoeck and Ruprecht, 1960, esp. 26–47; Anthony Brennan, '"That within which passes show:" The Function of the Chorus in *Henry V*', *Philological Quarterly* 58 (1) (1979): 40–52; D. J. Palmer, '"We shall know by this fellow": Prologue and Chorus in Shakespeare', *Bulletin of the John Rylands University Library of Manchester* 64 (2) (1982): 501–21; M. J. B. Allen, 'Toys, Prologues and the Great Amiss: Shakespeare's Tragic Openings', in Malcolm Bradbury and David Palmer, eds, *Shakespearian Tragedy*, New York: Holmes and Meier, 1984, 3–30; Charles H. Frey, 'Collaborating with Shakespeare', in Charles H. Frey, ed., *Shakespeare, Fletcher, and The Two Noble Kinsmen*, Columbia: University of Missouri Press, 1989, 31–44; Ludger Brinker, 'The Art of Marlowe's Prologues: Subtle Innovations within Traditional Patterns', *Cahiers Elisabéthains* 42 (1992): 1–15; Robert Weimann, 'Authority and Representation in the Pre-Shakespearean Prologue', in Elmar Lehmann and Bernd Lenz, eds, *Telling Stories: Studies in Honour of Ulrich Broich on the Occasion of His 60th Birthday*, Amsterdam: Gruner, 1992, 34–46; Jacek Fabiszak, 'The (Inter-)Theatricality of Marlovian Prologues', *Studia Anglica Posnaniensia* 29 (1994): 189–97; and Robert F. Willson, ed., *Entering the Maze: Shakespeare's Art of Beginning*, New York: Peter Lang, 1995, in which see, in particular, Willson's introduction (1–9), Barbara D. Palmer, 'Shakespearean Openings with a Flourish: Pageantry as Introduction' (27–35), and David M. Bergeron, 'The Beginnings of *Pericles*, *Henry VIII*, and *Two Noble Kinsmen*' (169–81). On the subject of beginnings and introductions generally, we have profited from, among other works, Edward Said, *Beginnings: Intention and Method*, New York: Basic Books, 1975; and A. D. Nuttall, *Openings: Narrative Beginnings from the Epic to the Novel*, Oxford: Clarendon Press, 1992.

4   This is the phrase of Martha Gause McCaulley, 'Functions and Content of the Prologue, Chorus, and Other Non-organic Elements in English Drama, from the Beginnings to 1642', *Studies in English Drama, First Series*, New York: University of Pennsylvania Press, 1917. However, for a recent anthology of essays that assert the importance of literary form, broadly conceived, to a study of Renaissance works – essays concerned with issues of history, society, and culture – see Mark David Rasmussen, ed., *Renaissance Literature and its Formal Engagements*, New York: Palgrave Press, 2002.

5   For understandable reasons, prologues have often been seen as vehicles for exposition alone. A *locus classicus* of this sentiment comes in Samuel Johnson's puzzlement over the bravura prologue to *Henry V*: 'The lines given to the chorus have many admirers; but the truth is, that in them a little may be praised, and much must be forgiven; nor can it be easily discovered why the intelligence given by the chorus is more necessary in this play than in many

others where it is omitted'. Samuel Johnson, from his 1765 *Works of Shakespeare*, quoted in *Shakespeare: 'Henry V'*, ed. Michael Quinn, London: Macmillan, 1969, 34. We can see such traditional reluctance to take prologues as more than information-carriers in G. K. Hunter's valuable entry in 'The Oxford History of English Literature' series, *English Drama 1586–1642: The Age of Shakespeare*, Oxford: Clarendon Press, 1997. For while Hunter calls upon over a dozen prologues from this period to confirm observations about the early modern stage, he rarely acknowledges the specificity of the prologue form, even though on several occasions his material apparently prompts him to admit the prologue's distinctive complexity. Of the prologue to Lyly's *Campaspe* (1583), for instance, Hunter notes 'The Prologue is, of course, an apology' before going on to acknowledge 'it also, however, sets up a somewhat adversary relation between the players and the audience' (139). Of the prologue to *Eastward Ho* (1605), he similarly notes 'The fact that the Prologue is good-humoured does not mean, of course, that the difference of viewpoint is without substance, or the values at issue wholly different from those in the poetomachia' (323). In each of these instances, Hunter seems reluctant to explore the range of complexities involved in the prologue he cites. Such, we would argue, has been largely typical of critical responses to the early modern prologue.

6 For the portmanteau phrase and concept 'cultural historicism', see Albert H. Tricomi, *Reading Tudor–Stuart Texts Through Cultural Historicism*, Gainesville: University Press of Florida, 1996, ix, 1–22. The importance of prologues to students of theatre and performance history cannot be underestimated. As early as the late twelfth-century *Seinte Resurreccion*, for instance, 'A staging prologue in verse . . . is particularly important as showing what locations would have been included.' William Tydeman, ed. *The Medieval European Stage, 500–1550*, Cambridge: Cambridge University Press, 2001, 169. For prologues that indicate such details as who the audience was presumed to be, the place of performance, characters, and plot, see also, in this study, 179–80 [C633], 302 [E24], and 309 [E42] (bracketed numbers refer to the volume's sections). Throughout the early modern period, prologues give us some of our best evidence regarding performance spaces and practice. Paul Whitfield White calls the prologue to Lewis Wager's *The Life and Repentance of Mary Magdalene* (1558) 'the first known English Protestant defense of the stage.' White, *Reformation Biblical Drama: 'The Life and Repentance of Mary Magdalene'; 'The History of Jacob and Esau'*, Renaissance Imagination, New York: Garland: 1992, 146, n. 31. And Rosalyn Knutson sees the playwright of *A Larum for London* (1599) coyly alluding to the physical textures of the Globe in the first two lines of the play's prologue: 'Round through the compass of this earthly ball / The massy substance hanging in the sky . . .'. As Knutson notes, 'About a year later, another dramatist with the Chamberlain's men thought these features of the playhouse were still a draw, and he alluded to them in *Hamlet*' (Rosalyn Knutson, 'Filling Fare: The Appetite for Current Issues and Traditional Forms in the Repertory of the Chamberlain's Men', *Medieval and Renaissance Drama in England*, 15 (2002): 57–76; 72).

7 R. A. Foakes and R. T. Rickert, eds, *Henslowe's Diary*, Cambridge: Cambridge University Press, 1961, 187, 207. Henslowe's willingness to pay these sums for prologues and epilogues strongly suggests that such speeches were valued for being regularly, rather than sporadically, presented. Here we diverge from a recent argument made by Tiffany Stern, who maintains that 'prologues and epilogues . . . were only spoken on the opening day'. (Tiffany Stern, *Rehearsal*

from Shakespeare to Sheridan, Oxford: Clarendon Press, 2000, 116). Some prologues were clearly, as Stern suggests, delivered on only one occasion: the
specificity of many prologues written for performances at court, for instance,
indicate their ephemerality. But Stern's model cannot account for the obvious
continuity of prologic form from the era of the Interludes (where, as we will see,
the prologue was often an extremely substantial speech necessary to understanding the play), the fact that many plays integrate their prologues with the
dramatic action that follows – as, for instance, does *Henry V* (1599) when the
prologue asks the audience to 'Admit me Chorus to this history' (Pro. 32), or
the fact that numerous prologues were unfolded into inductional byplay – such
as, for example, in *The Knight of the Burning Pestle* (1607). And leaving aside the
sheer literary and conceptual brilliance of many early modern prologues, perhaps the best evidence for their regular presentation at theatrical performances
comes from Henslowe's willingness to compensate playwrights at a greater per-
word rate for prologues and epilogues (which, in the single-performance model,
would become self-consuming artifacts, worthless once given) than for the
scripts of plays themselves. While we differ with Stern about the regularity of
the prologue's performance, we wish to stress the importance of her research to
the present study.

8 Autrey Nell Wiley, *Rare Prologues and Epilogues 1642–1700*, London: George
Allen and Unwin Ltd, 1940, xxix.

9 Thomas L. Berger, William C. Bradford, and Sidney L. Sondergard, eds, *An
Index of Characters in Early Modern English Drama: Printed Plays, 1500–1660*, Cam-
bridge: Cambridge University Press, 1998; this is the second, revised edition of
Berger and Bradford, eds, *An Index of Characters in English Printed Drama to the
Restoration*, Englewood, CO: Microcard Editions Books, 1975. In compiling the
figures that follow, we have cross-referenced the *Index*'s list of 'Prologue' plays
(81–2) with the conjectured dates supplied there from the *Annals of English
Drama, 975–1700*, ed. Alfred Harbage, Samuel Schoenbaum, and Sylvia Stoler
Wagonheim, New York: Routledge, 1989. The decade-by-decade breakdown is
as follows (some percentages have been rounded to the next highest integer):

Decade	Surviving plays	Number with prologues	Percentage with prologues
1560–9	25	14	56
1570–9	18	9	50
1580–9	25	16	64
1590–9	91	29	31
1600–9	136	50	37
1610–19	117	43	37
1620–9	99	33	33
1630–9	160	74	46
Totals	671	68	40

Of course, the presence of prologue figures within dramatic fictions themselves
– *A Midsummer Night's Dream* provides a familiar example – obviously testifies to
the imperfect nature of this method of calculation (that is, by inflating their
number). Yet the absence of a more exact tabulation, along with the existence
of (a) prologues without plays, and (b) plays with multiple prologues (such as,

for instance, *The Jew of Malta*) counted only once by the *Index*, leads us to offer this tentative reckoning.

10 See G. Blakemore Evans, ed., *Romeo and Juliet*, Cambridge: Cambridge University Press, 1984, 208.

11 J. B. Leishman, ed., *The Three Parnassus Plays*, London: Ivor Nicholson and Watson, 1949.

12 Anon., *The Birth of Hercules*, ed. R. W. Bond, Oxford: Oxford University Press, 1911, 1.

13 See Sir John Suckling, *The Goblins*, London, 1646, 2; and Philip Massinger, *The Unnatural Combat*, London, 1639, A2r.

14 See Wiley, *Rare Prologues and Epilogues*, 1–8. Wiley identifies the probable author as Abraham Cowley (rather than the 'Francis Cole' of the quarto), and suggests that this small imprint offered 'probably the first prologue and epilogue to receive separate publication' in England (2).

15 On the physical highlighting of such wisdom in early modern printed books, see G. K. Hunter, 'The Marking of *Sententiae* in Elizabethan Printed Plays, Poems, and Romances', *The Library* 5th Series 6 (1951): 171–88.

16 On Jonson's relation to the epigraph, see Robert S. Miola, 'Creating the Author', *The Ben Jonson Journal* 6 (1999): 35–48.

17 On this opening in Olivier's *Hamlet* and its counterpart in *Much Ado*, see Neil Forsyth, 'Ghosts and Courts: The Openings of *Hamlets*', *Shakespeare Yearbook* 8 (1997): 1–17; 2–3, 17 n. 3.

18 On the dramatic induction in the early modern era, see Thelma N. Greenfield, *The Induction in Elizabethan Drama*, Eugene: Oregon University Press, 1969; and Steven C. Young, 'A Check List of Tudor and Stuart Induction Plays', *Philological Quarterly* 48 (1969): 131–4.

19 E. K. Chambers, *The Elizabethan Stage*, 4 vols, Oxford: Clarendon Press, 1923, vol. 2, 547, n. 1.

20 On ring posies and their significance in early modern England, see Juliet Fleming, 'Wounded Walls: Graffiti, Grammatology, and the Age of Shakespeare', *Criticism* 39 (1997): 1–30; and Fleming, *Graffiti and the Writing Arts of Early Modern England*, London: Reaktion Books, 2001, 138–43.

21 Prologues to the Tudor interludes tend to be much longer than prologues written after 1590. To cite only a few examples, the lines for several prologues to interludes and plays are given below:

Play and date	*Lines given to prologue*
The Longer Thou Livest (1559)	70
Enough is as Good (1560)	92
Cambises (1561)	36
Like Will to Like (1568)	36
The Conflict of Conscience (1572)	70
The Tide Tarrieth No Man (1576)	56
Jack Juggler (1583)	83

22 In Francis Beaumont and John Fletcher, *Comedies and Tragedies*, London, 1647, 165.

23 D. J. Palmer is one of many critics who have seen Richard as 'Prologue to his own tragedy'. Palmer, 'We shall know by this fellow' (508). Palmer continues:

'It is as though Richard assumes the orotund impersonal manner of a Prologue to toss it aside contemptuously and reveal himself as he takes the audience into his private confidence' (509). See also Wolfgang Clemen, *Shakespeare's Soliloquies*, London: Methuen, 1987, 15–19.

24 Manfred Pfister, *The Theory and Analysis of Drama*, trans. John Halliday, Cambridge: Cambridge University Press, 1991, 74.

25 [Cicero], *Ad C. Herennium (De Ratione Dicendi/ Rhetorica ad Herennium)*, trans. Harry Caplan, Cambridge, MA: Harvard University Press, 1984, 12–13, par. 7.

26 Chambers, *The Elizabethan Stage*, vol. 2: 547, n. 1. We can gesture only briefly here toward the role that humanism took in the development of early English drama. For various studies which explore the influence of the humanist tradition on many of the plays examined in these pages, see G. K. Hunter, *John Lyly: The Humanist as Courtier*, Cambridge, MA: Harvard University Press, 1962; Wolfgang Riehle, *Shakespeare, Plautus, and the Humanist Tradition*, Cambridge: D. S. Brewer, 1990; and Howard B. Norland, *Drama in Early Tudor Britain, 1485–1558*, Lincoln: University of Nebraska Press, 1995.

27 On the 'resources of kind' and renaissance genres, see Rosalie L. Colie, *The Resources of Kind: Genre-Theory in the Renaissance*, Berkeley: University of California Press, 1973.

28 See 'Donatus on Comedy', trans. S. Georgia Nugent, in Nugent, 'Ancient Theories of Comedy: The Treatises of Evanthius and Donatus', *Shakespearean Comedy*, ed. Maurice Charney, New York: New York Literary Forum, 1980, 259–80. The other three parts of comedy, according to Donatus, are *protasis*, *epitasis*, and *catastrophe* (273).

29 Trans. in Nugent, 'Ancient Theories of Comedy', 273–4.

30 See Emily Kearns, 'The Prologues of *Comoedia sacra* and Their Classical Models', *Medieval and Renaissance Texts and Studies* 86 (1991): 403–11.

31 Thomas Heywood, *A Woman Killed with Kindness*, in *Drama of the English Renaissance*, vol. 1: The Tudor Period, ed. Russell A. Fraser and Norman Rabkin, Upper Saddle River, New Jersey: Prentice-Hall, 1976, 513.

32 *Sir Thomas More*, ed. Vittorio Gabrieli and Giorgio Melchiori, Manchester and New York: Manchester University Press, 1990.

33 Nathaniel Woodes, *An Excellent New Comedy Entitled 'The Conflict of Conscience'*, London: 1581, t.p.

34 William Wager, *The Longer Thou Livest and Enough is as Good as a Feast*, ed. R. Mark Benbow, Lincoln: University of Nebraska Press, 1967.

35 Here we should point out that our survey departs from David Bevington's suggestions regarding the casting of *Clyomon and Clamydes* (1570); Bevington suggests (*From 'Mankind' to Marlowe: Growth of Structure in the Popular Drama of England*, Cambridge, MA: Harvard University Press, 1962, 196) an economical doubling of the prologue with Subtle Shift – an arrangement that would contradict what we see in these other interludes.

36 On the tradition of the dramatic Vice, see Bernard Spivack, *Shakespeare and the Allegory of Evil: The History of a Metaphor in Relation to his Major Villains*, New York: Columbia University Press, 1958; and R. Weimann, 'Mingling Vice and "worthiness" in *King John*', *Shakespeare Studies* 27 (1999): 109–33.

37 Wiley, *Rare Prologues and Epilogues*, xxxiv.

38 Unless otherwise noted, our information regarding actors' biographies comes from Edwin Nungezer, *A Dictionary of Actors and of Other Persons Associated with the*

Public Representation of Plays in England before 1642, New Haven: Yale University Press, 1929.

39 See the plot as reproduced, with transcription, in W. W. Greg, *Dramatic Documents from the Elizabethan Playhouses*, 2 vols, Oxford: Clarendon Press, 1931, vol. 2: Plot III.

40 T. J. King, *Casting Shakespeare's Plays: London Actors and their Roles, 1590–1642*, Cambridge: Cambridge University Press, 1992, 31. The distribution of roles for this play is, of course, notoriously difficult to parse. See the discussion in David Bradley's *From Text to Performance in the Elizabethan Theatre: Preparing the Play for the Stage*, Cambridge: Cambridge University Press, 1992.

41 We would note that these figures come from King's Table 7, 101; they differ from the estimates he gives on 31.

42 See Foakes and Rickert, eds, *Henslowe's Diary*, 241.

43 Henry Glapthorne, *Pöems*, London, 1639, 28.

44 We point this out in part because the approximate date squares with the appearance in print of a similar 'prologue' by Thomas Heywood as published in his *Pleasant Dialogues and Dramma's* [sic], London, 1637. Its discursive title tells the story: 'A young witty Lad playing the part of Richard the third: at the Red Bull: the Author because he was interes[t]ed in the Play to encourage him, wrote him this Prologue and Epilogue. The Boy the Speaker'. We may be no more certain that Heywood's prologue was delivered than we are concerning Glapthorne's. But it seems significant that each of their prologues involves a younger man (in Heywood's case, a boy) juxtaposed with the image of manhood. Heywood's prologue, like that of Glapthorne, has his speaker work through invidious comparison:

> If any wonder by what magic charm,
> *Richard* the third is shrunk up like his arm:
> And where in fullness you expected him,
> You see me only crawling, like a limb
> Or piece of that known fabric, and no more,   5
> (When he so often hath been view'd before.)
> Let all such know: a Rundlet ne're so small
> Is called a vessel: being a Tunne; that's all.
> He's termed a man, that shows a dwarfish thing,
> No more's the Guard, or Porter to the King.   10
> So Pictures in small compass I have seen
> Drawn to the life, as near, as those have been
> Ten times their bigness: Christmas loaves are bread,
> So's your least Manchet: have you never read
> Large folio Sheets which printers over-look,   15
> And cast in small, to make a pocket book?
> So *Richard* is transform'd: if this disguise
> Show me so small a letter for your eyes,
> You cannot in this letter read me plain,
> He'll next appear, in texted hand again.   20

Where Glapthorne's prologue maintained the actor-as-ship trope and stressed the ritual of passage for Fenn, Heywood – who does not seem to know the boy's name of whom he writes – is more interested in capitalizing on the discrepancy of size between the young actor and the length of his role. '[T]exted hand' in the final line refers to an engrossed (rather than diminutive) letter.

45   Kevin Dunn, *Pretexts of Authority: The Rhetoric of Authorship in the Renaissance Preface*, Stanford: Stanford University Press, 1994, 1–16.

46   See Vladimir Mayakovsky, *How to Make Verse*, trans. Valentina Coe, Willimantic, CT: Curbstone Press, 1985.

47   John Fletcher, *The Woman Hater*, London, 1648, A2.

48   James William Gousseff, 'The Staging of Prologues in Tudor and Stuart Plays', Dissertation: Theatre – Northwestern University, June 1962, UMI 63–1290: 580–1. In *The Elizabethan Stage*, E. K. Chambers gathers a number of remarks from contemporary texts that suggest the prologue appeared after three soundings of a trumpet, was bearded, wore a long black cloak, and genuflected before the audience. See vol. 2, 542, 547 and notes; vol. 3, 72; vol. 4, 367.

49   [James Shirley], *The Coronation*, London, 1640, A2. This play is credited to John Fletcher on the title page. Female characters appear to have more frequently delivered prologues as the century unfolded. See Autrey Nell Wiley, 'Female Prologues and Epilogues in English Plays', *PMLA: Publications of the Modern Language Association of America* 48 (1933): 1060–79, and also Alan Dessen and Leslie Thomson, *A Dictionary of Stage Directions in English Drama 1580–1642*, Cambridge: Cambridge University Press, 1999, 172, who cite a '*Prologue delivered by an amazon with a Battleax in her hand*' before the play of *Landgartha* (1682–3), A4v.

50   On this prologue's relationship to a time in which 'cultural relations of writing in the private, and playing in the public, theatres came to constitute an emerging scene of uncertainty and friction', see Weimann, *Author's Pen and Actor's Voice*, 62–3; cit. at 63. See also, on this turbulent time, Matthew Steggle, *Wars of the Theatres: The Poetics of Personation in the Age of Jonson*, Victoria, BC: English Literary Studies, University of Victoria, 1998; and James P. Bednarz, *Shakespeare and the Poet's War*, New York: Columbia University Press, 2001.

51   Gousseff, 'The Staging of Prologues', 590.

52   Gousseff, 'The Staging of Prologues', 581.

53   Tom Clayton, '"So quick bright things come to confusion": or, What Else Was *A Midsummer Night's Dream* About?', in *Shakespeare: Text and Theatre (Essays in Honor of Jay L. Halio)*, ed. Lois Potter and Arthur F. Kinney, Newark: University of Delaware Press, 1999, 62–91; cit. at 84–5.

54   In addition to the prologue to *Troilus and Cressida*, one could note the brief description in Dekker's *The Gull's Hornbook*: 'Present not yourself on the Stage (especially at a new play) until the quaking prologue hath (by rubbing) got colour into his cheeks, and is ready to give the trumpets their Cue that he's upon point to enter', cit. in Chambers, *Elizabethan Stage*, vol. 4, 367.

55   On the practice of posting playbills, see Chambers, vol. 2, 113, 514, 547; vol. 3, 373, 501; vol. 4, 199, 205, 228, 267, 283, 303. On such forms as playbills, handbills, and title pages used for advertisement, see the section on 'Advertising' in Emmett L. Avery and Arthur H. Scouter, *The London Stage 1660–1700: A Critical History*, Carbondale, IL: Southern Illinois University Press, 1968, lxxv–lxxxviii; and Ifan Kyrle Fletcher, 'British Playbills before 1718', *Theatre Notebook* 17 (1962–3): 48–50. For the later practice of offering separately printed prologues and epilogues for sale during a play's run in the theatre, see Judith

Milhous and Robert D. Hume, 'Dating Play Premières from Publication Data, 1660–1700', *Harvard Library Bulletin* 22 (1974): 374–405.

56 For the prologue's moment of greatest acceptance, see Pierre Danchin, *The Prologues and Epilogues of the Restoration, 1660–1700*, 4 vols, Nancy: Publications de l'Université Nancy II, 1981– ; see, especially, the editor's introduction, vol. 1: xxiii–xliii. On the form's appearance in today's theatre, one might note the respective prologues to the first and second part of Tony Kushner's *Angels in America*. Kushner has each speak for a vanishing kind of authority: one is a rabbi who laments the passing of the old ways and generations, the other, the world's oldest living Bolshevik. Kushner's notes indicate that the same actor is to play both characters.

57 Emma Smith, ed., *King Henry V*, Shakespeare in Production, Cambridge: Cambridge University Press, 2002, 83. Smith notes several historical experiments with the prologue and chorus, including William Macready's 1839 production, which had the prologue and chorus as 'the figure of Time, standing on a pedestal at the side of an enormous framework of painted clouds and bearing a scythe and hourglass' (84).

58 James N. Loehlin, ed., *Romeo and Juliet*, Shakespeare in Production, Cambridge: Cambridge University Press, 2002, 87. All subsequent quotations are from this page.

2 Prologue as threshold and usher

1 The available literature on prologues, prefaces, and beginnings of various sorts has taken up these forms of beginning in many ways. Yet for all the insights that we owe to criticism on the early modern prologue – detailed above in note 3, pp. 157–8 above – there remain at least three desiderata which the following chapters seek to address: Focusing on the uneasy conjunction, in the prologue, of service and authority, we suggest that it is best possible to do so by viewing in interconnection (1) the prologue as usher and go-between, as an institution mediating among those who write and those who deliver texts, as well as those who receive both the texts and their delivery; (2) further, such mediation needs to be studied as a process and event in culturally, and, specifically, theatrical space. There, the prologue's service and authority are conjoined with a specific site that vitally shares in, and literally foregrounds, the Elizabethan platform stage's *platea* dimension; (3) finally, and most crucially, such space is functionally marked by a liminal position and movement in that the prologue inhabits, and helps spectators cross, a threshold. While all three aspects intricately overlap, the threshold function, for reasons that will explain themselves, deserves to be given priority. Tied to both a highly specific Elizabethan use of theatrical space and a language marked by a recurring imagery of ushering and culinary service, the prologue's liminality has scarcely begun to receive critical attention. For its dramaturgy, its epistemology, and cultural significance we have adopted a critical language developed in a complementary approach to Shakespeare's epilogues and endings; see the last chapter in Weimann's *Author's Pen and Actor's Voice*, 216–45. For the practice of ushering in Elizabethan England, we have benefited from not only the studies cited below but also from more general studies of service in this era. See, for example, Ann Kussmaul, *Servants in Husbandry in Early Modern England*, Cambridge and New York: Cambridge

University Press, 1981; and Susan Dwyer Amussen, *An Ordered Society: Gender and Class in Early Modern England*, Oxford: Blackwell, 1988. For useful accounts of literary representations of service, and of the language and paradigms of service, see Mark Thornton Burnett, *Masters and Servants in English Renaissance Culture*, Basingstoke: Macmillan, 1997; Michael Neill, 'Servant Obedience and Master Sins: Shakespeare and the Bonds of Service', in Neill, *Putting History to the Question: Power, Politics, and Society in English Renaissance Drama*, New York: Columbia University Press, 2000, 13–48; and Lynn Magnusson, '"Power to hurt": Language and Service in Sidney Household Letters and Shakespeare's Sonnets', *ELH* 65 (4) (1998): 799–824.

2 Jonson, *The Entertainment at Althrope*, in *Ben Jonson*, ed. C. H. Herford, Percy Simpson and Evelyn Simpson, 11 vols, Oxford: Clarendon Press, vol. 7, 129, l. 250.

3 Act 4, Scene 1, ll. 185–7.

4 Jasper Mayne, *The City Match*, London, 1639, 53 (5.2).

5 Nathan Field and John Fletcher, *Four Plays, or Moral Representations, in One*, in *Comedies and Tragedies Written by Francis Beaumont and John Fletcher*, London, 1647, 25, ll. 76–7.

6 E. K. Chambers, *The Elizabethan Stage*, 4 vols, Oxford: Clarendon Press, 1923, vol. 1, 205.

7 Thomas Thomas, *Latin–English Dictionary*, London: R. Boyle, 1587, s.v. 'Antemoulo, onis'.

8 Randle Cotgrave, *A dictionarie of the French and English tongues*, London: 1611, s.v. 'Audiencier'.

9 Paul V. B. Jones, *The Household of a Tudor Nobleman*, University of Illinois Studies in the Social Sciences 6, Urbana, IL: University of Illinois, 1917, 155. On the usher in early modern England, see also Appendix C: 'The Gentleman Usher', in George Chapman, *The Gentleman Usher*, ed. John Hazel Smith, Lincoln: University of Nebraska Press, 1970, 131–7.

10 Stephen Greenblatt, *Marvelous Possessions: The Wonder of the New World*, Chicago: University of Chicago Press, 1991, 119–51; cit. at 139.

11 We take this phrase from *Pericles*, 4.6.18.

12 Bruce R. Smith, *The Acoustic World of Early Modern England: Attending to the O-Factor*, Chicago: University of Chicago Press, 1999.

13 Smith, *Acoustic World*, 272, 273, 274.

14 Smith, *Acoustic World*, 271.

15 Smith, *Acoustic World*, 276.

16 Smith, *Acoustic World*, 277, 279.

17 Quoted in Chambers, *Elizabethan Stage*, vol. 4, 367.

18 David Schalkwyk, *Speech and Performance in Shakespeare's Sonnets and Plays*, Cambridge: Cambridge University Press, 2002, 81–2.

19 Terence Hawkes, *Shakespeare in the Present*, London and New York: Routledge, 2002, 86, 89.

20 Gérard Genette, *Paratexts: Thresholds of Interpretation*, trans. Jane E. Lewin, Cambridge: Cambridge University Press, 1997, 1. For an application of Genette's vocabulary to Jonson's prefatory instances, see Paul D. Cannan, 'Ben Jonson, Authorship, and the Rhetoric of English Dramatic Prefatory Criticism', *Studies in Philology* 99 (2) (2002): 178–201.

21 Genette, *Paratexts*, 1–2.

22 Genette, *Paratexts*, 344.

23 Genette, *Paratexts*, 347.

24 Genette, *Paratexts*, 361. The larger thought from which this phrase is drawn reads as follows: 'the interview is – to put it lightly – part of a social game that no one can evade, or, to put it more seriously, part of a collaborative intellectual venture between writers on the one hand and the media on the other hand', quoted in *Paratexts*, 361.

25 Arnold van Gennep, *The Rites of Passage*, trans. Monika B. Vizedom and Gabrielle L. Cafee, Chicago: University of Chicago Press, 1960, 21.

26 Van Gennep, *The Rites of Passage*, 3.

27 Victor Turner, 'Variations on a Theme of Liminality', in *Secular Ritual*, ed. Sally F. Moore and Barbara G. Myerhoff, Assen, The Netherlands: Van Gorcum, 1977, 36–52.

28 Turner, 'Variations on a Theme of Liminality', 37. See also A. D. Nuttall, who notes of Shakespeare's beginnings, 'he finds his way, via various versions of what I have called the *in medias sententias* opening, to an entry not so much into the midst of (known) things as *between things*, or between whole orders of things. The ordinary indeterminacy of Elizabethan and Jacobean staging, with its rudimentary scenery and correlatively high demands upon the imagination of the audience, is made the vehicle of an ontological indeterminacy'. *Openings: Narrative Beginnings from the Epic to the Novel*, Oxford: Clarendon Press, 1992, 239.

29 Marjorie Garber, *Coming of Age in Shakespeare*, London and New York: Methuen, 1981; Edward Berry, *Shakesepare's Comic Rites*, New York: Cambridge University Press, 1984; Brian Vickers, 'Rites of Passage in Shakespeare's Prose', *Shakespeare Jahrbuch* 1986, 45–67; reprinted in Vickers, *Returning to Shakespeare*, London and New York: Routledge, 1989, 21–40. See also Arthur Holmberg, '*The Two Gentlemen of Verona*: Shakespearean Comedy as a Rite of Passage', *Queen's Quarterly* 90 (1983): 33–44; and Mark Thornton Burnett, 'The "Heart of My Mystery": *Hamlet* and Secrets', in *New Essays on Hamlet*, ed. Mark Thornton Burnett, New York: AMS Press, 1994, 21–46.

30 Garber, *Coming of Age in Shakespeare*, 26.

31 Garber, *Coming of Age in Shakespeare*, 8.

32 For an exception to this tendency, see William C. Carroll, '"The Form of Law": Ritual and Succession in *Richard III*', in *True Rites and Maimed Rites: Ritual and Anti-Ritual in Shakespeare and His Age*, ed. Linda Woodbridge and Edward Berry, Urbana and Chicago: University of Illinois Press, 1992, 203–19; Carroll argues that the failure of various cultural rituals in the play (including rituals involving failed *passages*) reflects the tensions, in late-Elizabethan England, over the question of succession.

33 Garber, *Coming of Age in Shakespeare*, 31–2.

34 Van Gennep, *Rites of Passage*, 39, 189.

35 Victor Turner, *From Ritual to Theatre: The Human Seriousness of Play*, New York: Performing Arts Journal Publications, 1982, 44.

36 Stephen Greenblatt, 'Liminal States and Transformations', in *Rites of Passage: Art for the End of the Century*, ed. Stuart Morgan and Frances Morris, London: Tate Gallery Publications, 1995, 28–30; cit. at 28.

37 M. C. Bradbrook, *English Dramatic Form: A History of its Development*, New York: Barnes and Noble, Inc., 1965, 22. On the question of audience response in early modern drama, see Kent Cartwright, *Shakespearean Tragedy and Its Double:*

The Rhythms of Audience Response, University Park: Pennsylvania State University Press, 1991.

38 M. M. Mahood, *Bit Parts in Shakespeare's Plays*, Cambridge and New York: Cambridge University Press, 1992, 33.

39 Anthony B. Dawson and Paul Yachnin, *The Culture of Playgoing in Shakespeare's England: A Collaborative Debate*, Cambridge and New York: Cambridge University Press, 2001.

40 Reprinted in Hyder E. Rollins, ed., *A Pepysian Garland*, Cambridge, MA: Harvard University Press, 1922, 35.

41 See, for instance, Roslyn Knutson's *The Repertory of Shakespeare's Company, 1594–1613*, Fayetteville: University of Arkansas Press, 1991, and her more recent study of 'guild' identities in *Playing Companies and Commerce in Shakespeare's Time*, Cambridge: Cambridge University Press, 2001; Andrew Gurr, *Playgoing in Shakespeare's London*, 2nd edition, London and New York: Cambridge University Press, 1996; and Vincent Petronella, 'Shakespeare's Dramatic Chambers', in Thomas Moisan and Douglas Bruster, eds, *In the Company of Shakespeare: Essays on English Renaissance Literature in Honor of G. Blakemore Evans*, Madison, NJ, and London: Fairleigh Dickinson University Press, 2002, 111–38.

42 See Andrew Gurr, *The Shakespearian Playing Companies*, Oxford: Clarendon Press, 1996; and Robert Weimann, 'Le Declin de la Scène "Indivisible" Elisabéthaine: Beaumont, Fletcher et Heywood' in *Dramaturgie et Société*, Paris: Centre National de la Recherche Scientifique, 1968, vol. 2, 815–7.

43 See, for example, Charles J. Sisson, *Le goût public et le théâtre Elisabéthaine jusqu'à la mort de Shakespeare*, Dijon: Darantière, 1928, esp. 35–51, and Alfred Harbage, *Shakespeare's Audience*, New York: Columbia University Press, 1941, 143–6.

44 Michael D. Bristol, *Carnival and Theatre: Plebeian Culture and the Structure of Authority in Renaissance England*, New York and London: Routledge, 1985, 3.

45 Louis Montrose, *The Purpose of Playing: Shakespeare and the Cultural Politics of the Elizabethan Theatre*, Chicago: University of Chicago Press, 1996, 33.

46 Montrose, *Purpose of Playing*, 33–4.

47 See Steven Mullaney, *The Place of the Stage: License, Play, and Power in Renaissance England*, Chicago: University of Chicago Press, 1988, and Montrose's remarks on this study in *Purpose of Playing*, 34–5, n. 25.

48 The dumb show constitutes a large and largely unexplored activity in the early modern theatre. But see Dieter Mehl, *The Elizabethan Dumb Show: The History of a Dramatic Convention*, London: Methuen, 1965; Sidney R. Homan, 'The Uses of Silence: The Elizabethan Dumb Show and the Silent Cinema', *Comparative Drama* 2 (1968): 213–28; Lee Sheridan Cox, *Figurative Design in 'Hamlet': The Significance of the Dumb Show*, Columbus: Ohio State University Press, 1973; and Frederick Kiefer, 'A Dumb Show of the Senses in *Timon of Athens*', in Moisan and Bruster, eds, *In the Company of Shakespeare*, 139–58.

49 Weimann, *Author's Pen and Actor's Voice*, 83.

50 On this trope's deployment during the early modern era, see Christopher Hill, 'The Many-Headed Monster in Late Tudor and Early Stuart Political Thinking', *Change and Continuity in Seventeenth-Century England*, Cambridge, MA: Harvard University Press, 1975, 181–294; and C. A. Patrides, '"The Beast with Many Heads": Views on the Multitude', *Premises and Motifs in Renaissance Thought and Literature*, Princeton: Princeton University Press, 1982, 124–36.

3 Authority and authorization in the pre-Shakespearean prologue

1 Marjorie Garber, *Shakespeare's Ghost Writers: Literature as Uncanny Causality*, New York and London: Methuen, 1987, 13.
2 Edward Said, *Beginnings: Intention and Method*, New York: Basic Books, 1975, 23.
3 Said, *Beginnings*, 83, 84, 16.
4 Sören Kierkegaard, *The Concept of Irony: With Constant Reference to Socrates*, cited in Said, *Beginnings*, 88.
5 Thomas Hobbes, *Leviathan*, ed. C. B. Macpherson, New York: Pelican, 1968, 217–18.
6 Leeds Barroll, *Politics, Plague and Shakespeare's Theatre: The Stuart Years*, Ithaca: Cornell University Press, 1991, 8.
7 Jean-Christophe Agnew, *Worlds Apart: The Market and the Theatre in Anglo-American Thought, 1550–1750*, Cambridge: Cambridge University Press, 1986, 9, 11.
8 See Douglas Bruster, 'The Structural Transformation of Print in Late Elizabethan England', Chapter 3 in *Shakespeare and the Question of Culture: Early Modern Literature and the Cultural Turn*, New York: Palgrave Macmillan, 2003, 65–93. An earlier version of this essay was published in *Print, Manuscript, Performance: The Changing Relations of the Media in Early Modern England*, ed. Arthur F. Marotti and Michael D. Bristol, Columbus: Ohio State University Press, 2000, 49–89. More recently, John Pitcher has extended some of this essay's arguments in 'Literature, the Playhouse and the Public', in John Barnard and D. F. McKenzie, eds, *The Cambridge History of the Book in Britain*, vol. 4: 1557–1695, Cambridge: Cambridge University Press, 2002, 351–75.
9 Robert Weimann, *Authority and Representation in Early Modern Discourse*, Baltimore and London: Johns Hopkins University Press, 1996, 11.
10 Brian Cummings, *The Literary Culture of the Reformation: Grammar and Grace*, Oxford: Oxford University Press, 2002, 10, 11.
11 See, for instance, David Bevington, *Tudor Drama and Politics: A Critical Approach to Topical Meaning*, Cambridge, MA: Harvard University Press, 1968; Paul Whitfield White, *Theatre and Reformation: Protestantism, Patronage and Playing in Tudor England*, New York: Cambridge University Press, 1993; and Greg Walker, *The Politics of Performance in Early Renaissance Drama*, Cambridge: Cambridge University Press, 1998.
12 Timothy J. Reiss, *Knowledge, Discovery and Imagination in Early Modern Europe: The Rise of Aesthetic Rationalism*, Cambridge and New York: Cambridge University Press, 1997, 15. On modernity's changes reflected in the domain of empiricism and the law, see Barbara J. Shapiro, *A Culture of Fact: England 1550–1720*, Ithaca: Cornell University Press, 2000.
13 Weimann, *Author's Pen and Actor's Voice*, 48–9.
14 Rosalie L. Colie, *The Resources of Kind: Genre-Theory in the Renaissance*, Berkeley: University of California Press, 1973, 19.
15 Timothy J. Moore, *The Theater of Plautus: Playing to the Audience*, Austin: University of Texas Press, 1998, 8. As Moore points out: 'More than one-sixth of Plautus's corpus – and over one-quarter of some plays – is made up of monologues'.
16 Moore, *The Theater of Plautus*, 10–11; cit. at 11.
17 Titus Machius Plautus, *Menaechmi: A Pleasant and fine Conceited Comædie, taken out of the most excellent wittie Poet Plautus*, trans. W. W., London: Thomas Creede, 1595, A4r–A4v.

18 On the *sermo simplex*, see Ernst Robert Curtius, *European Literature and the Latin Middle Ages*, trans. Willard R. Trask, orig. publ. 1948; London and Henley: Routledge and Kegan Paul, 1953, 148–51; on *sermo humilis* see Erich Auerbach, *Literary Language and Its Public in Latin Antiquity and in the Middle Ages*, trans. Ralph Manheim, orig. publ. 1958; New York: Pantheon Books, 1965, 25–81. On the body in Rabelaisian discourse, see Walter J. Kaiser, *Praisers of Folly: Erasmus, Rabelais, Shakespeare*, Cambridge, MA: Harvard University Press, 1963, and, of course, M. M. Bakhtin, *Rabelais and His World*, trans. Helene Iswolsky, Cambridge, MA: MIT Press, 1968.

19 The phrase is that of Joseph Hall, in his *Virgidemiarum*, 1.3.44. See Weimann's discussion of this passage in *Author's Pen and Actor's Voice*, 101 ff.

20 On Kemp's physical praxis, see David Wiles, *Shakespeare's Clown: Actor and Text in the Elizabethan Playhouse*, Cambridge: Cambridge University Press, 1987; and Max W. Thomas, *'Kemps Nine Daies Wonder*: Dancing Carnival Into Market', *PMLA* 107 (1992): 511–23.

21 *Terence in English*, trans. R. Bernard, Cambridge: John Legat, 1598, 4.

22 *The Castle of Perseverance*, in *Medieval Drama*, ed. David Bevington, Boston: Houghton Mifflin, 1975, 799. Subsequent references to this text will be cited parenthetically.

23 *Mankind*, in *Three Late Medieval Morality Plays*, ed. G. A. Lester, London: A. and C. Black, 1999, 4–5.

24 *Everyman*, in *Three Late Medieval Morality Plays*, ed. G. A. Lester, London: A. and C. Black, 1999.

25 Thomas Lupton, *All For Money*, ed. M. E. P. Concolato, Napoli: Linguori Editore, 1985, ll. 92–8. We have collated this text with the Tudor Facsimile Text, ed. John S. Farmer, 1910; repr. New York: AMS Press, 1970.

26 For Robert Wilson's extemporizing mother-wit we have the authority of Stowe's 1615 *Annals*, in which Stowe describes him as having possessed 'a quick, delicate, refined, extemporal wit'. See G. K. Hunter, *English Drama 1586–1642: The Age of Shakespeare*, Oxford: Clarendon Press, 1997, 34. See also F. P. Wilson, *The English Drama, 1485–1585*, ed. George Hunter, Oxford: Clarendon Press, 1969. For more extensive information on Wilson, some of it highly speculative, we need to go back to F. G. Fleay, *A Biographical Chronicle of the English Drama, 1559–1642*, 2 vols, New York: Burt Franklin: 1891, vol. 2: 278–83. On the politics of Wilson's *The Cobler's Prophesie*, see Irene Rose Mann, 'A Political Cancel in *The Cobler's Prophesie*', *Library* 23, (1942): 94–100. See also Frank Kermode, 'The Playwright's Prophecy: Robert Wilson's *The Three Ladies of London* and the "Alienation" of the English', *Medieval and Renaissance Drama in England* 11 (1999): 60–87.

27 Robert Wilson, *The Three Ladies of London*, in *Dodsley's Select Collection of Old English Plays*, ed. W. C. Hazzlitt, 15 vols, London: Reeves and Turner, 1874–6, vol. 6.

28 For an argument about the Queen's men and their 'plain' style of protestant performance, see Scott McMillin and Sally-Beth MacLean, *The Queen's Men and Their Plays*, Cambridge and New York: Cambridge University Press, 1998.

29 Richard Southern, *The Staging of Plays before Shakespeare*, London: Faber and Faber, 1973, 545, 549. The question of venue appears crucial in light of what Ruth Lunney calls 'the rhetoric of theatrical space' – which, of course, is part of and affects the 'perspective frame' of 'theatrical experience' (Lunney, *Marlowe*

and the Popular Tradition: Innovation in the English Drama before 1595, Manchester: Manchester University Press, 2002, 104, 159). See, in this connection, Alan Dessen, *Shakespeare and the Late Moral Plays*, Lincoln: University of Nebraska Press, 1986. For more recent contextualizations, see, among other studies, William Ingram, *The Business of Playing: The Beginnings of the Adult Professional Theatre in Elizabethan London*, Ithaca: Cornell University Press, 1992; John Astington, 'The London Stage in the 1580s', *The Elizabethan Theatre* 11 (1990): 1–15; and, for the 1590s and after, Rosalyn Knutson, *Playing Companies and Commerce in Shakespeare's Time*, Cambridge: Cambridge University Press, 2001.

30 Douglas Bruster, *Drama and the Market in the Age of Shakespeare*, Cambridge: Cambridge University Press, 1992, 1.
31 G. K. Hunter, 'The Beginnings of Elizabethan Drama: Revolution and Continuity', *Renaissance Drama* 16 (1986): 44.
32 Agnew, *Worlds Apart*.
33 Agnew, *Worlds Apart*, x–xi.
34 William Shakespeare, *King John*, ed. L. A. Beaurline, The New Cambridge Shakespeare, Cambridge: Cambridge University Press, 1990, 99.

4 Frivolous jestures versus matter of worth: Christopher Marlowe

1 See Thomas Lupton, *All For Money*, ed. M. E. P. Concolato, Napoli: Linguori Editore, 1985, l. 31.
2 Ruth Lunney, *Marlowe and the Popular Tradition: Innovation in the English Drama Before 1595*, Manchester and New York: Manchester University Press, 2002, 104; cf. 14–16.
3 Throughout our text is that of *The Revels Plays of Christopher Marlowe*; here: *Tamburlaine the Great*, ed. J. S. Cunningham, Manchester: Manchester University Press, 1981, 113–14.
4 Christopher Marlowe, *Tamburlaine. Parts One and Two*, ed. Anthony B. Dawson, London: A. and C. Black, 1997, xi.
5 Clifford Leech, *Christopher Marlowe: Poet for the Stage*, ed. Anne Lancashire, New York: AMS Press, 1986, 42.
6 Prologue ('Chorus'), l. 6; see Christopher Marlowe, *Doctor Faustus*, ed. David Bevington and Eric Rasmussen, Manchester: Manchester University Press, 1993.
7 On the Tantalus myth, and tantalization, as centrally informing Marlowe's literary practice, see Fred B. Tromly, *Playing with Desire: Christopher Marlowe and the Art of Tantalization*, Toronto: University of Toronto Press, 1998.
8 *The Oxford Book of Medieval Latin Verse*, ed. F. J. E. Raby, Oxford: Oxford University Press, 1959, 369–70; cit. Robert S. Knapp, *Shakespeare: The Theatre and the Book*, Princeton: Princeton University Press, 1989, 44.
9 Douglas Bruster 'The Structural Transformation of Print in Late Elizabethan Enland', in *Shakespeare and the Question of Culture: Literature in Early Modern England and the Cultural Turn*, New York: Palgrave Macmillan, 2003, 65–93; 67, 75.
10 Thomas Hobbes, *Leviathan*, ed. C. B. Macpherson, Harmondsworth: Penguin, 1968, 218.
11 This stance antedates and yet prepares for a new 'allegory of genius' that informs the imminent 'shift of authority from stage to page'. See Timothy Murray,

Theatrical Legitimation: Allegories of Genius in Seventeenth-century England and France, New York: Oxford University Press, 1987, 15 and (mainly on Jonson), 23–104.

12 The printer, who 'was not working from a theatre manuscript', may actually have been Thomas Orwin printing for Richard Jones; see *Tamburlaine the Great,* ed. Cunningham, 89–90. But, since the latter is named in the Stationers' Register entry for the play (14 August 1590), we shall continue to refer to Jones as Marlowe's printer.

13 Of course, 'jestures' is a now obsolete spelling of what is typically rendered 'gestures', and we have retained this spelling to indicate a pun latent in the preface. Current from at least the early sixteenth century through the first half of the seventeenth, this spelling, 'jestures', asks the reader of Jones's preface to think about the connections between theatrical *gestures* (in modern spelling) and comic *jests*, especially as the latter were relayed by playhouse jesters. This pun was more than fortuitous: both 'gestures'/'jestures' and 'jests' (as a noun) come from the same root. According to the *Oxford English Dictionary*, 'gesture'/'jesture' was related to Old French *geste* or *jeste*, 'action', which derived from medieval Latin *gestūra*, a noun of action which in turn came from Latin *gerēre*, 'to carry on (war, etc.), perform'. Nor was a play on these words original with, or confined to Jones during this period. Thomas Drant had spoken of 'the jester's gesturings / and glosing words' in his 1567 translation of Horace's *Ars Poetica* (Thomas Drant, trans. *Horace his arte of poetrie, pistles, and satyrs Englished*, London, 1567, ll. 973–4). And the first sentence of *Tarltons newes out of Purgatorie* (1590) offers the precise conjunction in a dichotomy of seeing and hearing the renowned comedian: 'Sorrowing as most men do for the death of Richard Tarlton, in that his particular loss was a general lament to all that coveted, either to satisfy their eyes with his Clownish gesture, or their ears with his witty jests . . .'. (*Tarltons newes out of Purgatorie. Onely such a jest as his jigge.* Published by Robin Goodfellow, London, 1590, 'Prologue'.) We adduce these instances and chains of etymology not to imply any deep philological self-consciousness on the part of Jones, but instead to point out that, conscious or otherwise, his use of 'jesture' took advantage of an accepted, variant spelling and pun, and, in doing so, may have (like the *Tarlton* pamphlet) enlisted the readers' imaginations (and experiences of playgoing) to suggest a continuity between comedic improvisation and theatrical practice itself.

14 Richard Dutton, 'The Birth of the Author', *Texts and Cultural Change in Early Modern England*, ed. Cedric C. Brown and Arthur F. Marotti, London: Macmillan, 1997, 154 ff.

15 Dutton, 'The Birth of the Author', 159.

16 Lukas Erne, *Shakespeare as Literary Dramatist*, Cambridge: Cambridge University Press, 2003.

17 Dutton, 'The Birth of the Author', 166.

18 Bruster, 'The Structural Transformation of Print in Late Elizabethan England', 67.

19 Bruster, 'Structural Transformation', 72, 75.

20 Bruster, 'Structural Transformation', 63, 79, 87–8.

21 Fredson Bowers, ed., *The Complete Works of Christopher Marlowe*, 2 vols, Cambridge: Cambridge University Press, 1973, vol. 1, 75. But in no case would the printer's disapproval of those 'fond and frivolous' elements have referred to the scornful taunts addressed to Mycetes or Bajazeth in Part I, as F. P. Wilson

(*Marlowe and the Early Shakespeare*, Oxford: Clarendon Press, 1953, 28) once suggested. Rather, these 'graced deformities' have their origins in the demands of the playhouse, not the culture of humanistic literacy; as David Bevington notes, 'Marlowe's company would hardly have countenanced a public renunciation of its popular Vice comedy in *Tamburlaine*, only to return to it in *Doctor Faustus*' (*From 'Mankind' to Marlowe: Growth of Structure in the Popular Drama of Tudor England*, Cambridge, MA: Harvard University Press, 1962, 201).

22 Lest too dogmatic a binary be presumed here, we would refer the reader to 'Space (in)dividable: locus and platea revisted', Chapter 7 in Weimann's *Author's Pen and Actor's Voice*, 180–215, for an account of the radical overlapping and interaction of these entities.

23 Jill L. Levenson, '"Working Words": The Verbal Dynamic of *Tamburlaine*', in *'A poet and a filthy play-maker': New Essays on Christopher Marlowe*, ed. Kenneth Friedenreich, Roma Gill, and Constance B. Kuriyama, New York: AMS Press, 1988, 99–115, cit. At 112.

24 For an examination of the peculiarly effective words of Marlowe's most famous lyric, 'The Passionate Shepherd', see Bruster, *Quoting Shakespeare: Form and Culture in Early Modern Drama*, Lincoln: University of Nebraska Press, 2000, Chapter 2, 'Quoting Marlowe's Shepherd', 52–87.

25 See Joseph Porter, *The Drama of Speech Acts: Shakespeare's Lancastrian Tetralogy*, Berkeley: University of California Press, 1979.

26 See D. Allen Caroll, ed., *Greene's Groatsworth of Wit, Bought With a Million of Repentance*, Binghamton: Medieval and Renaissance Texts and Studies, 1994, ll. 935–55.

27 In view of the vexed chronology of Marlowe's plays, the most plausible dates we hold to be either approximately 1589–90 (the latter year first proposed by Tucker Brooke) or, alternatively, a date that 'puts *The Jew* chronologically last' (as Leech suggests in *Christopher Marlowe*, 167; and see his Chapter 2, 'The Texts and the Chronology', especially 22–4.)

28 See Tucker Brooke, *The Life of Marlowe and The Tragedy of Dido Queen of Carthage*, New York: Gordian Press, 1966, 123, 115.

29 Our text is *Dido Queen of Carthage and The Massacre at Paris*, ed. M. J. Oliver, Cambridge, MA: Harvard University Press, 1968.

30 Garrett A. Sullivan, Jr, *The Drama of Landscape: Land, Property, and Social Relations on the Early Modern Stage*, Stanford: Stanford University Press, 1998, 2.

31 Emily C. Bartels, *Spectacles of Strangeness: Imperialism, Alienation, and Marlowe*, Philadelphia: University of Pennsylvania Press, 1993, 39, 185.

32 We could compare, with this specification, Puck's vow to 'put a girdle round about the earth / In forty minutes' (*A Midsummer Night's Dream* 2.1.175–6), a claim that subsumes distance into time rather than spatial measure. On the growing consciousness of such forms of measurement in early modern drama, see Sullivan, *The Drama of Landscape*.

33 Richard Wilson, 'Visible Bullets: Tamburlaine the Great and Ivan the Terrible', *Christopher Marlowe and English Renaissance Culture*, ed. Darryll Grantley and Peter Robert, Aldershot: Scolar Press, 1996, 56, 58. Bartels's phrase cited, ibid., 55.

34 Eugene Waith, 'Marlowe and the Jades of Asia', *Studies in English Literature* 5 (1966): 66; cit. *Tamburlaine the Great*, ed. Cunningham, 25.

35 *The Letters of Charles and Mary Lamb*, ed. E. V. Lucas, New York: Macmillan, 1913, 1: 133; cit. in *The Jew of Malta*, ed. Bawcutt, 17. See T. S. Eliot,

'Christopher Marlowe', *Selected Essays*, London: Faber and Faber, 1951, 123.
Developing further Eliot's reading, Leech considers the play as 'a kind of
achieved dark comedy', where 'we are kept at a considerable distance from the
pain of it' (*'The Jew of Malta*: Black Comedy or Comic Tragedy', *Christopher
Marlowe*, 165, 173.) The 'distance', or partial absence of empathy, results, we
submit, from the protagonist's threshold position between the presentation of,
and his own representation in, the play.

36 *The Complete Works of Christopher Marlowe*, ed. Bowers, vol. 1: 256.

37 Our text is *The Jew of Malta*, ed. N. W. Bawcutt, Manchester: Manchester University Press, 1978.

38 In Heywood's 'Prologue spoken at Court', the play is introduced as an old play,
'writ many years agone', in 'that age' that was no longer Heywood's. Even
more revealing, in his Epilogue at the Cockpit, standards of verisimilar mimesis
are invoked, such as those associated in sculpture with 'Pygmalion', in painting
with 'Apelles'. At the same time, a poetic concept of lifelike representation that
is not Marlowe's is implicated: 'our actor did not so, / He only aimed to go,
but not out go'. See the material printed in Bawcutt's Appendix A, 191–4; and
Weimann's revisionary reading of Heywood's position in *Author's Pen and Actor's
Voice*, 128–34.

39 See Weimann, *Author's Pen and Actor's Voice*, 62–70.

40 Although Aristotle's *Poetics* does not, of course, mandate 'unities' of time, place,
and action, the effect of Continental commentary on classical poetics – one
could invoke the phrase *les unités scaligeriennes* – was to imply Aristotle's endorsement of their obligatory nature.

41 Patrick Cheney, *Marlowe's Counterfeit Profession: Ovid, Spenser, Counter-Nationhood*,
Toronto: University of Toronto Press, 1997, esp. 25, 151.

42 Stephen Greenblatt, 'Marlowe, Marx, and Anti-Semitism', *Learning to Curse:
Essays in Early Modern Culture*, London: Routledge, 1990, 53.

43 See the chapter 'Laughter and Terror: Herod and Pilate', in Weimann's *Shakespeare and the Popular Tradition in the Theatre*, Baltimore: Johns Hopkins University
Press, 1978, 64–72.

44 Bartels, *Spectacles of Strangeness*, 21.

45 See Victor Turner, *From Ritual to Theatre: The Human Seriousness of Play*, New
York: Performing Arts Journal Publications, 1982, 37–41. For further terribly
comic/tragic uses of threshold occasions in the early modern theatre, see the
section 'Liminality: cultural authority "betwixt-and-between"' in Weimann,
Author's Pen and Actor's Voice, 240–5.

46 Ludger Brinker, 'The Art of Marlowe's Prologues: Subtle Innovations Within
Traditional Patterns', *Cahiers Elisabéthains* 42 (1992): 1–15; cit. at 10.

47 Brinker, 'The Art of Marlowe's Prologues', 8.

48 Cheney, *Marlowe's Counterfeit Profession*, 139.

49 Lines 20–3. The 'letters' may allude to the spurious *Letters of Phalaris* and the
Renaissance debate on whether, in Bawcutt's words, 'letters and learning weakened [. . .] military effectiveness'.

50 *The Jew of Malta*, ed. Bawcutt, 65.

51 For stimulating examinations of the relationship of the early modern to that of
modernity as a whole, and the Enlightenment in particular, see Hugh Grady,
'Renewing Modernity: Changing Contexts and Contents of a Nearly Invisible
Concept', *Shakespeare Quarterly* 50 (3) (1999): 268–84; and 'Shakespeare's Links

to Machiavelli and Montaigne: Constructing Intellectual Modernity in Early Modern Europe', *Comparative Literature* 52 (2) (2000): 119–42.

5 Kingly harp and iron pen in the playhouse: George Peele

1 For this phrase, see Thomas Middleton, *Micro-cynicon. Sixe Snarling Sayres*, London, 1599, 'His defiance to Envy'.

2 See James Shapiro, *Rival Playwrights: Marlowe, Shakespeare, Jonson*, New York: Columbia University Press, 1991.

3 Throughout we use *The Life and Work of George Peele*, gen. ed. Charles Tyler Prouty, 3 vols, New Haven: Yale University Press, 1952–70 (hereafter referred to as the Yale edition); for this citation, see 3: 192–3. Prouty's edition is still a foundational resource for information about Peele's life and works. See also the entry by John Wilson in *Major Tudor Authors: A Bio-Bibliographical Critical Sourcebook*, ed. Alan Hager, Westport, CO: Greenwood Press, 1997, 376–80.

4 For discussions of the 'pavilion', 'booth', or 'tent' used in the scene, see Richard Hosley, 'The Discovery-Space in Shakespeare's Globe', *Shakespeare Survey* 12 (1959): 35–46; William A. Armstrong, 'Actors and Theatres', *Shakespeare Survey* 17 (1964): 191–204; see also the comments by Elmer Blistein, the editor of the Yale edition of the play, vol. 3: 256.

5 From the Geneva Bible (London, 1599).

6 John Fletcher and Nathan Field, *Four Plays, or Moral Representations, in One*, in John Fletcher and Francis Beaumont, *Comedies and Tragedies*, London, 1647, 39.

7 A. R. Braunmuller, *George Peele*, Boston: Twayne Publishers, 1983, 108. Several of our own readings are indebted to this fine study of a much-neglected dramatist.

8 So Sidney: 'And may not I presume a little further, to show the reasonableness of this word *vates*, and say that the holy David's Psalms are a divine poem? If I do, I shall not do it without the testimony of great learned men, both ancient and modern' (Sir Philip Sidney, *An Apology for Poetry*, ed. Forrest G. Robinson, Indianapolis: Bobbs-Merrill Educational Publishing, 1970, 11–12).

9 Thomas Nashe, Introduction to Greene's *Menaphon*, in Nashe, *Works*, 5 vols, Oxford: Blackwell, repr. 1958, ed. R. B. McKerrow, vol. 3: 323.

10 Here one might compare Ludger Brinker on the prologue to *Doctor Faustus*: 'Marlowe . . . employs rather deliberately a moral–epic form of the prologue to emphasize one aspect of the tragedy here: the objective world of religion and morals (which we encounter again at the end of the play) which spans over all of Faustus's actions' (Ludger Brinker, 'The Art of Marlowe's Prologues: Subtle Innovations Within Traditional Patterns', *Cahiers Elisabéthains* 42 (1992): 1–15; cit. at 7).

11 See D. H. Horne's critical biography of Peele, Yale edition vol. 1: 3–146. See also Edwin H. Miller, *The Professional Writer in Elizabethan England*, Cambridge, MA: Harvard University Press, 1959.

12 On the folk basis of *The Old Wives Tale*, see Jackson I. Cope, 'Peele's *Old Wives Tale*: Folk Stuff into Ritual Form', *ELH* 49 (1982): 326–38; and Roger de V. Renwick, 'The Mummer's Play and *The Old Wives Tale*', *Journal of American Folklore* 94 (1981): 433–55. See also Elizabeth Porges Watson, 'Folklore in Arcadia: Mopsa's "tale of the old cut" Re-cut and Set', *Sidney Journal* 16 (2) (1998): 3–15. For a more general account of the play's structure and technique, see Joan

C. Marx, "'Soft, who have we here?'": The Dramatic Technique of *The Old Wives Tale*', *Renaissance Drama* 12 (1981): 117–43.

13 Mary Ellen Lamb, 'Scholars and Nurses: Negotiating Conflicts between Learned and Popular Cultures Within the Early Modern Subject', paper delivered at Shakespeare Association Meeting, Washington, DC, 28 March 1997, 9. Our thanks go to Dr Lamb for permitting us to make use of her manuscript.

14 Lamb, 'Scholars and Nurses', 1. For an account of the masculine culture of the schoolroom – an account which Lamb may be seen as calling into question – see Walter Ong's discussion of Latin learning as a masculine rite of passage. Ong argues that Latin in the schools constituted something of a 'puberty rite' for boys during the early modern period. He holds that the sexual segregation of the grammar schools, their strict corporeal discipline, insistence upon obedience and imitation, and emphasis on the epic/heroic values of classical literature led to a hardening of the individual student 'for the extra-familial world in which he would have to live' (Walter J. Ong, 'Latin Language Study as a Renaissance Puberty Rite', *Studies in Philology* 56 (1959): 103–24, 123). Latin thus came to be perceived as the language of manhood, English remaining the mother tongue. This diglossic structure, William Kerrigan argues, led to the articulation of a bifurcated 'linguistic ego' in early modern authors brought up in the 'rigid, masculine world' of the grammar school: 'As the boy was separated from women, so he was divorced from the mother tongue' (William Kerrigan, 'The Articulation of the Ego in the English Renaissance' in *The Literary Freud: Mechanisms of Defense and the Poetic Will*, vol. 4 in *Psychiatry and the Humanities*, ed. Joseph H. Smith, New Haven: Yale University Press, 1980, 269). Lamb's revision of such a paradigm has recently found support in the research of Marjorie Curry Woods; see her 'Boys Will Be Women: Musings on Classroom Nostalgia and the Chaucerian Audience(s)', in *Speaking Images: Essays in Honor of V. A. Kolve*, ed. R. F. Yeager and Charlotte C. Morse, Asheville, NC: Pegasus Press, 2000, 143–66.

15 Patricia Binnie, ed., *The Old Wives Tale*, Manchester: Manchester University Press, 1980, 26; Frank S. Hook, editor of the play in *The Life and Works of George Peele*, 3 vols, New Haven: Yale University Press, 1970, 3: 336.

16 See the catalogue provided by Sylvia Lyons-Render, 'Folk-Motivs in George Peele's *The Old Wives Tale*', *Tennessee Folklore Society Bulletin* 26 (1960): 62–71. But note Hooks' reservations, *Life and Works of George Peele*, vol. 3: 339, n. 35.

17 John Wilson, 'George Peele' in *Major Tudor Authors*, 378.

18 See Yale edition 3: 341, editor's note.

19 Harold Jenkins, 'Peele's *Old Wives Tale*', *Modern Language Review* 34 (1939): 177–85.

20 For an argument positing a relationship between Peele's comedy and continental improvisation, see A. S. Moffett, 'Process and Structure Shared: Similarities Between *Commedia dell'arte* and *The Old Wives Tale* of George Peele', *New England Theatre Journal* 4 (1993): 97–105.

21 Peter Burke, *Popular Culture in Early Modern Europe*, revised reprint, Aldershot: Scholar Press, 1994, 23–7.

22 Burke, *Popular Culture in Early Modern Europe*, 28.

23 Mary Ellen Lamb, 'Apologizing for Pleasure in Sidney's *Apology for Poetry*: The Nurse of Abuse Meets the Tudor Grammar School', *Criticism* 36 (4) (1994): 499–519; 'Gloriana, Acrasia, and the House of Busirane: Gendered Fictions in

the *Faerie Queene* as Fairy Tale', in *Worldmaking Spenser: Explorations in the Early Modern Age*, ed. Patrick Cheney and Lauren Silberman, Lexington: University of Kentucky Press, 2000, 81–100; 'Engendering the Narrative Art: Old Wives' Tales in *The Winter's Tale, Macbeth*, and *The Tempest*', *Criticism* 40 (4) (1998): 529–53; and 'Taken by the Fairies: Fairy Practices and the Production of Popular Culture in *A Midsummer Night's Dream*', *Shakespeare Quarterly* 51 (3) (2000): 277–312. See also Lamb's forthcoming study, *The Production of Popular Culture by Shakespeare, Spenser and Jonson*, London: Routledge, 2004.

24 Inga-Stine Ewbank, '"What words, what looks, what wonders?": Language and Spectacle in the Theatre of George Peele', *The Elizabethan Theatre* 5 (1993): 124–54.

25 David Bradley, *From Text to Performance in the Elizabethan Theatre: Preparing the Play for the Stage*, Cambridge: Cambridge University Press, 1992, 91. For the function of the 'plotter', see 40–7, 75–94. Despite the obvious discrepancies between the presenting and the represented positions in the play, 'the Presenter's unreliability' (Susan T. Viguers, 'Peele's *The Battle of Alcazar*', *Explicator* 43 (2) (1985): 9–12) is not, we think, part of a deliberately complex scenario, but rather, part and parcel of the text's instability, its 'unfinished scenes and second thoughts' (Bradley, *From Text to Performance*, 90). Characteristically, such instability is especially marked in the Presenter's dumb shows; see our remarks on the Prologue and Chorus of *Henry V* in Chapter 7 here, and Gunter Walch, 'Tudor-Legende und Geschichtsbewegung in *The Life of King Henry V*: Zur Rezeptionslenkung durch den Chorus', *Shakespeare Jahrbuch* 122 (1986): 36–46.

26 See Werner Senn, *Studies in the Dramatic Construction of Robert Greene and George Peele*, Bern: Francke, 1973, 58.

27 A. R. Braunmuller, *George Peele*, 72–4.

28 Louis Adrian Montrose, 'Gifts and Reasons: Contexts of Peele's *Araygnment of Paris*', *ELH* 47 (1980): 433–61; 457.

29 See Edward Said, *Beginnings: Intention and Method*, New York: Basic Books, 1975, 16.

30 Jonas Barish, *The Antitheatrical Prejudice*, Berkeley and Los Angeles: University of California Press, 1981, 135–6. But for an antihistrionic (rather than antitheatrical) emphasis different from that in Barish's important study, see Weimann, *Author's Pen and Actor's Voice*, 34–6. See also John Gordon Sweeney III, *Jonson and the Psychology of Public Theatre: 'To coin the spirit, spend the soul'*, Princeton: Princeton University Press, 1985; and Clifford Davidson, 'Judgment, Iconoclasm, and Anti-theatricalism in Jonson's *Bartholomew Fair*', *Papers on Language and Literature* 25 (1989): 349–63.

31 *Romeo and Juliet*, ed. T. J. B. Spencer, New Penguin Shakespeare, Harmondsworth: Penguin, 1967, 171.

6 From hodge-podge to scene individable: John Lyly

1 See Thomas Hobbes, *Leviathan*, ed. C. B. Macpherson, Harmondsworth: Penguin, 1968; and Martin Heidegger, 'The Age of the World Picture', in *The Question Concerning Technology and Other Essays*, trans. William Lovitt, New York: Harper and Row, 1977. Weimann elaborates on this all too brief reference in *Authority and Representation in Early Modern Discourse*, ed. David Hillman, Baltimore: Johns Hopkins University Press, 1996, 2, 193.

2   *The Complete Works of John Lyly*, ed. R. Warwick Bond, 3 vols, Oxford: Clarendon Press, 1902, vol. 3, 115. Subsequent references to Lyly refer to this edition and will appear in the text.

3   Susan Wells, *The Dialectics of Representation*, Baltimore: Johns Hopkins University Press, 1985, 19–36.

4   Jacques Derrida, 'Sending: On Representation', *Social Research* 49 (1982): 294–326.

5   Joel B. Altman, *The Tudor Play of Mind: Rhetorical Inquiry and the Development of Elizabethan Drama*, Berkeley: University of California Press, 1978.

6   See Northrop Frye, *Anatomy of Criticism*, Princeton: Princeton University Press, 1957, 88–92; Angus Fletcher, *Allegory: The Theory of a Symbolic Mode*, Ithaca: Cornell University Press, 1970, 2–23.

7   An impact cogently demonstrated by Joel Altman in *The Tudor Play of Mind*.

8   *John Lyly: The Humanist as Courtier*, Cambridge, MA: Harvard University Press, 1962, esp. 159–84.

9   Peter Saccio, *The Court Comedies of John Lyly: A Study of Allegorical Dramaturgy*, Princeton: Princeton University Press, 1969, 5–6, 189–224; cit. at 189–90.

10 See Stephen S. Hilliard's dissertation, 'Dramatic Allegory in the Mythological Plays of John Lyly and His Contemporaries', Princeton University, 1967. Our reading of the prologue cannot accept Michael R. Best's ingenious idea (argued in 'A Theory of the Literary Genesis of Lyly's *Midas*', *Review of English Studies* 17 [1966]: 133–49) that 'If *Midas* is the charger of second-rate fare, the several dishes could be interpreted as representing two (or more) earlier plays, which Lyly regarded as superior, a 'feast', and which were 'minced' together to form the play as we have it' (133 ff.). While the internal evidence for this (untypical dualism of the main plot, unexplained inconsistencies in the subplot) appears to us to be inconclusive, the external evidence (the play's involvement in the Marprelate controversy) needs to be taken seriously, even though we do not think that it 'uniquely supports and explains the nature of the revision' (137) and the conflation of *ur-Midas I* and *ur-Midas II*.

11 Saccio, *The Court Comedies of John Lyly*, 192.

12 See Gayatri Chakravorty Spivak, 'Can the Subaltern Speak?' *Marxism and the Interpretation of Culture*, ed. Cary Nelson and Lawrence Grossberg, Urbana: University of Illinois Press, 1988, 271–318, cit. at 276.

13 The quotations are from A. L. Rowse, *The England of Elizabeth: The Structure of Society*, London, 1950, 243, and J. B. Black, *The Reign of Elizabeth: 1558–1603*, Oxford: Clarendon Press, 1959, 2nd edition, 268, respectively.

14 Michel Foucault, *The Order of Things: An Archaeology of the Human Sciences*, New York: Random House, 1970, 17 ff.; 65.

15 Alan Hager, *Shakespeare's Political Animal: Schema and Schemata in the Canon*, Newark: University of Delaware Press, 1990, 72; but see his full chapter on Lyly and Marlowe, 'The Politics of Literary Expropriation', 67–75.

16 Louis Montrose, *The Purpose of Playing: Shakespeare and the Cultural Politics of the Elizabethan Theatre*, Chicago: University of Chicago Press, 1996, 104, 101.

17 Stephen Greenblatt, *Renaissance Self-Fashioning: From More to Shakespeare*, Chicago: University of Chicago Press, 1980, 327.

18 Philip Sidney, *The Prose Works of Sir Philip Sidney*, ed. Albert Feuillerat, 4 vols, Cambridge: Cambridge University Press, 1962, vol. 3: 38–9.

19 Sidney, *Prose Works*, 40.

20 Stephen Mullaney, *The Place of the Stage: License, Play and Power in Renaissance England*, Chicago: University of Chicago Press, 1987, 21.
21 Paul Griffiths, *Youth and Authority: Formative Experience in England, 1560–1640*, Oxford: Clarendon Press, 1996.
22 Mullaney, *The Place of the Stage*, 49.
23 *Greene's Groats-worth of Wit, Bought with a Million of Repentance*, 1592, duplicated in Samuel Schoenbaum's *William Shakespeare: A Documentary Life*, New York: Oxford University Press, 1975, 115–16. As E. A. J. Honigman suggests, not unjustifiably so, the 'Tiger's hart' is part of considerable evidence of an 'ungentle' Shakespeare, 'sharp and businesslike'. See *Shakespeare's Impact on his Contemporaries*, Totowa: Barnes and Noble, 1982, 7, 9, 11, 22.
24 Walter Cohen, *Drama of a Nation: Public Theatre in Renaissance England and Spain*, Ithaca: Cornell University Press, 1985, 180.
25 Coburn Freer, *The Poetics of Jacobean Drama*, Baltimore: Johns Hopkins University Press, 1981, 57.
26 Robert S. Knapp, *Shakespeare: The Theatre and the Book*, Princeton: Princeton University Press, 1989, 16.

7 *Henry V* and the signs of power: William Shakespeare

1 For an argument regarding the centrality of legitimation to early modern playwrights, see Paul Yachnin, *Stage-Wrights: Shakespeare, Jonson, Middleton, and the Making of Theatrical Value*, Philadelphia: University of Pennsylvania Press, 1997; for a more specific account of Shakespeare's own struggles for legitimacy, see Katherine Duncan-Jones, *Ungentle Shakespeare: Scenes from His Life*, London: Arden Shakespeare, 2001, especially Chapter 4 'Spear-shaking Shakespeare', 82–103.
2 *King Henry V*, ed. Andrew Gurr, 'The New Cambridge Shakespeare', Cambridge: Cambridge University Press, 1992, 6.
3 Warren D. Smith, 'The *Henry V* Choruses in the First Folio', *Journal of English and Germanic Philology* 53 (1954): 38–57; cit. at 57.
4 R. A Law, 'The Choruses in *Henry the Fifth*', *University of Texas Studies in English* 35 (1956): 11–21; cit. at 15.
5 G. P. Jones, '*Henry V*: The Chorus and the Audience', *Shakespeare Survey* 31 (1978): 93–104; cit. at 95, 96; this reading is indebted to that of Warren D. Smith (note 3).
6 Anthony S. Brennan, 'That Within Which Passes Show: The Function of the Chorus in *Henry V*', *Philological Quarterly* 58 (1979): 40–52; cit. at 43.
7 Edward I. Berry, '"True Things and Mock'ries": Epic and History in *Henry V*', *Journal of English and Germanic Philology* 78 (1979): 1–16; cit. at 6.
8 Gunter Walch, 'Tudor-Legende und Geschichtsbewegung in *The Life of King Henry V*: Zur Rezeptionslenkung durch den Chorus', *Shakespeare Jahrbuch* 122 (1986): 36–46; cit. at 46. Translation by Robert Weimann.
9 Lawrence Danson, '*Henry V*: King, Chorus, and Critics', *Shakespeare Quarterly* 34 (1983): 27–43; cit. at 28.
10 *The Complete Works of John Lyly*, ed. R. Warwick Bond, 3 vols, Oxford: Clarendon Press, 1902, vol. 3, 115.
11 See Jean Alter, *A Sociosemiotic Thoery of Theatre*, Philadelphia: University of Pennsylvania Press, 1990, 31–2.

12   Michael Goldman, *Shakespeare and the Energies of Drama*, Princeton, NJ: Princeton University Press, 1972, 58, 61, 63.

13   Antony Hammond, "'I must be your imagination then": The Prologue and the Plural Text in *Henry V* and Elsewhere', *Fanned and Winnowed Opinions: Shakespearean Essays Presented To Harold Jenkins*, ed. John W. Mahon and Thomas A Pendleton, London: Methuen, 1987, 138, 149, 144.

14   See Goldman, *Shakespeare and the Energies of Drama*: 'the Chorus sounds very much like the King'. See also Danson, '*Henry V*', 30–3.

15   Joel Altman, "'Vile Participation": The Amplification of Violence in the Theatre of *Henry V*', *Shakespeare Quarterly* 42 (1991): 1–32; cit. at 3.

16   Graham Holderness, *Shakespeare's History*, Dublin: Gill and Macmillan, 1985, 136–7.

17   Annabel Patterson, 'Back by Popular Demand: The Two Versions of *Henry V*', *Renaissance Drama* n.s. 19 (1988): 29–62; cit. at 56.

18   Stanley Wells, *Modernizing Shakespeare's Spelling*; with Gary Taylor, *Three Studies in the Text of Henry V*, Oxford: Clarendon Press, 1979, 98, 131. See also William Shakespeare, *Henry V*, ed. Gary Taylor, 'The Oxford Shakespeare', Oxford: Clarendon Press, 1982, 22.

19   Here, we find Taylor's reading as well as his reasoning absolutely convincing: Since 'there can be little question of the reporter inventing these lines', the 'origin of these interpolations need not affect their *authority*' (*Three Studies*, 151–2; emphasis in original). While, predictably, *The Norton Shakespeare* prints 'PISTOL *Coup' la gorge*' (4.6.39), other recent editors of *Henry V* continue to dispute the Quarto's authority and reject the 'comic catchphrase insertion which would lose all its comedy if immediately enacted' (*King Henry V*, ed. Gurr, 177; see also *King Henry V*, ed. T. W. Craik, 'The Arden Shakespeare', London, 1995, 98; 309.) For a critical approach to this scene, see Anthony Brennan, *Henry V*, London: Harvester, 1992, 92–5.

20   Patterson, 'Back by Popular Demand', 53.

21   See Patterson, 'Back by Popular Demand', and Peter W. M. Blayney, *Nicholas Okes and the First Quarto*, Cambridge: Cambridge University Press, 1982; further, Joseph Loewenstein, 'Plays Agnostic and Competitive: The Textual Approach to Elsinore', *Renaissance Drama* n.s. 19 (1988): 90–1.

22   See Alexander Schmidt, *Shakespeare Lexicon and Quotation Dictionary*, 2 vols., 1902, repr. New York: Dover Publications, 1971, vol. 1, 440.

23   Beckerman, *Shakespeare at the Globe*, New York: Macmillan, 1962, xi; nor does this necessarily conflict with the assumption that, by a few months, even weeks, 'the weight of the evidence excludes *Henry V*' from the Globe plays, xiv.

24   Ruth Lunney, *Marlowe and the Popular Tradition*, 104, 204 n. 11.

25   See Patterson, 'The Two Versions of *Henry V*', 45–59. As Holderness notes, it 'is possible that the play testifies to a brief but significant moment of unity shortly after Essex' departure, with the empress and her general reconciled in expectation of victory' (*Shakespeare's History*, 142).

26   Cornelius Castoriadis, *The Imaginary Institution of Society*, trans. Kathleen Blamey, Cambridge, MA: MIT Press, 1998, 238.

27   Here, representation in Shakespeare's play needs to be seen in conjuncture with that in Lyly's and Marlowe's theatre (see Chapters 4 and 6 of the present study) or, for that matter, in early modern narrative (see Weimann, *Authority and Representation in Early Modern Discourse*, 139–79).

28 See Holderness, *Shakespeare's History*, 189–90, emphasis in original.
29 Greenblatt, *Shakespearean Negotiations*, Berkeley: University of California Press, 1988, 63.
30 Mark Thornton Burnett, '*Doctor Faustus* and the Form and Function of the Chorus: Marlowe's Beginnings and Endings', *CIEFL Bulletin* n.s. 1 (June 1989): 33–45; cit. at 36.
31 Marjorie Garber, '"What's Past is Prologue": Temporality and Prophecy in Shakespeare's History Plays', in *Renaissance Genres*, ed. Barbara K. Lewalski, Cambridge, MA: Harvard University Press, 1986, 301–31.
32 Cited in William Shakespeare, *King Henry V*, ed. J. H. Walter, 'Arden Shakespeare', London: Methuen, 1954, 6. See, in this connection, Brian Rotman, *Signifying Nothing: The Semiotics of Zero*, New York: St Martin's Press, 1987; Rotman defines zero as a 'meta-sign for the absence of certain signs' (57). Resembling in this function both the vanishing point in Renaissance painting and the imaginary money in the rising mercantile economy, such a meta-sign 'disrupts the code in question by becoming the origin of a new, radically different mode of sign production; one whose novelty is reflected in the emergence of a semiotic subject able to *signify* absence' (57). Referring to *King Lear*, where 'the double image of "nothing" and "everything" was itself too interestingly subversive and enticing', Rotman hints at the hostility of the medieval church to 'the nihilistic consequences, the heretical and atheistic dangers of believing in and talking about "nothing"' (64). Historically, Shakespeare (who may have known Baret's *Alvearie*, as he almost certainly used Robert Recorde's *Arithmetic*) must have been acquainted with the transition from Roman numerals to the new decimal notations involving the use of a 'crooked figure' like zero. See also David Willbern, 'Shakespeare's Nothing', in *Representing Shakespeare: New Psychoanalytic Essays*, ed. M. M. Schwartz and C. Kahn, Baltimore: Johns Hopkins University Press, 1980, 256: '. . . through a metaphoric shift from geometry of shape [the architectural 'O'] to mathematics ['O' as number, zero] – bridged by the shared image of shape ['a crooked figure'] – Shakespeare transmutes impotence into omnipotence. The actors who are nothing in themselves become representative "ciphers to this great accompt . . .".'
33 For Holinshed and Hall and also for Daniel's 'panegyric of *Henry V*', see *Narrative and Dramatic Sources of Shakespeare*, ed. Geoffrey Bullough, 8 vols, London: Routledge and Kegan Paul, 1962, vol. 4: 349 ff. But the comparison with the Holinshed also reveals an astonishing frankness in certain passages, where Shakespeare's imagery of 'famine, sword and fire' – 'Leash'd in like hounds' – finds a remarkable precedent in Holinshed. Cf. Raphael Holinshed, *Chronicles of England, Scotland, and Ireland*, repr. New York: AMS Press, 1965, vol. 3, 104. For directly paraphrased passages from Holinshed, see *Three Studies in the Text of Henry V*, Taylor, 306–8; for a summarized comparison of the two texts, *King Henry V*, ed. Gurr, 231–4. In this connection, see Annabel Patterson's important reassessment of Holinshed, *Reading Holinshed's 'Chronicles'*, Chicago: University of Chicago Press, 1994.
34 Berry, 'True Things and Mock'ries', 4. The *OED* defines the verb as 'to cover with that which beautifies'.
35 For a critique of Foucault's paradigm of early modern representation, see Weimann, *Authority and Representation in Early Modern Discourse*, 190–2.

36 See Christopher Braider, *Refiguring the Real: Picture and Modernity in Word and Image, 1400–1700*, Princeton: Princeton University Press, 1993, 3.

37 Vassilis Lambropoulos, *The Rise of Eurocentrism: Anatomy of Interpretation*, Princeton: Princeton University Press, 1993, xi–xii, 28; et passim.

38 John Guillory, *Poetic Authority: Spenser, Milton, and Literary History*, New York: Columbia University Press, 1983.

39 Gardiner's remarks are contained in *The Actes and Monuments of John Foxe*, ed. Stephen Reed Cattley, London: Seeley and Burnside: 1838, vol. 6: 31, 41.

40 Sir Henry Wotton, from a letter to Sir Edmund Bacon first printed in 1661; quoted here in modernized version from *The Riverside Shakespeare*, 2nd edition, ed. G. Blakemore Evans *et al.*, Boston: Houghton Mifflin, 1997, p. 1968.

41 Erich Auerbach, *Mimesis: The Representation of Reality in Western Literature*, trans. Willard R. Trask, Princeton: Princeton University Press, 1953, Chapter 13.

42 Bullough, *Narrative and Dramatic Sources of Shakespeare*, vol. 4, 363–4.

Index

References to specific prologues are indexed under author's name (where known) or play title.

Merely Players?: Actors' Accounts of Performing Shakespeare

Jonathan Holmes

Merely Players?: Actors' Accounts of Performing Shakespeare marks a significant departure in Shakespeare studies by placing the Shakespearean performer in the role of critic. It draws on three centuries' worth of actors' written reflections on playing Shakespeare and recognises these individuals as valuable commentators in the field of Shakespeare studies. The book features the testimonials of various performers throughout history, including:

- Ellen Terry
- Henry Irving
- John Barrymore
- Flora Robson
- Michael Redgrave
- Juliet Stevenson

In bringing together the dual worlds of academia and performance, *Merely Players?* offers a unique resource for the Shakespeare scholar and theatre-lover alike.

hb: 0–415–31957–9
pb: 0–415–31958–7

Available at all good bookshops
For ordering and further information please visit:
www.routledge.com

Accents on Shakespeare

General Editor: Terence Hawkes

Books in the *Accents on Shakespeare* series provide short, powerful, 'cutting-edge' accounts of and comments on new developments in the field of Shakespeare studies. In addition to titles aimed at modular undergraduate courses, it also features a number of spirited and committed research-based books.

The *Accents on Shakespeare* series features contributions from such leading figures as: Philip Armstrong, Michael Bristol and Kathleen McLuskie, Dympna Callaghan, Christy Desmet and Robert Sawyer, Ewan Fernie, Wes Folkerth, Hugh Grady, Terence Hawkes, Jean E. Howard and Scott Cutler Shershow, John J. Joughin, Tiffany Stern and Sarah Werner.

Available at all good bookshops
For a full series listing, ordering details and further information please visit:
www.routledge.com